Partners in Furs

In this innovative study the authors investigate the effects of the fur trade on the social patterns of the Algonquian peoples living in the Eastern James Bay region from 1600 to 1870. Of central concern are the problem areas of winter hunting arrangements, land tenure system, and patterns of leadership; but historical setting, ecological factors, and the relations of the Algonquians to other groups are also discussed.

The pattern and course of contact between traders from Europe and the Indian populations are described and both English and French sources are used to reveal the competition between the two groups of traders and its impact on the native people. As the Hudson's Bay Company was the one permanent European presence during the period, this ethnohistorical study makes extensive use of unpublished HBC papers. The authors also examine such issues as the rise of a homeguard population at the trading posts, the trading captain system, the development of family hunting territories, and the issue of dependence and interdependence.

Partners in Furs provides new insight and makes a significant contribution to current scholarly inquiry into the impact of the fur trade on the native populations.

DANIEL FRANCIS is a freelance historical researcher and writer based in Vancouver.
TOBY MORANTZ is a Canadian Research Fellow in the Department of Anthropology, McGill University.

Partners in Furs

A History of the Fur Trade in Eastern James Bay 1600–1870

DANIEL FRANCIS AND
TOBY MORANTZ

McGill-Queen's University Press
Montreal & Kingston • London • Buffalo

© McGill-Queen's University Press 1983
Reprinted 1985, 1989

ISBN 0-7735-0385-4 (cloth)
ISBN 0-7735-0386-2 (paper)

Legal deposit 1st quarter 1983
Bibliothèque nationale du Québec

Printed in Canada

This book has been published with the help of a grant from
the Social Science Federation of Canada, using funds
provided by the Social Sciences and Humanities Research
Council of Canada. Publication has also been assisted by the
Canada Council under its block grant program.

A French translation of this book, entitled *Traite des
fourrures dans l'est de la baie James, 1600–1870*, has been
published by the Direction générale du patrimoine of the
Ministère des Affaires culturelles, Quebec.

Canadian Cataloguing in Publication Data

Francis, Daniel.
  Partners in furs

  Includes index.
  ISBN 0-7735-0385-4 (bound). – ISBN 0-7735-0386-2 (pbk.)

  1. Fur trade – Quebec (Province) – James Bay region –
  History. 2. Indians of North America – Quebec (Province)
  – James Bay region – Trapping. I. Morantz, Toby
  Elaine, 1943– II. Title.

  HD9944.C22F73   380.1'439   C82-094718-0

To the People of James Bay
Past, Present, and Future

Contents

Tables

Illustrations

MAPS AND PLANS

FIGURES

Preface

From the outset the authors of this book were conscious of an attempt to appeal to three different audiences. First, we intended to produce a local history of eastern James Bay which the people who live in that region would find useful and interesting. This objective required, we believed, a detailed description of incidents and personalities that would be of significance to inhabitants of the area, many of whose ancestors figure largely in our story. Secondly, we wanted to engage in a more theoretical discussion of the conduct of the fur trade in Canada and its impact on the Indian people. We make no apologies for having a particular point of view in this regard; we only hope the general reader will bear with the occasional echo of academic debates. Thirdly, we tried to produce an entertaining historical study of a little-known region of the country for readers with an interest in Canada's past.

In entitling this history *Partners in Furs*, we are not suggesting that the fur trade was an equal partnership. There is surely no need to belabour the obvious point that the merchant traders did not share their profits or their power with the Indian people. What struck us, though, is that on their home ground the Indians were not the defenceless, passive producers they have often been characterized as being. The title is meant to emphasize our belief that the Indian people were crucial to all aspects of the fur trade and were responsible to a considerable degree for establishing its procedures. In James Bay this was clearly true in the eighteenth century, though less so in the nineteenth century, for reasons the reader will discover. The history terminates in 1870; later events, which have done so much to colour opinions about the relationship of Indian peoples to Canadian society, have no bearing on it. In fact this study suggests strongly that the fur trade in Canada should not be viewed in monolithic terms, either geographically or temporally.

Partners in Furs combines historical and ethnohistorical methods. The latter term is used in the narrow sense of referring only to reconstructing (or constructing a reasonable facsimile of) societal organization from historical materials originally intended by the writers for other purposes. The historical method refers to rendering an account of the situations and events, the motives, and processes whereby change occurred. Since this is the first detailed history of eastern James Bay, emphasis has been placed on making available the historical data at the risk of appearing to ignore other dimensions. The ecological dimension, for example, so important to a complete understanding of the social and historical processes of any fur-trade history, is much more difficult to extract from the written records and must await further archaeological investigation. In our opinion the most serious gap in the sources is the near-absolute absence of the James Bay peoples' own narratives and points of view. In some instances oral history accounts of an event could be utilized and were. Most of the oral histories collected by the Cree Way Project (1975) and Preston (1975) seemed to refer to more recent events and thus were not incorporated in the history as such. However, they were invaluable in helping us to understand how the Cree people viewed their past. Although this history of eastern James Bay is very much a non-Indian account, given the sources and the historical records used, it is hoped the people of James Bay will consider it as a reference point from which to develop more of their own narratives of their life in the past.

Readers may notice that the seventeenth century is not covered in as much detail as the following two centuries. Much of this period, except for the Iroquois raids, is treated extensively in the published literature. Therefore, it seemed unnecessary to review fully these events, particularly since, strictly speaking, most took place outside the eastern James Bay area. Because the later history is to be found only in nonpublished sources, more emphasis in our history was given to this period.

Two principal collections of archives were used during our research, with unequal productiveness. In the Archives des Colonies are the papers and documents relating to New France, copies of which are on deposit in the Public Archives of Canada. They were searched for information on the early French involvement in eastern James Bay. Since these documents are generally concerned with official business and since the posts the French operated in the area were outposts, very little was found that directly shed light on French activities and almost nothing regarding Indian life. The James Bay people to the east visited from time to time the post at Chicoutimi. However, we decided not to include data on that post because it would have been impossible to do justice to it without entangling ourselves in the history of the other posts of the Domaine du Roi. As a result, the French presence in eastern James Bay is not fully documented in the following pages. Several scholars are now studying the history of this southeasterly region, what we might call the Montagnais area, and it is assumed that their work will redress the imbalance.

The archives of the Hudson's Bay Company, on deposit in the Provincial Archives of Manitoba and available on microfilm at the Public Archives of Canada, has provided most of the historical data on which this study is based. These records include daily journals and year-end account books of each fur-trading post in the area, as well as correspondence between the posts and correspondence between the bay and London headquarters. Unfortunately no documents were found that describe the North West Company's activities in the interior of the James Bay region. We do not apologize for our extensive reliance on the Hudson's Bay Company records, since they furnish information and details otherwise unavailable, but we are aware of the dangers inherent in this dependence. We caution our readers to keep this in mind when reading the history.

Some comments must be made about the maps. Geographical place-names in Quebec are complicated to sort out. There are the historic names with their various spellings and present-day names with Cree, French, and English renderings. Generally, in the text the historic names are used but the official name is indicated at least once. The maps, showing zones 1 and 2, also distinguish between historic and modern official names where necessary. Unfortunately the size of the maps has imposed severe limitations on the extent of information represented on them.

The reader's attention is drawn to Pike Lake Post and Lake Nicabau on the zone 2 map. In each case the general area is correct but the location of the actual lakes is the result of guesswork. So too is the pinpointing of the specific sites of the inland posts.

The research and writing of this study were carried out under the auspices of the James Bay Ethnohistory Program, part of a larger program of multidisciplinary research organized and financed by the Direction de l'archéologie et de l'ethnologie (now known as the Service du Patrimoine autochtone) of the Ministère des Affaires culturelles of the Province of Quebec. Since its inception in January 1975, the James Bay Ethnohistory Program has carried out historical research and produced a number of studies, some of an academic, historical, and anthropological nature and others more descriptive for use as resource materials in the schools of the James Bay Cree. An important part of the program was the financial assistance given to aid in the collection of oral history accounts by the Cree Way Project, a highly successful curriculum development program instituted at Rupert House by John Murdoch.

Acknowledgments

This study would not have been possible without the existence of the inestimably valuable archives of the Hudson's Bay Company. We wish to express our appreciation to the Hudson's Bay Company for its kind permission to consult and quote from its microfilm collection on deposit at the Public Archives of Canada in Ottawa.

We also wish to acknowledge our gratitude to the Ministère des Affaires culturelles, Quebec, for having generously financed most of the work for this history. More recently the Ministère has underwritten the cost of preparing the graphic work. We are most appreciative of the significant contribution of Charles Martijn to this history. In addition to his role as our liaison with the Ministère des Affaires culturelles, we were the grateful beneficiaries of his keen, critical mind which challenged us to refine our ideas and broaden our horizons.

The instructiveness and clarity of the graphs and maps are due entirely to the unsparing efforts of Jacqueline Anderson, cartographer at Concordia University. Her uncompromising professionalism and dedication have been greatly appreciated. Ably assisting her in the preparation of the maps were Deborah Trim and Jo-Ann Droghini. We owe special thanks to Laurence Hogue and her staff at the Direction de l'Environnement at Hydro-Québec who willingly and generously helped in some production aspects of the maps. Similarly we thank Laurent Girouard, also of the Direction de l'Environnement, who initiated Hydro-Québec's cooperation.

A number of people read, criticized, and made useful suggestions to improve an earlier draft of this work. For this we express our gratitude to Adrian Tanner of Memorial University, André Sévigny of Parks Canada, Stewart Raby of the Federation of Saskatchewan Indians, Keith Crowe of the Department of Indian Affairs, Arthur Ray of the University of British Columbia, and Alan Cooke of McGill University's Centre for

Northern Studies. We also wish to thank John Murdoch of Cree Way Project and Richard Preston of McMaster University for their instructive comments on some previous related studies.

For the chapter on the environment, help was desperately sought and willingly provided by Fikret Berkes of the Grand Council of the Crees and of Brock University; Pierre Normandeau, Jacques Gingras, and Pierre Guimont of the James Bay Development Corporation; and Jean-Pierre Ducruc of Environment Canada. For help on the prehistory we were the grateful recipients of the expertise of David Denton of McGill University's Centre for Northern Studies, James Chism of Archéologie Illimitée, and Marcel Laliberté of CERAN. We thank all of them for their help though we take full responsibility for the overview presented in chapter 1.

We also wish to thank Annie Whiskeychan of Rupert House, Marguerite MacKenzie of Memorial University, and David Cooter of the Université du Québec à Chicoutimi for their help with linguistic problems we encountered.

Others beside ourselves were involved, at times, in researching the archival records – Teresa Wiebe, Claire-Andrée Tremblay, Carol Sheedy, and Susan Marshall. We thank them for their interest and diligence. Many of the staff of the Public Archives of Canada were extremely helpful over the several years of research, but Peter Bower (now of the Manitoba Provincial Archives), Gary Maunder, and Ginette Cyr were bothered by us more than were the others. We would also like to extend a special thanks to Shirlee Anne Smith, archivist of the Hudson's Bay Company Archives, and staff members Garron Wells and Judith Beattie for their kind attention to our many and varied requests.

Similarly, we are indebted to our typist, Eveline Dallas, for her good humour in the face of handwritten scrawls, for her fast and accurate work, and above all for her quick mastery of eighteenth-century English. Finally, we wish to thank Audrey Hlady for her impressively thorough editing and general helpfulness and David Norton of McGill-Queen's University Press for guiding this work to publication.

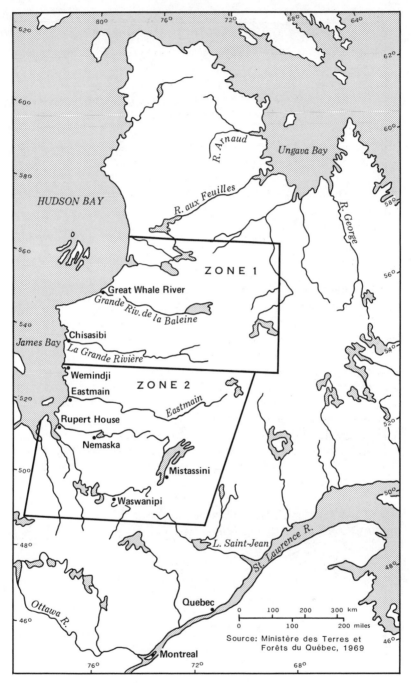

Present-day location of James Bay Cree bands and settlements

Zone One: Eastern Hudson Bay, historic and modern place-names

Source: Ministère des Terres et Forêsts du Québec, 1976
Hudson's Bay Company Archives 1700–1870

i. BELCHER

HUDSON BAY

Lower Seal Lake

Upper Seal Lake

Lac Guillaume–
Delisle
(Richmond
Gulf)

Clearwater
Lake

Richmond Fort
Little Whale River
(Little Whale R.)

Petite R. de la Baleine

Great
Whale River

Grande R. de la Baleine
(Great Whale R.)

L. BIENVILLE

Kaniapiskau

L. Caniapiscau

R. au Phoque (Seal R.)

Pte. Wastikun (Wastikun Pt.)
(Cape Jones)

Pte. Louis XIV

Big River/Fort George

L. Kanaaupscow

La Grande Rivière
(Fort George)

James Bay

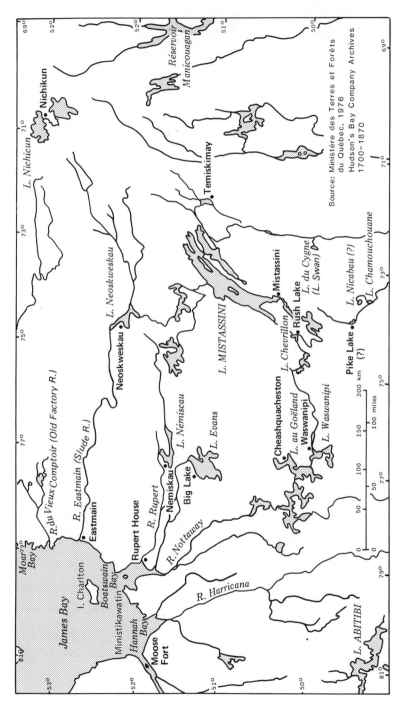

Zone Two: Eastern James Bay, historic and modern place-names

Source: Ministère des Terres et Forêts
du Québec, 1976
Hudson's Bay Company Archives
1700–1870

Partners in Furs

CHAPTER ONE

The Land and the People: An Introduction

Eastern James Bay is an inhospitable country. The land is rugged and impenetrable to all but the most resourceful travellers. The rivers drop through thunderous cataracts to a swampy coastal plain, blank and featureless. The climate is one of extremes, ranging from the hot, mosquito-plagued days of summer to the deadly cold of mid-winter. All in all it is among the most intimidating country in the Canadian Shield. Human inhabitants have always found it difficult to wrest a living from such a harsh environment. Stripped of its soil cover by massive glaciers ages ago, the land is a desolate mixture of bog and rock. Agriculture is impossible; hunting is the only feasible human activity. The earliest inhabitants were hunters and fishermen. The land provided just enough to survive but it was not generous; there was not enough in any one spot to stay for long. The quest for food was ceaseless and the people of eastern James Bay developed a technology and a social organization suited to the rigorous demands of their country. These people are the subject of this book.

The territory occupied by these people includes the coastlines of Hudson Bay and James Bay from Richmond Gulf (Lac Guillaume-Delisle) in the north to the bottom of Rupert Bay in the south and embraces the land fronting on this shoreline inland to the lakes and headwaters of the rivers which drain it. We have chosen to call this huge area eastern James Bay, since it encompasses the hunting territories of most of the Indian people who visited the early fur-trade posts situated on the east coast of James Bay. The original posts, Eastmain House and Rupert House, in time became the centre of a network of trading posts to the north and east. Some of the new posts, Richmond Fort and Little Whale River for example, were located outside the strict limits of eastern James Bay. However, their history cannot be appreciated apart from their parent posts and so it is included here.

LANDFORMS

Eastern James Bay falls within Canada's subarctic region and forms part of the Canadian Shield, that vast expanse of Precambrian gneisses and granites. The present contours of Hudson Bay and its environs took shape within the last ten thousand years after the retreat of the last Wisconsinian Laurentide ice sheet into northern Canada. Hudson Bay underlay the central zone of this huge glacier, which covered most of Canada east of the Rocky Mountains as well as parts of the northeastern United States. The tremendous weight of the ice caused a downwarping in the Hudson Bay area, depressing the land. When the glacier receded northward, the Atlantic waters immediately rushed in and flooded an area much larger in size than is covered by the present-day Hudson Bay. The Tyrrell Sea, as it is known – named after the first geologist to investigate it – spilled over extensively into the lands bordering Hudson and James bays, into Manitoba, Ontario, Keewatin, and Quebec. Along the Quebec shores of James and Hudson bays the Tyrrell Sea extended in some places as much as 240 kilometres inland (Hardy 1976, 192). Elson estimates that 148,000 square kilometres of Quebec were covered by the Tyrrell Sea (1969, 248).

Most scientists place the beginning of this marine inundation at about seventy-nine hundred years ago. The shrinking of the Tyrrell Sea to its present contours of Hudson and James bays was a gradual process caused by an isostatic rebound once the ice disappeared. This rebound caused the land to lift and the water to retreat (Lee 1968, 527), leaving a low-lying margin of land surrounding the bays. Probably by about two thousand years ago the present boundaries of Hudson Bay and James Bay had emerged.

In general terms the interior of the Quebec-Labrador peninsula is a rough tableland of moderate relief which slopes upward from the north and drops away quite suddenly in the other directions. Inland from James Bay the tableland rises abruptly out of the coastal lowlands to an elevation of approximately 233 metres, then climbs gradually inland. In this region the headwaters of the major rivers flowing into eastern James and Hudson bays are found. Along the rivers the quite abrupt change in elevation between the plain and the upland is marked by turbulent rapids and falls, which made penetration of the land beyond the east coast difficult for early traders. Neither did the low flat plain invite exploration by Europeans. At least one-quarter of the surface is under water (Lehoux and Rosa 1973, 1), and much of it has not yet developed an efficient drainage system. Hence swamps, bogs, and muskeg are common. The land is also strewn with ponds, lakes, and streams and the rivers are swift flowing and blocked by numerous rapids. As we shall see, the first traders preferred to keep to coastal waters, which, however, presented other difficulties. Along the south coast and in Rupert Bay mudflats formed by silt deposited by the larger rivers extend offshore. Most water traffic must keep well out into the bay to avoid grounding in the mud. North of Rupert Bay the shore is fringed with countless islands of rock and sand. The water within this labyrinth of small islands is shallow and treacherous. Ice forms here early in the winter and lingers well into the spring, making coastal navigation still more difficult. Such a short navigational season was an important factor in thwarting the Hudson's Bay Company's attempts to extend its trade along the southeast coast of Hudson Bay.

The coastal plain which forms the east coast of James Bay narrows as it progresses northward until in the vicinity of Cape Jones it disappears altogether and the interior upland comes out to the coast. Here the shoreline changes character once again and takes on a bolder aspect which extends all the way to Richmond Gulf, the limits of this study. In places granite cliffs stand up directly from the water's edge. Elsewhere they stop anywhere from half a kilometre to five kilometres inland and sandy terraced beaches run down to the shore. The coastline is much smoother here than in James Bay, being almost unbroken by deep bays or prominent points of land. Except in the estuaries of the Great and Little Whale rivers this stretch of coast offers no safe harbours for sea-going traffic (Low 1900, 9d).

VEGETATION

Eastern James Bay is situated in the broad belt of coniferous boreal forest which stretches across the top of North America from Alaska to Labrador, and across Eurasia from Norway to Siberia. This boreal forest, occupying the subarctic climatic zone, consists primarily of black and white spruce with sizeable components of tamarack, aspen, and poplar. On the north it is bounded by the unforested tundra, the tree line extending across northern Quebec from Richmond Gulf to the bottom of Ungava Bay. To the south lies the deciduous forest of a more temperate climate (Rowe 1972, 21–9; Zarnovican 1976, 12).

In general as one proceeds northward through the study area the forest cover thins out. Closed forest gives way to open parklike woodland, and then to expanses of barren ground broken only by stands of spruce along the shores of rivers and lakes. The relative scarcity of timber in the northerly region, in addition to the bitterly cold climate, made the area inhospitable to permanent settlement by traders.

The native peoples of Canada's forest regions have always depended for many purposes on the vegetation of the area. Traditionally they put the products of the forest to many ingenious uses: canoes, toboggans, snowshoes, baskets, wigwams, cradleboards, medicines, and so forth. The forest regions also provide a suitable habitat and food supply for the animals which the Indians have at all times hunted to feed and clothe themselves.

CLIMATE

The climate also determined the life-style of the people who inhabited the James Bay area. The amount of precipitation and sunlight, the range of temperature, and the length of days and seasons limit the number and variety of plants and these in turn limit the animals of an area.

Eastern James Bay is situated in the same latitudes as much of the populated area of Europe, and yet its climate is both cooler and more moist. The presence of Hudson Bay itself, 480,000 square kilometres in extent, is the most important determinant of weather conditions in this area. In the fall and early winter air moving eastward across the bay picks up moisture which it dumps on the eastern coast as it rises to clear the interior plateau. By January the bay is frozen over and arctic air from the Northwest Territories passes over it unmodified. In the spring and early summer the bay remains ice-covered, cooling the air which passes over it and delaying the return of warmer temperatures to the eastern shore. The general result is that the eastern James Bay area experiences heavier snowfalls and colder temperatures than any other area of comparable latitude in North America.

Winter is definitely the longest season. The first signs of its approach occur in October, and by the end of November snow has covered the ground, the major rivers are frozen, and drifting ice pans cover the bay (Lehoux and Rosa 1973, 8). Early in winter the weather tends to be snowy, cloudy, and unsettled. After the bay has frozen over, the air is drier and colder and there is less precipitation along the east coast.

January is the coldest month: average temperatures range between minus twenty and twenty-three degrees Celsius but minus forty is not uncommon (Thompson 1968, 285). When traders established themselves in James Bay, communications between posts were confined to a single mail packet at this time of year. As well as the possibilities of getting lost or freezing to death in a storm, the traders had to risk the ice. The force of wind and tide sometimes causes fissures to form in the shore ice perpendicular to the shoreline. Poorly refrozen and covered with fresh snow, these channels can swallow up an unsuspecting traveller and his sled (Biays 1964, 97).

The return of spring to the eastern side of Hudson Bay is delayed by the persistent ice cover, but in James Bay the season arrives sooner with the help of warmer air from the south and west (Thompson 1968, 277). By

mid-May the ice along the coast is breaking up and by l'
the last snow generally has disappeared from the groun
ing into James Bay which rise to the south and west frequen.
ence flooding at this time of year, a spring high water pattern common .
all rivers and with important biological consequences. While their mouths
are still clogged with ice, their headwaters have thawed and the runoff
causes jamming and extremely high water. Along the east coast the ice
breakup is usually less dramatic, since most of the rivers have their
sources well up in the highlands where the altitude delays the approach of
spring (Larnder 1968, 332–4).

By mid-July the ice has left James Bay and temperatures climb to an
average daily maximum of near twenty degrees Celsius. However, navigation is still obstructed by ice from Hudson Bay, which is sometimes
driven south and clogs the passage northward. The safest time of year for
coastal shipping is the latter half of August and September, before winter
begins to set in once again. Nevertheless the Hudson's Bay Company
could not wait that long and shipped the furs procured by sloop to Moose
Fort (present Moose Factory) at the end of July. Whaling activities north
along the coast of Hudson Bay, which often set out from Eastmain House,
got under way in July as well.

ANIMAL HARVEST

Throughout the period under study the James Bay people were general-
ized hunters, fowlers, and fishermen, and to a much lesser extent gatherers. The nature of their environment did not permit the people to focus on
only one or two species, for none were entirely dependable or sufficient as
a food source. When the European fur-trading companies arrived in the
region, the people did not become trappers in the sense that acquiring
pelts for trade superseded hunting for food. Trapping always was subordi-
nate to their subsistence pursuits, much to the annoyance of the traders.

The animals prized above all others by most of the James Bay people,
according to the historical records, were the caribou, or "deer" as the
Hudson's Bay Company men referred to them. Not only was the meat a
favourite food, but the carcass supplied essential raw materials for clothing, tools, and utensils. Two subspecies of caribou inhabit the subject area.
Woodland caribou, the larger of the two, pass the summers on open
ground towards the tops of hills, retreating to the surrounding forests for
the winter. Barren ground caribou, on the other hand, occupy the barrens
to the north of the forested regions. Caribou are a gregarious animal. In
James Bay they gather in small bands of ten to fifteen. At times they
wander near the coast and so historically were hunted by the coastal
people, but generally they remain quite a distance inland.

Although moose were completely absent from James Bay from the time the Hudson's Bay Company records began circa 1700 to the end of our study in 1870, it is necessary to make some comments because of the commonly held assumption by biologists and social scientists that they were then present. The Jesuits who worked in the Saguenay–Lake St Jean region mentioned moose in that area, for example in 1671–2 (Thwaites 1896, 56: 159), though there is strong historical evidence that the moose populations there radically declined in the early 1700s. As for the James Bay region, two early sources report that moose were present before 1700 (ibid., 183; Oldmixon 1931, 383–4, 386). However, if this animal had at one time inhabited James Bay, it disappeared by the eighteenth century. Throughout the James Bay records of the Hudson's Bay Company from the first years of the 1700s to 1870 moose is never mentioned. That the company servants knew the difference between moose and caribou is certain, as both animals appear in lists from more western posts. Even historical records up to 1900 do not indicate the presence of moose. The James Bay people, particularly those in the north, state that moose have appeared in the area only in their lifetime.

Beaver flesh was, next to caribou, the most sought-after food. Beaver were more plentiful in the southern regions of James Bay and inland rather than in the coastal areas. They inhabit slow streams and rivers, marshes, and small lakes and feed on willow, alder, and birch trees. Their lodges are constructed of mud and branches, but they also excavate burrows in nearby banks into which they escape in the event of a flood or an attack. Aside from man, beaver have few serious predators and unlike some other mammals do not seem to be subject to cycles. Still, epidemics, overhunting, and poor hunting conditions meant that the numbers harvested annually fluctuated and were not predictable. When hunting the beaver, the Indians usually stopped up the burrows before breaking into the main lodge using ice chisels. Another hunting method was to set nets under the ice near the lodge. Sometimes the animals were shot but usually they were killed by a blow to the head. Steel traps did not come into use until late in the eighteenth century and then only sparingly.

Beaver fur is at its best during the middle to late winter. As spring progresses, the hairs become looser and thinner and therefore less valuable in trade (Ruttle 1968, 22). Throughout the fur-trade period beaver was the most important fur in James Bay. The attraction of the northern trade was not only the quantity of beaver pelts it promised, but also their quality. The beaver has a pelt consisting of two layers, an outer layer of long guard hairs and an undercoat of soft velvety fur called the duvet. The demand for beaver fur from North America was largely a creation of the European fashion of beaver felt hats, which required more of the duvet than of the outer fur. In the cold northern climate of North America, such as the James Bay area, the people wore beaver skins as clothing. For this purpose skins were scraped and greased and the long guard hairs dropped out during prolonged wearing, leaving the duvet exposed. This so-called coat beaver was cheaper for hat manufacturers to process than skins with guard hairs still intact (known as parchment beaver because they were simply sun-dried). Coat beaver was more in demand in Europe, especially after the 1670s when there was a glut of parchment beaver on the market (Innis 1956, 14; Borins 1968, 6; Rich 1967, 45–6).

Another highly prized trade fur was marten. These animals seemed in our period to be more prevalent along the coast than inland and were found as far north as Upper Seal Lake (Petit Lac des Loups Marins) about fifty-six degrees latitude. Today, they have disappeared from the Fort George area. Their fur becomes prime earlier in the winter than the beaver's, usually by late November or early December, after which time the individual hairs loosen and become brittle (Ruttle 1968, 16). Marten trapping by wooden deadfalls or snares is not strenuous work compared with hunting beaver and it was engaged in by the Indian women, young boys, and elderly men as well as the hunters. However, marten are subject to quite radical fluctuations in population size and periodically the people reported them to be very scarce. Marten were not favoured as food by the Indians, though they were eaten when necessary.

Fox, otter, and lynx (called "catts") were the next most important animals hunted and traded by the Indians, though in fewer numbers than that of the beaver or the marten. Foxes feed on mice and lemmings and, like marten, they periodically experience drastic population changes. It is not known if otters undergo cycles but it is less likely, as they are amphibious mammals subsisting mainly on fish (Weinstein 1976, 61). As the lynx feed chiefly on hare, their cycle follows that of the hare, though it lags behind it by two or three years (J. Gingras, personal communication). Whereas the otter and lynx were eaten regularly, the fox was eaten only in times of starvation.

The black bear was highly valued by the Indians for both its meat and its religious significance. The company accepted bear skins in trade but the numbers exchanged amounted to no more than thirty or forty per year. The preferred hunting season was the fall when the animals were at their fattest. Occasionally polar bears were sighted and shot near the mouths of the southern rivers and of course were more common in the north.

The snowshoe hare (usually referred to as "rabbit" in the records) was a particularly important subsistence animal for the James Bay people, though by itself it was not a sufficient food resource. Nocturnal in its habits, the hare travels to its feeding grounds along established runways, making it easy to snare. It too is subject to cyclical population changes, a peak occurring roughly every ten years (Weinstein 1976, 65–7). Other animals important to the Indians' livelihood – lynx, fox, wolf, and marten – also depended on the hare, so depletion of its numbers had adverse repercussions throughout the food chain. This animal seems to have been available in all regions of the James Bay territory. It feeds on grasses and the lower branches of trees and shrubs and was snared by men, women, and children throughout the year.

Other animals taken in small numbers for trade were muskrats ("musquash"), minks, groundhogs ("weenusk"), wolves, and wolverines ("quaquahatches"). Porcupines were hunted for food and their quills used in decoration.

Even more than hare, fish was a staple item in the diet of the James Bay people. The main species used and identified by the Englishmen were whitefish ("tikomeg" in the records), salmon trout (speckled trout), sturgeon, sucker, char, and jack (pike). Among the Fort George people today whitefish is the most important group (ibid., 71), and seems to have been so in historic times as well. Fishing was carried on at all times of the year, though the most important fishing season was the early fall when the people accumulated a supply of smoke-dried fish for the winter. If the fall fishery failed, their winter subsistence and fur-hunting activities were seriously hampered.

Although seals were to be found as far south as the Eastmain River, they do not seem to have figured greatly in the diet of the James Bay people; it is expected the northern Indians used them to a greater extent. The favoured hunting season was spring when the animals climb onto the fast ice along the coast to bask in the sun, moult, and give birth (Mansfield 1968, 379). Occasionally seals were traded at the posts for some tobacco or brandy. Like the Indians, the Hudson's Bay Company was interested in the seal for its blubber, which could be rendered into oil.

White whales, or belugas, were a summer source of food and oil for the Indians of the Richmond Gulf–Whale rivers area. Their preference was for dried whale flesh. The records indicate that the northern Indians congregated at one of the Whale rivers in July, and if they could successfully hunt whales, they remained there during the summer. If, however, the whales were "shy" and did not enter the rivers or the weather was poor, the people returned inland to look for caribou. The beluga came to the estuaries of the large rivers in July to feed and remained into September before migrating back northward.

Birds were also an important part of the diet of the James Bay people and for some of them, those living near the coast, an important basis of their relationship with the Hudson's Bay Company. Ptarmigan and geese were the two species extensively used. Two species of ptarmigan, willow and rock, inhabit eastern James Bay. During the summer the willow prefers the more moist, vegetated areas of the lowlands, whereas the rock ptarmigan frequents the drier upland regions. The birds feed on buds and twigs and, like so many of the other smaller animals, experience periodic population fluctuations. Whereas the English traders hunted their supply of ptarmigan, or "partridges" as they called them, with guns and nets, the Indians seem to have had to rely on bows and arrows because they could not afford the amounts of powder and shot required.

Geese were an important subsistence animal in the spring and fall when they visit the shores of James Bay on their way to and from their northern nesting grounds. Two species of goose, the Canada goose and the lesser snow goose, predominate. The marshes of Rupert Bay attract the greatest numbers of both species, but Canada geese were hunted all along the eastern coast as far as Cape Jones. The James Bay coast, indented by numerous bays with great concentrations of eelgrass and other marine plants, is considered by biologists to be a very important staging and feeding ground during migration (Curtis 1977, 704). The James Bay people participated in intensive goose hunts, as they do today.

Although the records are virtually silent on the use of plant life, except for birch bark, we know that the James Bay people used a variety of plants for medicinal purposes and for eating, particularly blueberries. Berries and roots, however, made up a very minor part of the diet in relation to the consumption of meat, fish, and fowl.

THE PEOPLE

The descendants of the Indian people who are the subject of this history refer to themselves today as the Cree. There is not a corresponding term in their language. Rather, they have a variety of designations which identify groups of people according to geographic and ecological considerations. For example, Wiinibeyk Iiyuu are the people who live and hunt along the coast, whereas Nuuhcimiihc Iiyuu are those from the inland areas. The Cree are members of eight bands, each of which has formed its own community – Great Whale River, Chisasibi (formerly at Fort George), Wemindji, Eastmain, Rupert House, Nemaska, Waswanipi, and Mistassini. The people are further identified by their membership in these communities.

The designation Cree is not a historic one. The first written reference to the people being Cree speakers was made in 1853 in the correspondence of the missionary E.A. Watkins (Church Missionary Society [CMS] reel A-97). No doubt this identification of the eastern James Bay people with the Cree language (a division of Algonquian) began with the missionaries at Rupert House and Fort George who used Cree prayer books translated at Moose Factory in western James Bay. Historically there is little evidence of strong intergroup ties between the east and west coast peoples. Stronger ties seem to have existed between those living on the coast and those inland. Nevertheless, in 1911 the anthropologist Alanson Skinner identified the Indians of the east coast as Cree. But in 1923 F.G. Speck, another early anthropologist, declared this classification to be artificial because the eastern people did not have a political or social affiliation with their western neighbours. He preferred to identify the eastern James Bay people with the Montagnais who live in central Quebec and along the north shore of the St Lawrence River because their dialects were similar (457–8), a view which is supported by linguists today. However, since both the Anglican Church and the federal government through their education policies fostered an association between the eastern James Bay people and the Cree to the west, the former people also came to be known as Cree. These same educational policies also aided in separating the James Bay Cree and the Montagnais, for the Cree have received their schooling in English and the Montagnais, in French.

As a result of modern political and social pressures there exists today, among the Cree, a consciousness of nationality and ethnicity which does not seem to have existed in the past. If it did, it was not perceived by the Englishmen serving in the bay. Unlike the journals for other parts of the Hudson's Bay Company's empire which named linguistic and local groups, the ones detailing activities in the eastern James Bay region almost never named the Indians other than by their association with a trading post, such as "Rupert House Indians" or "Fort George Indians." These designations were always English ones. An exception were the Mistassini Indians who were identified as such in the Jesuit *Relations* of 1642–4 and 1671–2, before the establishment of any European trading posts, and who have maintained this identity to the present. Other local groups were ascribed Indian names by the Jesuits, probably on the basis of their geographical location, but the names were not repeated. In the *Relation* of 1660 an Indian traveller just returned from Hudson Bay reported that there were nine bands of Kilistinons, an early name for Cree, living on or near "the great bay of the North." The most easterly group was the Pitchibourenik who apparently inhabited the area around the Eastmain and Rupert rivers (Thwaites 1896, 45: 229). This group was also identified by Father Charles Albanel when he reached the east coast of James Bay in 1672, though he called them the Pitchiboutounibuek (ibid., 56: 203). In 1679 Louis Jolliet located them along the Eastmain River (Public Archives of Canada [PAC] Map Coll. H2-1102), and in a memoir dated from 1691–9 the Pitchibouronny are mentioned as a nation who dwelled to the east of the bottom of the bay (Archives des Colonies [AC] C11A 125(1): 289). Then the name disappears from the records as the English speak only of "Indians."

Since the various groups of James Bay Indians were known to Hudson's Bay Company officials only with reference to their geographical location and since Cree was not a seventeenth or eighteenth or nineteenth century name for the people, we have chosen to refer to each group as it appears in the historical accounts. It is, however, clear that these people were the ancestors of the James Bay Cree.

It is difficult to gauge just how culturally and linguistically homogeneous the inhabitants of James Bay were about one to two hundred years ago, since the English traders did not dwell on these subjects. We know that when Richmond Fort was opened in 1750, the master there complained that the language spoken by the people living to the north was different from that usually encountered in eastern James Bay, a statement repeated in the Fort George records of 1818 (B.182/a/6: 3; B.77/e/2a: 3; unless otherwise indicated, references are to Hudson's Bay Company records). On the whole, however, it does not seem to have been a problem for the company. Linguists working in James Bay today are in agreement that all Indians of the Quebec-Labrador peninsula speak the same language, Montagnais, which they divide into three major dialects (MacKenzie 1977; Pentland 1978). It is expected that future linguistic studies will be instrumental in determining population movements among the James Bay Cree and in identifying various linguistic groups. As for culture, Preston finds that today there is "a surprisingly uniform culture in spite of the lack of any obvious or explicit unifying cultural structures." He attributes this fact to their "linguistic and geographic-ecological continuity" (1975, 2). It is thought that this assessment also pertains to the past.

At this date a full account of the prehistory of the James Bay people is not possible. Archaeological research in this vast region began very recently and primarily in the northern limits of the territory as salvage archaeological work in the wake of Quebec's giant hydro-electric project. It is known, though, that man could have inhabited the James Bay region only when the Tyrrell Sea had retreated and vegetation and animals had become established. The earliest site located is one on Lake Caniapiscau, far inland, dated at 3485 ± 95BP (before the present). Considering that man would have been in the more southerly regions of James Bay before that, archaeologists suggest that portions of James Bay probably were inhabited a minimum of five thousand years ago (Martijn 1969, 62).

It used to be thought that the eastern subarctic, because of its geographical location, had remained a culturally isolated region throughout prehistoric times. New evidence now necessitates a revision of this assumption. As an example, finds of pottery dating from a number of widely distributed sites, dating back to the Middle Woodland, Late Woodland (Iroquoian), and early historic periods, indicate that regular contact was maintained with more southerly neighbours over the course of many centuries (Martijn, personal communication).

The approximately one hundred sites either tested or fully excavated provide a picture of small mobile hunting groups of several families exploiting a wide range of animal resources but principally beaver and caribou (Laliberté 1981b, 96; 1980, 60). Working inland from the coast at Lake Caniapiscau, Denton also found camp size relatively small, varying between ten to twenty persons (two to four families) and this in an area where big game (caribou) was of considerable importance (1981, 3–4).

Typical of the sites excavated along the La Grande Rivière is one dating from about AD 1000 on the north shore of Lake Kanaaupscow. Laliberté points to the vestiges of the house structure and the small quantity of stone flakes left over from tool-making as indications that the site was inhabited for a short period by perhaps no more than a single nuclear family. He suggests it was an autumn hunting camp when beaver was the principal food source, supplemented by hare, caribou, and bear (1981a, 180).

Camp sites have been discovered which show evidence of larger assemblages of people. One notable site, which is provisionally dated from earlier than one thousand years ago, is located on the left bank of a small tributary of the La Grande Rivière in the LG-3 reservoir zone. Séguin excavated thirty-two concentrations of burnt bone, which she suggests correspond to sites of habitation that would have housed in total some three hundred people. She proposes that this site was a meeting place occupied during several weeks in the summer (1980, 58).

Another camp, larger than the others, is also from this same region. There Mandeville unearthed a longhouse structure measuring 9.5 by 1.7 metres which may have housed thirty individuals (1980, 42). This site has been dated to the beginning of the seventeenth century. A slightly smaller one, also bearing a similar date but from Lake Kanaaupscow, was described by Laliberté as having held some fifteen to twenty people who had used it as a base camp for hunting beaver and other animals (1980, 37–45). The largest single structure uncovered in the entire region under archaeological investigation comes from Lake Caniapiscau where Denton found a 32- by 6-metre longhouse with six aligned hearths (1981, 10). One-third of this longhouse seems to have been preserved for ceremonial purposes. Denton proposes that an exceptional caribou kill made this very large gathering possible during the summer months. It, too, has been dated to the early seventeenth century.

These large gatherings seem to be the exception. On the whole, the archaeological record for northern James Bay indicates that considerably smaller winter hunting groups were the norm. Thus, what the archaeological and historical records show, so far, is a continuity not only in population, but in life-styles as well. There even appears to be a striking similarity between the present, as represented by ethnographers, and the past, as reconstructed from the historical records. The James Bay people of up to one thousand years ago were not specialized hunters. They seem to have exploited to their best advantage the variety of animals and plant life available to them. Accordingly, throughout the long winter period they shifted their camps as the level and type of resources demanded. With the almost exclusive dependence on fish during the summer, a usually reliable food source, greater numbers were able to associate in close proximity and participate in social and cultural events.

Along with other Algonquian-speaking peoples, the James Bay Indians had a religious system of beliefs and practices based on each man establishing his own relationship with a spiritual realm of good and evil forces (Speck 1935; Tanner 1979). Not only human beings but all living things had a spiritual essence and each hunter had to learn to placate the spirits so they would allow the animal to be killed. Consequently hunting practices took on religious significance, as did other aspects of daily life. The religious and supernatural beliefs and practices of the eighteenth and nineteenth centuries mentioned in the archival records include the concept of windigo, the respect for beaver and caribou spirits, the shaking tent ceremony, conjuring to harm and conjuring to cure, prophecies, fear of strange sounds and occurrences, and feasting with ritual practices. Not mentioned but surely ancient practices as well are such observances as the care taken in placing the bones of food animals in the trees or otherwise disposing of them and the songs sung to these animals in anticipation of, or in gratitude for, hunting success (Preston 1975, 219).

Similarly the records provide little information about the material culture of the people. It is one of the arguments of this study, however, that at contact the James Bay Indians did not instantly discard their own technology in favour of the Europeans'. For instance, the arrival of the white traders did not seem to alter Indian modes of transportation. On the contrary, it was the Indians who supplied the Hudson's Bay Company servants with two indispensable pieces of equipment: the birchbark canoe and snowshoes. As well, toboggans and sleds drawn by men or women were used in winter to transport goods and canoes. The design of these vehicles was not uniform throughout the area but reflected regional styles and practical considerations as did the snowshoe.

This brief introduction to the land and the people in eastern James Bay creates a setting in which the Europeans arrived early in the seventeenth century. From that point the historical record begins and, with it, our narrative.

CHAPTER TWO

Strangers Encroach on James Bay

The first recorded meeting between Indian and European in James Bay took place early in 1611. The previous summer Henry Hudson had guided his ship, the *Discovery*, into the bay which eventually would carry his name. In search of an inland passage to the Pacific Ocean, the English explorer and navigator had sailed south along its east coast and down into James Bay before the approach of cold weather had caused him to seek winter harbour near the mouth of the Rupert River. In the spring, while the *Discovery* was still ice-bound, a local Indian visited the ship. A member of Hudson's crew, Abacuk Pricket, left the following version of the encounter:

To this savage our master gave a knife, a looking-glass, and buttons, who received them thankefully, and made signes that after hee had slept hee would come againe, which hee did. When hee came hee brought with him a sled, which hee drew after him, and upon it two deeres skinnes and two beaver skinnes. Hee had a scrip under his arme, out of which hee drew those things which the master had given him. He tooke the knife and laid it upon one of the beaver skinnes, and his glasses and buttons upon the other, and so gave them to the master, who received them; and the savage tooke those things which the master had given him, and put them up into his scrip againe. Then the master shewed him an hatchet, for which hee would have given the master one of his deere skinnes, but our master would have them both, and so hee had, although not willingly. After many signes of people to the north and to the south, and that after so many sleepes he would come againe, he went his way, but never came more. (Asher 1860, 114)

Evidently, from the first encounter the relationship between white and Indian in the bay was an economic one, though certainly not all the local inhabitants were as eager as this lone emissary to greet the sailors. Later in the spring Hudson, hoping to obtain some food, went looking for the local people. He discovered a camp of them but they refused to be approached, setting fire to the grass and shrubbery to keep the Europeans away. Unfortunately, no indications have survived of how the James Bay Indians interpreted these first meetings.

The rest of Hudson's story is both familiar and brief. Shortly after he set off on the return voyage to England, his crew mutinied and he, his son, and seven loyal crew members were set adrift in a small boat. No record exists of them ever being seen again.

Hudson's voyage proved that James Bay did not provide access to the "Western Sea" and so the region was ignored by European navigators for the next half a century. The single exception was Thomas James, another Englishman, who sailed into the bay in 1631. Like Hudson, James passed a winter there, encamped on an island which he named Charles Towne, on the occasion of the birthday of Prince Charles, and which came to be called Charlton Island. He apparently did not meet any of the local inhabitants and returned to England in the spring. James's voyage inspired no imitators, though it did earn him the honour of having the bay named after him.

The next visitors to the James Bay region came by land without, however, reaching the coast itself. In 1663 Indian emissaries from the north had come to Quebec for the second time in two years seeking a missionary (AC C11A 13: 268). This request may well have represented an attempt by these people to ensure French support against the Iroquois, who were making armed sorties into the area at this time. In response three French fur traders from New France, Guillaume Couture, Pierre Duquet, and Jean Langlois, were dispatched. Accompanied by forty-four canoes of Indians, they reached Lake Nemiscau via Lake Mistassini and the Rupert River in July 1663. There they traded with the local people but returned to New France instead of pushing on to James Bay because, in the words of Couture, the Indians "n'ayant jamais vue d'Européens les soupçonnaient et témoignaient avoir de la peine contre eux" (AC C11A 10(1): 2).

As the experience of these earliest European visitors indicates, when white men penetrated into James Bay they found that the Indian people were no strangers to the fur trade. They already possessed some of the standard items of exchange and knew how the trade was carried out. Information gathered later in the seventeenth century suggests that the James Bay people were at the outer edge of a network of trade which for many years had carried goods from the St Lawrence northward to the bay via a number of different Indian groups and, of course, had carried furs in the opposite direction back to the French. Several canoe routes linked James Bay to the south. The first was mentioned by Champlain in 1603. He learned from Indian informants that travellers ascended the Saguenay River as far as Lake St Jean, continued by various routes to Lake Mistassini, then descended the Rupert River to James Bay (Biggar 1922, 1: 124). Once the fur trade was established, this became the most

important route linking the Indians at the bay with the St Lawrence. The
Montagnais played the role of middlemen, and Jesuit accounts identify
Lakes Nemiscau and Nicabau as central trading spots for the northern
Indians and their southeastern neighbours (Thwaites 1896, 46: 275; 56:
183).

In the Jesuit *Relation* of 1657–8 Father Gabriel Druillettes described
five other routes used by different Indian groups to reach the "North
Sea." With the aid of Crouse we can identify those routes on modern
maps (1924, 139–69). Druillettes obtained his information "partly from two
Frenchmen who have made their way inland, and partly from several Savages who are eyewitnesses to the things which I am about to describe"
(Thwaites 1896, 44: 237). The two Frenchmen were probably Radisson and
Des Groseilliers. The first route sketched by Druillettes was a variation on
the Saguenay–Mistassini–Rupert River route already described by Champlain (ibid., 239–41; Crouse 1924, 147). Father Albanel would journey this
way in 1672 when he became the first European to travel overland from
New France to James Bay. The second route also began in the St
Lawrence. It involved ascending to the headwaters of the St Maurice
River from Trois-Rivières, crossing a network of rivers and lakes near
the height of land, and then following the Nottaway River down to the
bay (Thwaites 1896, 44: 241–3; Crouse 1924, 153).

The third route was followed annually by the Nipissing Indians who
arrived in James Bay to trade for furs with goods obtained from the
French via their Huron neighbours (Thwaites 1896, 45: 229). According
to Druillettes, the route taken by these trading parties followed the
Ottawa River and Lake Temiscaming to Abitibi Lake, the outlet of which,
Abitibi River, joins the Moose River just before it enters James Bay
(ibid., 44: 243, 324). After the destruction of the Huron and the dispersal
of the Nipissing, the Ottawa and Ojibwa Indians assumed the role of
middlemen and travelled north to trade at the bay (Heidenreich and Ray
1976, 12).

Druillettes's fourth route linked Lake Huron to James Bay via the
Spanish River, a series of lakes, and the Mattagami River (Thwaites
1896, 44: 243; Crouse 1924, 153). And finally, the Indians living along the
top of Lake Superior travelled north to Lake Nipigon and then through a
series of lakes and rivers to the Albany River, which drains into the west
side of James Bay (Thwaites 1896, 44: 243; Crouse 1924, 154).

The first Europeans to enter James Bay had no impact on this peaceable trading system. Rather, it was the Iroquois who first disrupted the
traditional trading patterns of the northern people. In the latter half of
the seventeenth century the Iroquois carried out a series of armed raids
into the vicinity of eastern James Bay. To understand their motivation it
is necessary first to describe the balance of power which formerly had

existed between Iroquois and Huron. In the first half of the century the Huron were the dominant middlemen in an extensive trade network through which furs gathered from the north, east, and west were funnelled by way of the Ottawa–St Lawrence River system to Quebec. The James Bay people had trade relations with the Huron via the Nipissing Indians, but most of their furs seem to have reached New France by way of the Saguenay route described earlier. To the south, across Lake Ontario in what is now New York State, the Iroquois were the middlemen in another competitive fur-trade network, one that supplied the Dutch via the Hudson River. It has been a matter of debate among scholars to what degree war between the Huron and the Iroquois can be explained by their respective involvements in the fur trade. The purely economic argument was formulated by George Hunt (1940) and more recently has been accepted by Robert Goldstein (1969). According to Hunt, by the 1640s the Iroquois' supply of furs was drying up and so to maintain their pivotal role in the Dutch trade they had to tap new sources of supply by absorbing the Huron trade empire (1940, 70). Subsequent military activity against other Indian peoples was intended to secure their position as the pre-eminent fur-trading tribe in eastern Canada (ibid., 99). Opposed to this unicausal explanation of Iroquois warfare is the multicausal explanation offered by Raoull Naroll, among others, who has disputed the degree to which Iroquois fur production was falling off and has suggested that "blood revenge" and a desire for prestige, both traditional causes of conflict among woodland peoples, were as significant as the need to enhance their position in the fur trade (1969, 58, 62). More recently Bruce Trigger has argued that the Iroquois raided neighbouring peoples to obtain European trade goods and later to obtain furs (1976, 2: 627).

In May 1649 a party of about one thousand Iroquois invaded Huronia, destroyed two villages, and drove the remaining inhabitants into exile. The Huron were now dispersed, their hold on the fur trade broken. Between 1650 and 1652 Iroquois warriors raided the country of the Attikamegue Indians between the Ottawa and St Maurice rivers, and the Algonquins of the Ottawa Valley retreated into the north country. After a brief period of peace between the French and the Iroquois in the mid-1650s, a respite which allowed the Iroquois to destroy the Erie Indians on their western flank, Mohawk raiders were back north of the St Lawrence. In 1657–8 they penetrated at least into the territory between Lake Abitibi and Lake St Jean, and by 1660 the James Bay country had become a refuge "where various Algonquin Nations sought a retreat, fleeing from the Iroquois" (Thwaites 1896, 45: 219).

As previously noted, the Jesuit Fathers of New France had been made aware of Hudson Bay by Indian informants and they knew that "upon this bay are found, at certain seasons of the year, many surrounding

Nations embraced under the general name of Kilistinons" (ibid., 46: 249). French sources indicate that in 1661 "des sauvages du fond de la Baye du Nort estans venus exprès à Québec pour chercher un missionnaire," and in response Fathers Druillettes and Claude Dablon left Quebec City to attempt to reach the northern "sea" by land (AC C11A 9: 295). Arriving at Lake Necouba (the modern Lake Nicabau), the priests found the Indian inhabitants harassed and terrified by Iroquois raids. A tribe of Indians called the Squirrel Nation had recently been decimated by an attack "so terrifying all the surrounding tribes that they have all dispersed in quest of other and more remote mountains" (Thwaites 1896, 46: 289). Dablon and Druillettes decided that in such a dangerous situation their mission was fruitless and they turned back to Quebec. "The panic is said to have spread even to the Sea-coast whither we were going," the priests reported, "and whither these barbarians fully intend this year to extend their cruelty, in order to push their conquests as far toward the North as they have done, of late years, toward the South" (ibid., 289–91).

That winter, 1661–2, a party of Iroquois captured a number of Indians engaged in funeral rites at Lake Nicabau. One of the captives escaped and brought word to the French that the invaders intended moving on to the "North Sea" and that "all the lands of the North, which had never before seen any Iroquois, have become so infested with them that there is no cavern in those vast regions of rocks dark enough to serve as a place of concealment, or any forest deep enough to be entrusted with one's life" (ibid., 47: 151–3).

Whether or not the Iroquois actually reached James Bay that summer, they had probably done so by 1665. In that year a party of about thirty, both Mohawk and Onondaga, destroyed or captured almost three times their number in an engagement at Lake Nemiscau (ibid., 50: 37ff). Father Albanel reported that seven years later he discovered at the lake "the remains of a large fort constructed of stout trees by the Iroquois, whence he guarded all the approaches and made frequent murderous sallies ... this caused the entire abandonment of the place, its original inhabitants departing thence" (ibid., 56: 183).

When Albanel reached James Bay in the summer of 1672, he encountered a group of Indian people he described as the "people of the sea" living between the Rupert and Eastmain rivers (ibid., 187–9). Since 1667 peace had existed between the French and the Iroquois, and Albanel told the Indians that "the Iroquois has ceased to disturb you" because of French influence (ibid., 193). In fact, however, the Iroquois do not appear to have withdrawn from the north. Peace lasted in New France until the next decade, yet in the spring of 1674 Father Crespieul, travelling in the Lake Mistassini region, wrote that the Iroquois were in the vicinity and "fear reigned everywhere" (ibid., 59: 39). Luckily for the Mistassini Indians this particular raiding party headed off in another direction, perhaps to James Bay where the previous winter a party of "Nodwayes" had slaughtered some Moose River Indians (Oldmixon 1931, 385). Apparently the northern sorties were unaffected by French diplomacy.

Early maps and local tradition indicate that the Iroquois invaded James Bay mainly down what is now the Nottaway River. The first map to show this river, the 1699 Franquelin map, identifies it as "the River of the Iroquois," and F.W. Hodge in his *Handbook of Indians of Canada* says that the word "Nottaway," or "Nadowa," was a term of hatred used by various Algonquian tribes to describe their enemies (1913, 325). Heidenreich confirms that the term, or its earlier variant "Nadouessiou," was applied by Algonquian speakers originally to the Sioux and later to the Iroquois (1976, personal communication). J.M. Cooper, in his article on the northeastern Indian hunters, writes:

The memory of their [Iroquois] raids around the southern end of James Bay is still vividly preserved in native tradition, and Edward Namē'kus, one of my most reliable and intelligent older native informants at Rupert House told me in 1932 that his grandfather had told him that the Nottaway River got its name from the fact that the Iroquois, nātawē'wuts, used to come down this river on their raids. (1946, 275)

Iroquois warriors travelled to the north in small groups, sometimes as few as thirty in a party. At first they came in the summer and returned south for the winter, but Albanel's account suggests that later they built small fortifications and remained in the area year round. One might speculate they were there to trap furs. The local oral tradition identifies a number of spots in the vicinity of Rupert House where battles are believed to have been fought. For example, one story tells of two brothers who succeeded in killing a large party of Iroquois invaders. The place where the dead bodies were piled is now known by the Rupert House people as *nottowao kan kaashtekaw* – "where the Nottaway Indian bones lie." Similarly, there is a rapid on the Nottaway River named from a story in which a lone woman is said to have tricked a party of Iroquois into canoeing over a high falls. And according to local tradition, the last battle between the Iroquois and the James Bay people occurred at a spot along the coast to the south of Rupert House where a party of Iroquois, attempting to surprise a group of local Indians playing ball, were discovered, attacked, and defeated (Cree Way Project 1975).

While scattered reports of Mohawk incursions can be cited well into the eighteenth century, they were different in kind and purpose from the early raids. Later raids were carried out by Mohawk from Caughnawaga acting as allies of the French. Their targets were the English trading posts on the bay and not the James Bay Indians. The earlier period of prolonged raiding ended in the 1680s. If Hunt's thesis is accurate, the Iroquois carried out sorties into the north as part of a master plan to establish themselves as the dominant middlemen in the French fur-trade system. Yet if this was the case, it seems unlikely that they would disperse and kill the very people who would be the chief suppliers of furs. More probably the raids were independently organized attacks by young Iroquois motivated by a desire for plunder and prestige. As such, they were of little importance to the Iroquois' military and economic position to the south and largely ended in the 1680s when war with the French resumed.

Ultimately, of course, the violent incursions of the Iroquois had much less of an impact on life in eastern James Bay than the visits of those other "invaders," the white man. By the second half of the seventeenth century enough knowledge had been accumulated from Indian informants and early explorers to allow traders to establish themselves in the bay. It was Radisson and Des Groseilliers who first conceived the notion of exploiting the northern fur areas by sending ships into Hudson Bay. We need not be concerned here with the much-debated question of whether the two adventurers actually reached James Bay, as they claimed (Adams 1961, 146). What is important is that they recognized the potential of a northern sea route. First in Quebec, then in France, they attempted to obtain financial backing for a voyage to the bay. Finally a group of merchants in England agreed to finance the project and in the summer of 1668 two ships, the *Eaglet* and the *Nonsuch*, set sail for Hudson Bay. The *Eaglet*, with Radisson aboard, was forced to turn back but the *Nonsuch*, captained by Zachariah Gillam and guided by Des Groseilliers, reached James Bay in September. The newcomers were conducted by some local Indians to the mouth of a river which was immediately christened the Rupert after the king's cousin, Prince Rupert, subsequently the first governor of the Hudson's Bay Company. Charles Fort (the forerunner of Rupert House) was constructed on the left bank of the river near its mouth, and the ship's crew settled in for the winter (Rich 1958, 62). The arrival of the first ship was still part of the oral tradition of the people some one hundred years later (Isham 1949, 315).

This visit by a ship from Europe was different from the earlier ones. Now the white man came, not in search of a passage to China, but rather intent on establishing trading settlements, claiming ownership of the land, and bartering for furs. The James Bay Indians accepted the newcomers, not because they were naive or helpless, but because the Europeans brought rare and useful items to trade for the most common of New World commodities, furs.

CHAPTER THREE

Competition for
Indian Furs, 1668–1693

The James Bay people needed no convincing to bring their furs to the new English fort at the mouth of the Rupert River. In the spring of 1669 three hundred men, women, and children arrived and the furs they brought were carried back to London in the *Nonsuch* that summer (Rich 1958, 62). The success of this first voyage proved the profitability of exploiting the fur resources of the north via Hudson Bay, and in May 1670 the English king granted to a group of English merchants and aristocrats calling itself the Hudson's Bay Company exclusive trading rights in the approximately 3 million square miles of North America draining into the great bay.

Knowing that Quebec fur traders were active in the hinterland behind James Bay, the fledgling Hudson's Bay Company attempted to ensure its control of the area by making treaties with the local people. The following instructions to the bayside governor date from 1680:

In the severall places where you are or shall settle, you contrive to make compact wth. The Captns. or chiefs of the respective Rivers & places, whereby it might be understood by them that you had purchased both the lands & rivers of them, and that they had transferred the absolute propriety to you, or at least the only free-dome of trade, And that you should cause them to do some act wch. by the Religion or Custome of their Country should be thought most sacred & obliging to them for the confirmation of such Agreements. (Rich 1948, 9)

There is no concrete evidence that such a "compact" was made at Charles Fort but it seems likely.

The Indians undoubtedly interpreted these pacts as expressions of mutual goodwill and as political and military alliances, which in part they were, but the company chose to interpret them also as business agreements by which the Indians surrendered their ownership of the land. These agreements were, however, meaningless because they were one-sided. The James Bay people could not sell or otherwise dispose of the land because they had no equivalent concept of ownership which allowed them to conceive of doing so. It is questionable whether Hudson's Bay Company officials themselves ever took these agreements seriously, since in the next century when France invoked similar "sales" in defence of territorial claims in North America, the company refused to recognize them (Rich 1958, 63). At any rate, a more effective way to claim the land was to occupy it and this the company eventually did.

In the fall of 1670 the first Hudson's Bay Company servants arrived at Charles Fort aboard the *Prince Rupert*. Among them was Thomas Gorst, whose journal contains an account of the post's construction. By mid-October the crew had built two dwelling houses. "Our English houses consisted of three roomes a peece & as many severall floors," wrote Gorst.

The Cellar held ye beer wee brewd there for our dayly drinking, together with the Beefe Pork and Butter. The Chamber held our dry Provisions as bread, flower, peas & Oatmeale and on the ground floore was our kitchin, Dyining roome & Lodgings – which were Standing Cabbins such as are used in his Maties shipps. The houses themselves are built of Timber cut into Sparrs set quite close to one another & calked with Mosse instead of Okam to keep out ye wind & ye weather. Thatched with a ranke sort of grasse growing in ye marshes much like ye Saggs wch are every where in our English brookes. Wee had a large Chimney built of bricks which wee carryed along with us, & wee spared not ye wood, that Country affording enough to keep alwayes Summer within, while nothing but Ice & snow are without doores. Wee had also erected a good Oven & feasted our selves at pleasure with Venson pasty. (Nute 1943, 288)

On 12 October a second ship, the *Wivenhoe*, arrived at the river after having visited the mouth of the Nelson River. The season being too far advanced to allow construction of another wooden house, the ship's crew "set up their Wigwam covered in stead of skins with old sailes" (ibid.). The winter passed uneventfully, the newcomers relying on the local Indians for supplies of venison, partridge, and rabbit. An Indian named Damaris was the first native to greet the Englishmen in the fall and during the winter Indians were frequent visitors at Charles Fort. In the spring of 1671 a small party travelled to the mouth of the Moose River where more furs were traded before the two company ships sailed for England.

Hudson's Bay Company servants were back in residence at Charles Fort in the autumn of 1672 and from that date the post was occupied year round. A man named Cuscudidah, apparently the leading Indian in the area at this time, informed the white traders that most of the Indians living inland were taking their furs to the French (Oldmixon 1931, 388). However, according to Oldmixon, in the spring a party of "about 50 Men,

Women and Children came in 22 Canoes to trade." These Indians were called Pishhapocanoes and came from the north (ibid., 390). The east coast people did not bring in nearly as many furs as did the Indians encountered at the mouth of the Moose River; therefore, in the summer of 1673 an outpost, to be called Moose Fort, was built on Hayes Island at the mouth of that river (Rich 1948, 358). In the summer of 1674 Charles Bayly, the first overseas governor for the company, went on a trading expedition up the west coast to the Shechittawan, now Albany River, and in 1679 another fort, later named Albany Fort, was built there, near the lower end of Bayly Island on the north side of the main channel (ibid., 345). Thus, by the end of its first decade, the Hudson's Bay Company had ringed the bottom of James Bay with a trio of fur-trade posts situated at the mouths of three major rivers.

For almost the first century of the company's existence its employees did not, because they could not, penetrate up the rivers from the bay into the fur-rich hinterland. They did not have the skill to manoeuvre canoes through the turbulent lacework of rivers and lakes which formed the highways of the new world. They did not have the knowledge to hunt and trap their fur-bearing prey, or even the caribou, hare, and geese which were the staples of the wilderness diet. And they were not accustomed to enduring long, physically punishing voyages in an extreme climate in pursuit of furs and food. All these abilities the Indians possessed; consequently they were necessary partners in the fur-trade enterprise.

The James Bay people played their role willingly because they desired the trade goods which the company bartered for their furs. Early records show that they were not naive traders, willing to accept beads and trinkets for valuable pelts. On the contrary, they had had experience trading with other Indian groups and were familiar with the variety of goods offered by the Europeans. They had supplemented their traditional weapons and utensils with guns, knives, hatchets, and kettles, and the establishment of permanent trading posts in their territory meant a reliable supply of these items. The Indians did trade, of course, for brandy and tobacco and decorative items such as beads, lace, combs, and mirrors, but these were luxuries, acquired only after their stock of ammunition and metal goods had been replenished (Oldmixon 1931, 380; Rich 1958, 70).

At this point in the history of the fur trade the relationship between Indian and white man was one of mutual dependency. Hudson's Bay Company servants relied on the Indians for food and furs, while the Indians relied on a supply of guns, ammunition, and the metal implements which enabled them to more efficiently harvest their wilderness environment. Given this state of interdependency, relations between the James Bay people and the company's servants were peaceful if not actually friendly. Instructions to the bayside posts from London reiterated the need for honesty in dealing with the local people, and if these instructions had not been carried out, it is doubtful whether the Indians would have supplied the fur traders with provisions as willingly as they had (Rich 1948). Perhaps an indication of the extent to which the Indians trusted the white man was the fact that in 1675 two of them agreed to spend a winter in London. One man did not survive the sea voyage but the other, Attash, returned to his people the next spring. For their part the postmasters seem to have been mistrustful of the Indians, who would later complain that the English were frightened of them and rebuffed them (AC C11A 8: 156). Such uneasiness is understandable. These Europeans were strangers in an alien land, dependent for survival on the goodwill of an unknown local population and unreliable sea links with Britain. If the Indians became hostile, the approximately sixty Englishmen at the three posts were hopelessly outnumbered. If the Indians became indifferent, if they deserted the posts, then the Englishmen were incapable of surviving on their own. Furthermore, in an attempt to make private trade impossible, company servants were forbidden to communicate with the local people, a regulation which must have struck the Indians as unusual and unfriendly.

If the company's policy was to keep the James Bay people at arm's length, postmasters were at the same time anxious to conciliate them. The company was in the initial stages of establishing what it hoped would become a permanent trading operation. To accomplish this aim the cooperation of the Indian hunters was essential. Furthermore, as French traders became numerous inland from James Bay, the Indians were given an alternate source of trade goods, and so the terms of trade could not be forced on them but instead became negotiable, within limits. The result was that the Hudson's Bay Company appears to have been responsive to Indian requests for certain types of goods and somewhat flexible in fixing their prices (Rich 1948, 8). European and Indian had certainly not reached across the barriers of culture to embrace as brothers, but they had established a peaceable, businesslike relationship.

As we have seen, when they arrived in James Bay, Hudson's Bay Company servants learned that the Indians there customarily traded their furs with the French, either by travelling to Canada or by dealing through Indian middlemen. In the summer of 1671 seventeen Indian "nations," some of which were believed to inhabit the coast of Hudson Bay, met at Sault Ste Marie and according to French sources voluntarily placed themselves under the sovereignty of the French king (AC C11A 13: 269). This agreement was probably motivated by a common fear of the Iroquois but it could well have allied the Indians and the French economically as well as militarily. By this period French traders from Tadoussac had penetrated up the Saguenay and established two posts, one at Lake St Jean (Thwaites 1896, 60: 322) and the other at Chicoutimi (AC C11A 7:

281). A single reference in the records of France suggests that a fort had been built on the Nemiscau (Rupert) River in 1661 as a result of the Indians' representations to the French for protection (AC C11A 13: 268). However, Albanel in his journey a decade later does not mention such a fort. After Father Albanel's overland voyage of 1672, a post was erected at Lake Mistassini as well (L. Jolliet map of 1679 in PAC Map Coll. H2-1101). By the spring of 1674 so many Indians were being intercepted up the Rupert River that Hudson's Bay Company officers considered moving their bayside headquarters from Charles Fort to the new post at Moose River, a move which was eventually made later in the decade. Essentially, however, the trading activity of the French was small scale and uncoordinated. It was in the next decade that a group of merchants from New France launched the first organized challenge to the Hudson's Bay Company in the north.

In 1679 the famed explorer Louis Jolliet made an overland voyage to James Bay. He was supported by a small group of Montreal-based merchants who had been squeezed out of the Great Lakes–Mississippi Valley trade and were interested in investigating the extent of the Hudson's Bay Company's activities in the north. Jolliet returned to New France with alarming reports as to the future of any French participation in the northern trade if the English were not evicted from the bay. "Il n'y a point de doute si on les laisse dans cette Baye qu'ils se rendent Maistres de tout le commerce du Canada devant dix ans," he warned (Delanglez 1944, 249). In 1682 the merchant group, led by Charles Aubert de La Chesnaye, formed the Compagnie du Nord and in 1685 received a charter from the king of France enabling it to trade into Hudson Bay (AC C11A 16: 184 and AC C11A 7: 309).

The new company's first step was to establish a post at Lake Nemiscau, commanded by Zacharie Jolliet. However, the advantage which the Hudson's Bay Company enjoyed in the northern trade was based on its ability to transport heavy trade items into the centre of the trading area relatively cheaply by sea. To counter this, the Compagnie du Nord required a coastal post, and so in 1682 the merchants sent Radisson and Des Groseilliers, now back in the French camp, to establish a post near the mouth of the Nelson River. For the next three years the Compagnie du Nord and the Hudson's Bay Company both maintained posts at this spot but eventually the French were forced to withdraw (Rich 1948, 367; AC C11A 125(1): 141).

Despite this setback, the Compagnie du Nord still desired a seaside post in the north. Therefore in 1686 it launched an audacious overland invasion of James Bay. Led by the Chevalier de Troyes, a force of 105 men with thirty-five canoes left Montreal late in March. The commander kept a daily record of his expedition (see Caron 1918; Frégault 1944).

A redrawn portion of the Jolliet map of 1679 showing the explorer's route to James Bay

Source: PAC Ph 900 1679

Baye de Hudson

Rivière des Assiniboüels

Rivière des Quiristinons

Rivière Penachtchéouen

Rivière Kechichéouen

anglois

anglois

Lac alimibegong
passage de tous
les Sauvages

R. des Monsoni

R. des Outabittibi

Nipissing

Amikoué

Michilimakinac

Lac Superieur

Sault
ste Marie

Missisagué

Lac Huron

Timiskaming
Mataoüan

chemin des outaoüacs

Lac

Lac

R. des Pachibourouniou

R. de Nemisco

anglois

Nemisco

an-
glois

R. Necouba

Montroyal

Lac Timagaming
ou l'ay basti
une maison

Lac
fran-
cois.

R. Katigaousisi.

Lac
St Jean

R. Periboca

Quebec

Chicoutimi

Tadoussac

Fleuve Saint Laurent

Sept isles

anticosti

gaspé
Isle Percée

Following winter as it retreated northward, the men, most of whom were French-Canadian voyageurs and not regular soldiers, paddled up the Ottawa River, across Lake Temiscaming, and down to Abitibi Lake where a fort was erected during the first week of June. From there the small army of canoes descended the Abitibi and Moose rivers, arriving in the vicinity of the Hudson's Bay Company post at the mouth of the Moose at daybreak, 21 June. De Troyes had encountered some of the local Indians but as they were alienated from Henry Sergeant, the postmaster at the company's Albany River post, who, they said, beat them, they did not raise an alarm. The previous summer Zacharie Jolliet had written from Lake Nemiscau advising his counterpart at Charles Fort of an impending attack from Quebec and recommending that he "retire with all your People as soon as you Can," but for some reason the warning had been ignored (Rich 1948, 312). The French were able to enter the back door of the bay and preserve the most crucial element of their attack – surprise (Caron 1918, 42–68).

It took de Troyes just over a month to capture all three English posts at the bottom of the bay. Moose Fort fell first. Occupied by seventeen men, the fort was a square structure of palisades eighteen feet high, flanked by bastions of earth and stone topped by five cannon. Such was the English lack of preparedness at the time of the attack that there were no sentinels on duty and the cannon were not loaded. The French occupied the post with relative ease and then moved eastward along the coast by canoe and longboat towards Charles Fort (ibid., 63–73). This fort was almost identical with the one at Moose River – a square palisaded structure flanked by four bastions. Inside the walls, slightly off centre, was a three-storey log redoubt, or internal fortress, also flanked by bastions about the height of a man (ibid., 74). Once again the French experienced little difficulty in occupying the post. By the end of July they had crossed the bay and captured Albany Fort after a short bombardment, as well as destroying the warehouse at Charlton Island which had served the Hudson's Bay Company as a central supply depot. De Troyes and his backers, the Compagnie du Nord, had actually hoped to capture Port Nelson (York Fort), the Hudson's Bay Company post at the mouth of the Nelson River, but this objective was now recognized to be impossible for a land expedition. The commander returned to New France, leaving Pierre Le Moyne d'Iberville in command of forty men and the three conquered forts, renamed Fort Sainte-Anne (Albany), Fort Saint-Louis (Moose), and Fort Saint-Jacques (Charles) (ibid., 83–98).

The James Bay people had been bystanders during these three small battles. The group de Troyes had encountered on the Moose River had wanted to join the French invaders – de Troyes did not trust them and refused their assistance – but their enthusiasm had more to do with a specific grievance against the Hudson's Bay Company than any sympathy for the Compagnie du Nord or the French king (ibid., 62). It is open to speculation where the Indians might have stood in the conflict. They had been trading with both the French and the English for the past few years, and what little evidence has survived indicates that, prices being equal, they preferred the French because the latter's familiarity with the Indian habitat made them more confident and approachable (AC C11A 8: 156). Nevertheless, Indian allegiance was probably to the trader who gave them the best price for their furs. Individual Indians may have developed preferences because of experiences they had had with a French or an English trader, but there is no evidence that as a body the local population supported one side of the conflict or the other. Of course, events happened so quickly that there was very little time for the Indians to choose sides. If the James Bay posts had been on guard and a more prolonged engagement had occurred, then perhaps the role of the local population would have been crucial and their preferences more obvious.

De Troyes's success in James Bay was not unqualified. The Compagnie du Nord had still not accomplished its aim of evicting the Hudson's Bay Company entirely from Hudson Bay, since the company continued to occupy the post at Port Nelson. This post tapped the fur supply of an enormous northwestern hinterland and its bountiful trade made the loss of the three James Bay posts less of a financial blow to the company. Furthermore, de Troyes's victories irritated the French traders at Tadoussac, who found that the people living inland from the east coast of James Bay began to take their furs down to the newly conquered posts there. The traders complained that the Indians no longer came down to the posts at Chicoutimi or Tadoussac now that the French were in the bay (AC C11A 10: 158).

It was Iberville's ambition to capture Port Nelson and during the early 1690s he busied himself making plans. Before he could attack the English, however, the English attacked him. In 1692 the Hudson's Bay Company dispatched an expedition under the command of James Knight to retake Albany Fort, by then the most prosperous of the three James Bay posts. Arriving in the bay too late in the season to launch an assault, Knight and his men wintered at Gilpin's, or Old Factory, Island on the east coast and the next summer, in July, easily occupied the undermanned fort at Albany. Later that summer a ship arrived from New France bringing supplies to the James Bay posts. It was attacked by the English and driven from the bay but not before its crew had landed and destroyed by fire the posts at the Moose and Rupert rivers (Rich 1958, 304).

Albany Fort now stood alone as the sole trading post in James Bay. The next year, 1694, Iberville realized his ambition of conquering Port Nelson (renamed Fort Bourbon), and Albany was left the only Hudson's

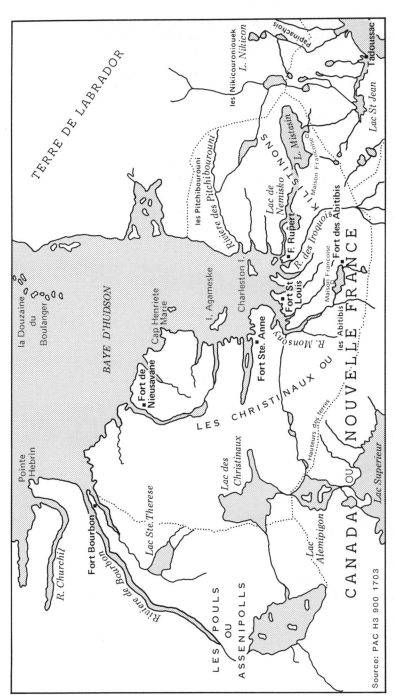

A redrawn portion of the Del'Isle map of 1703 showing the location of French posts on James Bay and Hudson Bay

Source: PAC H3 900 1703

Bay Company post in the whole of Hudson Bay. Interestingly enough, the French soon changed their mind about the relative importance of Fort Bourbon vis-à-vis James Bay, deciding the latter had the advantage of easier communications with New France (AC C11A 16: 187). However, the French continued to occupy Fort Bourbon and the English remained at Albany Fort until 1713 when according to the terms of the Treaty of Utrecht the French recognized the Hudson's Bay Company's claim to all of the bay and abandoned the Nelson River.

The reversion of Albany Fort to English control in 1693 marked the last time James Bay served as a battleground for European powers. For the next century competition in the area between rival countries and trading companies would be constant but, while sometimes violent, that competition would be commercial, not military.

CHAPTER FOUR

Trading on the East Main, 1693–1735

With the destruction in 1693 of Charles Fort, or Fort Saint-Jacques as the French called it, eastern James Bay was again deserted of European fur traders. Though French coureurs de bois still traded actively out of posts on Lakes Mistassini and Abitibi, there were no longer any posts on the eastern shore of the bay itself. This situation, however, was not allowed to continue for long – the eastern woodlands were too valuable a source for furs – and by the final years of the century Hudson's Bay Company servants were being dispatched from Albany Fort to winter on the shores of the east main, as the eastern James Bay region was called in those days.

The speed with which a regular east coast trade was established reflected the changing requirements of the European fur market. While twenty years before, parchment beaver from North America had been oversupplied and the softer, coat beaver was in demand, now the pendulum of the marketplace had swung back. In 1697 James Knight, the superintendent of the company's trade in James Bay, received the following instruction from his London superiors: "Wee proceed in Matters Relateing to our Trade & Begin wth that which is our greatest grievance Viz. the quantity of Coate Beavr. the Indians bring to the Factory, Wee have about 70 thousand of them upon our hands & can not sell them soe that wee referr it to yr. Principall Care to Suppress by all wayes Imaginable the Indians from Cloging Us therewith" (A.6/3: 29d). Actually the attempt to discourage the collection of coat beaver had begun as early as 1689 (Rich 1957, 61) and continued well into the next century. Besides simple persuasion, one of the "wayes Imaginable" that hunters were encouraged to bring the more marketable skins was to offer them specially imported European clothing and sheep skins (A.6/3: 29d). If coat beaver skins, which were worn before they were traded, could be replaced by other kinds of clothing, fewer of them would be produced.

TABLE 1

Content of the East Main Trade for Selected Years, 1700–1739

	1701	1707	1712	1717	1722	1725	1731	1736	1739
Beaver:									
parchment	1173½	1729	872	1973	1442½	1486½	2209½	1040	890
coat	1065	430	497	183	185	–	190	25	87
Cats (lynx)	8	20	9	71	116	23	196	360	186
Fox:									
grey	10	6	10	12	21	9	13	–	10
red	–	–	–	–	–	–	–	–	53
Marten	550	864	1600	1605	1150	2170	2214	800	2256
Otter	38	69	27	43	32	32	72	18½	77
Wolverine	–	1	9	6	4	9	8	9	15
Bear	–	–	16	10	15	15	31	31	12

Source: B.3/d/12–47.

Since, predictably, the Indians were not interested in the latest fashions from London, the company resorted to a more direct means of influencing them, which was to refuse to accept the unwanted beaver. In fact, London officials allowed company servants to burn the skins publicly as an indication of their worthlessness (A.6/3: 43d).

At the end of the seventeenth century, however, the company was faced with a greater problem than the oversupply of coat beaver and that was the oversupply of all types of beaver pelts and the gradual decline in the price of the commodity. London officials complained that "since we have Imported great quantitys of Beavr. it is become a drugg & sells at a very low rate." Their answer was to exploit alternate resources and most importantly "to Improve the small Furr trade nothing being more vendable than small Furrs" (Rich 1957, 232). "Small furrs" was the term applied to the pelts of a variety of fur-bearing animals other than beaver, animals such as otter, muskrat, lynx, fox, and especially marten. These animals were plentiful on the east coast of James Bay, and it was primarily to obtain their skins that company servants returned to the east main in the last years of the seventeenth century. Table 1 indicates that by 1712 the number of small furs, taken together, equalled the number of beaver pelts in the east coast trade and that by the early 1720s the number of small furs consistently exceeded the number of beaver. Not until the 1820s, however, did the actual value of small furs exceed that of beaver and even then the situation was temporary.

Company servants who were sent to winter on the east coast sailed to the mouth of the Eastmain, or Slude, River in September, hoping to be in time to meet with the Indians before they left for their winter territories inland. If the season was not too far advanced, the hunters were issued ammunition and encouraged to shoot geese for the company in the coastal marshes. Early in the century there were not more than half a dozen Englishmen in the Eastmain complement but by the 1730s the number had increased to eight. These men were all sailors or labourers and were commanded by the sloopmaster. One of these early traders was the famed explorer Henry Kelsey, who wintered on the east coast in 1701–3, and 1707–9.

For a brief period a miner was in residence at the post. Gotlob Augustus Lichtenberger was sent out to the bay in 1701 "to make Inspection into the Menerialls on the East Maine," especially mica deposits at the mouth of the modern Old Factory River (A.6/3: 48d). As early as the 1680s company officials in London had recommended the establishment of an outpost at this spot, but it is not clear from the records whether this advice was ever acted on (Rich 1948, 121–2). In any case, Lichtenberger does not appear to have made any useful discoveries and was not replaced after his death in 1712.

In the spring when the geese returned to the shores of James Bay, the local people came in to hunt and also to fish. Quantities of fish and geese, fresh and salted, were taken back to Albany each year and were another reason the eastern outpost was maintained. After the departure of the geese in June the trading establishment was closed for the summer, and the Hudson's Bay Company men sailed back to Albany to deliver the winter's furs and pick up more trade goods. Invariably the east main trade followed this annual pattern, though early on there were years when, because of lack of men or because the sloop was needed elsewhere, no company servants wintered on the east coast.

Before 1719 there does not appear to have been a building on the east coast. The men probably lived below deck on the sloop, either in the river or at a winter mooring spot on Gilpin's Island, thirty miles to the north. In 1719 some kind of habitation was constructed near the mouth of the "fishing creek" (now Fishing River or Rivière la Pêche) on the north shore of the Eastmain River (Hearne map in Rich 1954). Three years later, Joseph Myatt, chief at Albany Fort, warned his London superiors 'that it is Unanimously agreed by the Natives that an Enemy will Attempt to take your Factory at Slude River sooner or later" (A.11/2: 43d). The enemy in question was of course the French and their Indian allies to the south, who were regularly rumoured to be preparing assaults on James Bay. With the memory of de Troyes fresh in their minds, company officials agreed to the strengthening of the post, Eastmain House, during the winter of 1723–4, though another half a century passed before the post was occupied year round.

French traders from Canada were active in the hinterland behind James Bay throughout this period. At Lake Abitibi a post had been erected by de Troyes on his way to James Bay in 1686 and was supplied from a larger post on Lake Temiscaming. Further east there were alternately posts on Lakes Nicabau and Chamouchouane just over the height of land northwest of Lake St Jean (Normandin 1732, 115, 131, in Collection Margry). Further east again, a post on Lake Mistassini had been in operation off and on since the 1670s and on Lake Nemiscau the Compagnie du Nord erected a second post in 1695, which closed when the company dissolved in 1700 (AC C11A 16: 191). From these posts, and others which existed for brief periods, the "woodrunners" opposed the Hudson's Bay Company by intercepting the Indians as they carried their furs down to the bay.

The activities of the French were a constant aggravation to the company's men. In May 1706 two Indians from the Moose River area told Anthony Beale, governor at Albany, that "the French together with a great many Indians are coming downe to burn our Factory and Cutt our Throts and to this end they have wintered in a Lake up Rupuss River," but later that month another Indian reported that "the french & Indians that where comming against our Factory are hindered by those Indians that lies betweene them and us who will not Suffer them to pass through their Countrey notwithstanding they have offered them presents to that end" (B.3/a/1: 43d, 50d). The next spring the rumour was repeated (B.3/a/2: 30ff) and in the summer of 1709 an attack actually took place. A force of seventy French Canadians supported by thirty Mohawk from Quebec descended the Moose River and assaulted Albany Fort, at that time commanded by John Fullartine (A.6/3: 100d–1). Unfortunately for the French, the post had been alerted by a local hunter and its occupants were prepared. The attackers were repulsed, leaving sixteen of the Indians dead along with two Hudson's Bay Company servants (A.6/7: 35). This incident was the final armed attack by the French on a company post in the bay, though rumours of further attacks persisted for two decades.

After the signing of the Treaty of Utrecht in 1713 the English and French governments attempted to negotiate a boundary between Canada and what would be considered Hudson's Bay Company territory. Taking the company's side, the English government hoped for a boundary approximately following the height of land between the bay and the St Lawrence River. The French, on the other hand, wanted to confine the company to a narrow strip of land bordering Hudson Bay, reckoning that control of the headwaters of the rivers draining north meant control of the trade. Neither side would capitulate and negotiations broke down (Rich 1958, 485). The dispute would be settled by open competition, not diplomacy.

French activities inland from the bay increased. In 1716 Thomas McCliesh of Albany reported that a French post had been established "not above seven days paddling" up the Albany River (Davies 1965, 55).

A decade later Joseph Myatt at Albany complained, "I have reason to Believe this part of the Contry was never So Pestered with the wood Runners as at this time" (A.11/2: 58). The east main did not escape the opposition of the French. When Myatt had wintered there as sloopmaster in the early twenties, most of his trade had come from Indians living to the southeast, but by 1727 he unhappily reported, "All those southward Indians have left that place and gone to the French" (Davies 1965, 124). To staunch this flow of trade to the opposition Moose Fort was re-established in 1730, as will be discussed later. As far as the east main fur returns were concerned, however, the new post seems to have had little effect, since nine years later Richard Staunton wrote from Moose that "as for the southward Indians or Rupert Indians, if they do not go to Slude River they must certainly go to the French for there is but few comes here at present" (ibid., 303). Many of these "Rupert Indians" may have been patronizing the "two small factories of about three Frenchmen each" which William Bevan, master at Moose Fort, had heard lay about four days' paddle to the southeast of Moose (ibid., 183). One of these may have been the post at Lake Chamouchouane, described by Joseph Laurent Normandin, who in 1732 was sent from New France to survey the territory towards the height of land:

Cet établissement consiste en ce qui suit. Une maison scituée à 1 arpent ½ environ du bord du lac, batie de pieux de bout et couverte d'écorce d'épinettes, planchée de pieux doubles en haut.

Le plancher d'en bas de planches de boulots. Une chambre d'onze pieds de long sur 11 pieds de large et 6 pieds de hauteur.

Au dessus de cette chambre est un petit grenier qui a 3 pieds de haut, il est fait en chouron [sic] et couvert d'écorce d'épinettes.

Dans la d^e chambre est une porte et une fenestre du costé du Ouest. La fenestre a deux pieds de large sur deux pieds de haut et la porte est large de deux pieds et demy.

Au bout de la d^e maison du costé du Sud est une cheminée qui a 9 pieds de haut, maçonnée d'une terre sableuse.

Au Ouest de cette maison est un Magasin aussy de pieux de bout qui a 15 pieds de longeur sur 12 pieds de largeur. Le d^t magasin est garni de tablettes de planches de boulots et d'écorces afin d'empescher la poussière de tomber sur la marchandise.

Un comptoir large de deux pieds de la hauteur de trois pieds et demy, et la porte afin d'empescher que les Sauvages ayent communication avec l'endroit où est la marchandise.

Les planchers sont de pieux ronds et doubles enduits de mousse.

Un grenier de mesme espèce que celuy de la maison et couvert aussy d'écorces d'épinettes. (1732, 113–15, in Collection Margry)

While French competition did not keep the Hudson's Bay Company from prospering during this period, it did have notable effects on the conduct of the trade and the Indian role in it. The French were energetic in carrying the trade to the Indians, who were thus spared the long trip to the coast each spring. More importantly, having an alternative market for their furs allowed the Indians to be particular about the kind and price of trade goods. Joseph Myatt, governor of Albany, described the situation in 1727: "They choose rather to trade the goods up in the countrey then have the fatigue of comeing down here and are grown so nice and difficult in the way of trade that I admire to see it, a true signe as I take it that they have a glut of goods upon the countrey" (A.11/2: 58). The French offered better prices on some goods, notably cloth and gunpowder, but bulkier items such as guns were traded advantageously by the English. Company men complained that the Indians were taking their martens to the French, who reportedly gave a better price for them, and were bringing only their beaver skins to the bay (Davies 1965, 114, 183). London officials, however, did not want to engage in a price war with the opposition and told their postmasters that instead of matching prices in particular items they were to emphasize the overall advantage of trading with the company (A.6/5: 1).

Other effects of competition were less beneficial to the James Bay people. False rumours and threats could be as effective encouragements to trade as price changes, and their use led to an increased instability and a degree of violence in the woods. Hunters arriving at Albany Fort told of French threats that Indians discovered taking their furs to the English would be killed (B.3/a/13: 31d). On other occasions the coureurs de bois simply spread the news that the company's supply ship had not reached the bay and the English therefore had no goods to trade (B.3/a/13: 30d). The records do not divulge what similar stories the English traders may have told the Indians.

Competition also contributed to an increased consumption of liquor by the hunters. During the early decades of the Hudson's Bay Company's history there was almost no mention of alcohol in the records, except in cases of heavy drinking by European servants. As the trade rivalry intensified, however, brandy in increasing quantities was presented to the Indians as an inducement to patronize one side or the other, until by 1716 Thomas McCliesh wrote that brandy "is become so bewitching A Liquor Amongst all the Indians, Especially Amongst Those that Traded with the French" (A.11/2: 27). After 1710 brandy became an article of trade as well. Since the quantity of goods traded by the Indians was limited by their quite spartan needs and by what they were capable of transporting back inland, one of the attractions of liquor was that it could be consumed on the spot. By the mid-1720s brandy had become one of the Hudson's Bay

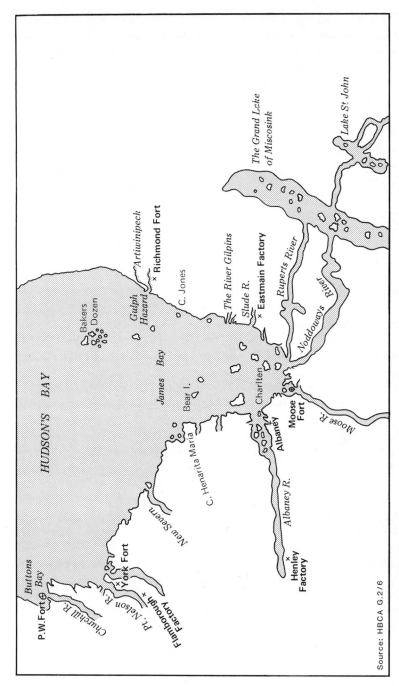

A redrawn portion of the Mynd map of c. 1750 showing the location of English posts on James Bay and Hudson Bay

Source: HBCA G.2/6

Company's most important trade items – "it beinge I find the stapelest Commoditie to acquire all sorts of small furrs," declared Richard Staunton in 1724 – and it would remain so into the next century (B.3/a/12: 23).

The company responded to the extension of French activity inland by extending their own operations along the coast of James Bay. It was the possibility of French attack that led to the strengthening of Eastmain House in 1723–4 and it was the fact of French opposition at the headwaters of the Moose River that caused the company to approve the construction of a post at the mouth of that river in the summer of 1730. The advisability of a post at this location had been pointed out by Myatt, at Albany, three years earlier in a letter to London:

We have had six canoes of strangers from Moose River ... to trade and they are all very desirous of having a factory or settlement at that place, for they dread paddling along shore betwixt Moose River and this place; for they are obliged to come here in the midst of summer by reason the ice lays so long upon that shore when there is neither fish nor fowl to be got, so that many times they are half-famished in coming here. (Davies 1965, 123)

Myatt also pointed out that a Moose River post might draw in the Rupert River hunters who had deserted Eastmain House for the French. The following summer William Bevan surveyed the mouth of the river, and London's permission having been granted, in the summer of 1730 construction began on Moose Fort (ibid., 130, 153). At first the post was plagued by incompetent leadership and ill-disciplined servants and on 26 December 1735, during a drunken party, the buildings were destroyed by fire (A.11/43: 9d). However, the fort was rebuilt and discipline restored, and Moose Fort has continued in operation to the present day.

By the mid-1730s the Hudson's Bay Company once again occupied three posts strung out around the bottom of James Bay. On the east main the small outpost aboard a sloop at Slude River had expanded into a full-fledged trading post, dealing with Indians from as far north as Richmond Gulf and competing with French coureurs de bois for the furs of the southeastern peoples. But this single establishment was as much as the company was at this time willing to risk in its eastern territory. No attempts were made to venture inland and for most of the century the woodlands back of the main remained unknown to the English. Aside from an unsuccessful attempt to settle Richmond Gulf, it would be forty years before a new set of competitors provoked the Hudson's Bay Company into extending its activities in eastern James Bay along the coast and up the rivers towards the height of land.

CHAPTER FIVE

The Fur Trade
in the Eighteenth Century

The fur trade was not an economic enterprise developed in the Old World and imposed on the New. Quite the contrary, trading practices were shaped in large part by the environment of the north and the cultures of the peoples who lived there. This chapter describes the trade during its first century at Eastmain House, how it affected the James Bay people and was in turn affected by them.

The trading period began early in June with the breakup of the ice in the rivers and the arrival by canoe of Indians who had spent the winter hunting inland. In the vocabulary of the trade these people were called inlanders and were distinguished from the Indians whose winter grounds were near the coast and who were called homeguard. The homeguard arrived at Eastmain House earlier than the inlanders did, sometimes as early as the beginning of March, to await the arrival of the geese, which they hunted every spring and fall in the coastal marshes. The homeguard traded their furs on arrival but they were not the main source of the post's returns, since their territory was not rich in fur-bearing animals. As postmaster Thomas Mitchell remarked, "The Chiefest of our Trade Coms from amongst ye In Land Indians," that is, those Indians who wintered to the east around the headwaters of the Big (the present La Grande Rivière or Fort George), Eastmain, Rupert, and Nottaway rivers (B.59/a/14: 15d). These were the people whose arrival heralded the commencement of the hectic, three-week trading season.

Early in the century the trading Indians arrived at the post in parties of three or four canoes, much smaller groups than those that descended to the posts on the west coast of Hudson Bay. By the 1780s, however, parties consisting of as many as thirty-three canoes visited, though they were not the norm. Groups of trading Indians were called gangs by the Hudson's Bay Company servants, who recognized one man as the leading Indian, or "captain," a term first used in James Bay by the Jesuits. Large groups

TABLE 2
Goods Presented to Trading Captains, Spring, 1784

	Cabbage, Capt	Shenap, Lt	Old French, Capt	Suck'a'pa'twa'-u'nish, Capt	Caumasey, Lt
Cloth, yd:					
fine	2	2	2	2	2
plain	4	3	4	4	3
Lace, orris, yd:					
broad	10	5	10	10	5
narrow	10	5	10	10	5
Serge, embossed, yd	1½		1½	1½	
Buttons, coat, doz	1½	1	1½	1½	1
Sash, worsted, yd	1	1	1	1	1
Hat, plain/laced, no.	1	1	1	1	1
Shirt, ruffled, no.	1	1	1	1	1
Feather, no.	1	1	1	1	1
Shoes, pump/turn soles, pr	1	1	1	1	1
Handkerchief, no.	1	1	1	1	1
Stockings, grey knitted, pr	1	1	1	1	1
Brandy, qt	3	2	3	3	3
Tobacco, lb	5	3	6	6	3
At his going away:					
gun, 3½ ft					
brandy, qt	2	2	4	x	x
tobacco, lb	4	4	9	6	4
powder, lb				8	5
shot – duck/Bristol/ partridge, lb				24	15
flints, no.				16	10

Source: B.59/d/1: 21.

included more than one captain, the average being five or six canoes per captain. From the mid-1760s to the mid-1780s the postmaster also designated a number of "lieutenants," but this position was abolished because of the extra expense it entailed. As a reward for bringing in hunters and as encouragement to continue doing so, leading Indians received gifts of brandy, tobacco, and, to distinguish them as leaders, an outfit of quasi-military clothing. Edward Umfreville, a Hudson's Bay Company servant at Severn House, described such a uniform:

a coarse cloth coat, either red or blue, lined with baize and having regimental cuffs; and a waistcoat and breeches of baize ... He is also presented with a white or check shirt; his stockings are of yarn, one of them red, the other blue, and tied

Sackitaw, Lt	Cobbitti-gooshish, Capt	Pauchache, Capt	Cau'mas'-cop'pe, Capt	A'rous'can, Capt	Wapachu, Capt	Wiskehagan, Capt
2	2	2	2	2	2	2
3	3	4	4	4	6	4
5	10	10	10	10	10	10
5	10	10	10	10	10	10
	1½	1½	1½	1½	1½	1
1	1½	1½	1½	1½	1½	1
1	1	1	1	1	1	1
1	1	1	1	1	1	1
1	1	1	1	1	1	1
1	1	1	1	1	1	1
1	1	1	1	1	1	1
1	1	1	1	1	1	1
1	1	1	1	1	1	1
3	4	4	4	4	6	4
3	6	6	4	4	6	6
					1	
x	4	4	6	4	6	4
4	8	8	8	8	20	8
4						
12						
8						

below the knee with worsted garters; his Indian shoes are sometimes put on, but he frequently walks in his stocking feet; his hat is coarse, and bedecked with three ostrich feathers of various colours, and a worsted sash tied round the crown; a small silk handkerchief is tied round his neck, and this compleats his dress. The Lieutenant is also presented with a coat, but it has no lining; he is likewise provided with a shirt and a cap, not unlike those worn by mariners. (1790, 59)

Table 2 lists the presents given to the captains and their lieutenants at Eastmain House in 1784.

The recognition of trading captains was not unique to the Hudson's Bay Company – "French captains" were often encountered – nor was it a

practice which developed on the east coast. Apparently it was transported there after Eastmain House was established and it was not until
1744 that the records indicate the first captain's suit was presented, while
at Albany such a reference dates back to 1727. By the 1780s as many as
ten or twelve captains and lieutenants were visiting the post, bringing
gangs from north, south, and east. Trading captains were recognized by
the postmaster according to certain criteria. First they were expected to
bring in a sizeable haul of furs each season. In 1767 the Eastmain master
was told:

When a leader comes to trade with You if you think his goods will amount to 500
Made Beaver Give Him a Captains Coat, Hat, Shirt and other things as usual ... a
Man that brings You 300 Made Beaver give Him a Lieutenants coat with other
things as usual and any one that brings 150 Made Beaver or near ought to have a
plain Coat, with Tobacco and Brandy given Him in proportion to the Goodness of
his Goods and so the rest. (B.3/b/5: 2)

Yet a profitable trade was not the only requirement made of a captain.
More importantly, he had to be a man of influence among his fellows, and
in this respect the Indians might be said to have chosen their own captains. Even Indians who were deemed untrustworthy or idle were made
captains if company officers believed they were influential with their fellows. For instance, throughout Richmond Fort's existence Shewescome,
an Indian the postmaster deemed an "Idle Lazey Fellow," was maintained as a captain because "he has so Great a Sway Over the Natives
here I am Obliged to be very kind to him, for what he says is a Law wth
them" (B.182/a/1: 48d). For their part, the Indians probably recognized
the captain as a spokesman who would represent their interests to the
English. It is likely that the captain slipped into this role before the trading period and that for the rest of the year he was simply one of several
leading Indians whose leadership was subsistence-oriented.

Unlike traditional Indian leaders who seem to have been recognized
only for specific tasks and for short periods of time (see Oldmixon 1931,
382), trading captains retained their position for life. The company's
motive here is unclear. Perhaps officers feared that if the privileges of
captaincy were taken away, the demoted hunter might begin patronizing
the opposition, taking other Indians with him. Or perhaps the company
felt obliged to conform to the Indians' respect for elderly hunters. In
Europe it was customary for individuals who acquired titles to continue
using them for the rest of their lives and possibly this custom was applied
by the English to the fur-trade system. Whatever the reason, captains
who enjoyed a long life kept their title for twenty or twenty-five years. Of
a total of thirty-five captains and lieutenants who patronized Eastmain

House during the trading captain system, nine held their position for this long.

A captain generally recruited his gang in the summer or fall, and then collected them in the spring before embarking on the trip to the coast. These remarks from the Moose Fort journal of 1761 describe the process: "The reason of his staying so long before he came down, was in order to have collected more Indians together (as I promised him last Summer that if he brot a good Trade ... I would make him a Captain) but that several who had promised him in the Winter to come with him down to Moose Fort had traded their goods up the Country" (B.135/a/33: 32d). Gangs varied in size from year to year, though hunters generally were consistent in their allegiance to a particular captain. Not all men joined a gang but those who did presumably did so to share in the gifts of brandy and tobacco given to a captain, to share in the social aspect of a trip to the post, and to benefit from an experienced negotiator with the white man.

The information in the daily journals on the trading captains visiting Eastmain House from 1744 to 1815 was sufficiently detailed to permit an analysis of the trading captain system (Morantz 1977; 1982), which has been useful in understanding the James Bay peoples' mode of adaptation to the fur trade. The trading captain system was a specialized and formalized institution, two characteristics not always associated with northeastern Algonquian speakers. Another characteristic not generally recognized by anthropologists as being typical was that often the trading gangs encompassed men of more than one hunting group. In other words, the gangs were not necessarily organized on the basis of close familial ties. The trading captain's persuasive abilities probably drew people to him, especially for groups of anywhere from ten to twenty canoes or twenty to forty men, a not infrequent occurrence. Smaller trading gangs of two to three canoes probably represented a single hunting (that is, cooperating) group. The facts that not all hunters were members of trading gangs and that the social structure does not seem to have been affected once the Hudson's Bay Company terminated the office of trading captain in the 1820s also show that the trading captain system was a task-oriented group which was grafted onto the existing and more traditional social system. Those men who previously had been referred to as captains were in the 1820s simply referred to as leading or principal men. In all likelihood, the trading captains themselves and not the overall social system suffered the greatest shock when the Hudson's Bay Company abolished formal captaincy.

The captain of the homeguard Indians had different responsibilities from his inland counterparts. First he ensured that members of the homeguard were present at the goose hunts in the spring and fall. Often he was engaged as an emissary by the company, taking presents to the upland

"French Indians" in an attempt to lure them to the coast (B.59/a/46: 31d). In one instance the Eastmain captain was sent among the northward Indians "to bring ye Natives into Beatter Methods to Catch furs and to be Carefull off them" (B.59/a/4: 39). As well, the homeguard captain was an ally of the English in the event of an attack either by the French or by hostile Indians. For all of this the homeguard leader was rewarded with the customary clothing and presents.

By no means all trading Indians arrived at Eastmain House in the company of an acknowledged captain. At mid-century, in fact, most hunters came independently. Later in the century, however, by the 1780s, when Canadian, that is, Montreal-based, competitors were well established inland, at least three-quarters of the canoes arriving at the coast were organized around a captain or a lieutenant. In the western fur trade Indian leaders were usually middlemen who did not hunt furs themselves but instead traded them from other Indians and transported them to York Fort (Davies 1965, xxvii). This class of Indian trader did not develop in eastern James Bay where the distances to be travelled were not as great, though occasionally hunters bringing their own furs to the post brought other hunters' as well. Such was noted by John Potts at Richmond Fort in 1754. He reported that before the establishment of this northern post an Indian captain named Cawpachisqua used to meet each summer at one of the Whale rivers with Indians who wintered northeast of Richmond Gulf where he collected their furs for delivery to Eastmain House the next spring (A.11/57: 38).

When only a few Indians arrived with their furs, the trading ceremony was not elaborate. The men were presented with brandy and tobacco, which they took to their tents erected nearby. The next day they returned to the post and traded. When a large gang arrived, headed by a captain, it was greeted by the postmaster before brandy and tobacco were presented, and the gang was sometimes housed in a tent provided by the company. After a period of socializing and ritual ceremony which might last a day or more, the inlanders returned to the post for trading. There is no description on record of the actual trading procedure at Eastmain House but it was probably similar to, though likely less elaborate than, that followed at York Fort, described by James Isham in his book *Observations on Hudson's Bay* (1949, 84–7). The main elements of the ceremony were speeches by the postmaster and the leading Indians, the smoking of a pipe, and the exchange of gifts, the captains presenting the master with furs which had been collected from their hunters. According to Abraham Rotstein, this ceremonial aspect of the trade in fact had political motives. He has argued that gift-giving represented the confirmation of a political alliance between Indian and trader and that the trade is best understood as at least in part a political institution (1967,

6–7). Whether Rotstein's analysis applies to western Canada (see Ray and Freeman 1978, 232), it definitely does not apply to eastern James Bay. Some Indians may have identified with one set of traders and been antagonistic to the other, but there is no evidence that they viewed the traders as political or military allies or both. Indeed the Indians felt no compunction about trading part of their hunt with a French trader and the rest with a Hudson's Bay Company one. This last point will be discussed later in the chapter.

Company regulations stipulated that Indians were not allowed within the room where the trade goods were stored and so trading took place through a window. In 1749 at Eastmain House an enclosed passageway was constructed which connected the trading window to the main gate in the log palisades surrounding the post, thereby restricting Indian access to the house even further (B.59/a/17: 21). The one exception was the captain who was permitted to inspect the merchandise in the trading room. When the trade was completed, the gangs left the post and returned inland. Trading gangs usually remained at the post for just two or three days, enough time to rest after the journey to the coast and to conduct the trade. Gangs from different regions might sometimes meet at the post, but it definitely was not used by the Indians as a gathering place or a centre for prolonged socializing. For one thing the Hudson's Bay Company discouraged the Indians from lingering at the post, since usually they had to be provisioned from the company stores. As well, the home-guard people sometimes took trading advantage of the inlanders and the officers were just as happy if the two groups did not mingle. An example of this concern was reported in 1743 when Postmaster Light explained in his journal why he traded only a portion of the inland Indians' furs that day: "I ... refer the rest for morning to keep the home Indians from Spungin on them" (B.59/a/7: 17d). From the Indians' point of view, the trading post was not a good place to socialize because their families did not accompany them.

Trade between the company and the Indians was conducted according to the official standard of trade which valued all goods in beaver skins, the value of a single prime beaver pelt being designated one made beaver (see table 3). For example, in 1750 (table 4) one gallon of brandy equalled four made beaver and one four-foot gun equalled twelve made beaver. As well, all other furs, such as bear, marten, otter, fox, were given a made beaver value according to the comparative standard of trade (tables 3 and 5). Both standards remained fairly uniform for much of the century, though we will see that in 1769 the fur standard was changed in an attempt to meet competition from Canada. According to Ray, the reason for this inflexibility was that the Indians themselves were resistant to the notion of price changes (1974, 62).

TABLE 3
Standard of Trade, Albany Fort and the East Main, 1715–16

Beaver being the Chiefest Commodity we receive in the trade of these goods
we therefore make it ye Standard whereby we rate all ye other Furrs and
Commodities we deal for in Tradeing ...
  4 Martins as 1 Beaver
  2 Otters as 1 Beaver unless they be Extraordnary and then we rate them
    at 1 per Br.
  2 Foxes as 1 Beaver unless they be Extraordnary & then we rate them
    Sometimes to 1 Beaver to 1½ Beaver and 2 Beaver
  2 Quaquahatches* as 1 Beaver
  1 Catt as 1 Beaver
  1 Moos Skinn as 2 Beaver
  2 Deers Skinns as 1 Beaver
  1 Woolf as 1 Beaver
  1 lb. Castorum† as 1 Beaver
  10 lb. Feathers as 1 Beaver
  4 Fathom Netting as 1 Beaver
  8 Pair Moose hoofs as 1 Beaver
  1 Black Bear as 2 Beaver
  1 Cubb as 1 Beaver

Source: B.3/d/24: 15d.
* Wolverine.
† Glands of the beaver which produce an oily substance used in perfumes and medicines.

While a definite "price" schedule existed, the trade was not always, or
even usually, carried on in accordance with it. As Rich has pointed out,
"The evidence was that the Governors kept the Standard of Trade as a
purely token basis for their accounts with the Company: the actual trade
was carried on at the best rate which the Indians would tolerate" (1958,
595). By using his own standard, what Ray and Freeman (1978, 95) have
called the "factor's standard," the postmaster could arbitrarily increase
the number of pelts required for a certain article, but since the Indians
over time must have learned the official standard and been aware of
deviations from it, it was more usual for postmasters to give short measures of goods as they were portioned out. The difference between what
the trader did receive for his goods and what he would have received if he
had adhered to the standard was called the overplus. The amount of overplus the trader could accumulate depended in part on the degree of competition threatening his post. Figure 1 shows that before the 1760s the

TABLE 4

Official Standard of Trade, Eastmain House, 1750

Trade goods	Quantity	Value in made beaver
Awl blades	1 doz	1
Beads	1 lb	1⅓
Blanket	1	6
Brandy	1 gal	4
Chisel, ice	1	½
Cloth	1 yd	2
Comb, ivory	1	2
Duffle	1 yd	1½
Firesteel	1	¼
Flints	20	1
Gartering	1 yd	⅙
Gunpowder	1 lb	⅔
Gun:		
4 ft	1	12
3½ ft	1	11
3 ft	1	10
Gunworm	1	¼
Hat, plain	1	2
Hatchet	1	½
Horn and powder	¾ lb	½
Horn and powder	½ lb	½
Kettle (different sizes)	1	avg. 1⅓
Knife	1	⅛
Lace, orris	1 yd	⅙
Net line	1	½
Needles	1 doz	1
Sash, worsted	1	½
Shot	1 lb	⅕
Tobacco:		
Brazil	1 lb	1
roll	1 lb	⅔
Twine	1 skein	1
Vermilion	1 oz	⅔

Source: B.3/d/58: 23–7.

TABLE 5

Comparative Standard of Trade,
Eastmain House, 1735 and 1775

	Made beaver value in 1735	Made beaver value in 1775
Bear:		
winter prime	2	3
common	–	2
cub	1	1
Castoreum, 1 lb	1	½
Lynx:		
old	2	2
cub	–	1
Fox:		
black	–	4
blue	–	½
grey	2	3
red	1	1
white	–	½
Marten:		
prime	⅓	½
common	–	⅓
Mink	–	¼
Musquash (muskrat)	–	⅙
Otter:		
prime	1	1
common	½	½
Weejack (fisher)	1	1
Wolf:		
old	1	2
cub	–	1
Wolverine	1½	2

Sources: B.3/d/43: 5; B.3/d/83: 8.

overplus at Eastmain House remained fairly steady at about one-third
the value of the total returns. French competition during this period was
constant but not extreme. However, when Canadian competitors became
active inland towards the end of the 1760s, the overplus declined, since
the Indians were in a position to drive a harder bargain (cf. Ray 1974,

Figure 1. Overplus as a percentage of total trade, Eastmain House, 1730–1780

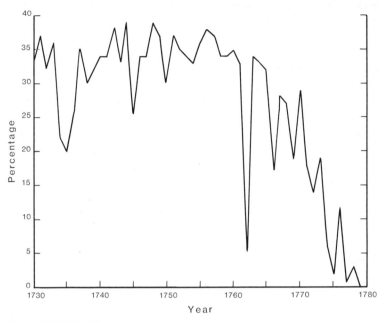

65). (We cannot account for the dramatic and atypical decline in the over-plus for 1762, a year when there was little competition. Nevertheless this single aberration does not negate the general trend.) Rich and Rotstein have both argued that the overplus was used by the Hudson's Bay Com-pany postmasters to finance the presents which they gave to the Indians, but this appears to have been true only in the obvious sense that overplus was part of the general revenues and presents were financed out of gen-eral revenues (Rich 1960, 43; Rotstein 1967, 113). According to Ray, profits from the overplus trade were not used to establish a gift fund of trade goods at the post (1976, 16). Furthermore it has been suggested (Ray and Freeman 1978, 240) that the overplus minus the gifts consti-tuted a highly significant element of the company's profit.

The practice of extending credit, or debt, to the Indians, a practice known as trusting, commenced sometime in the first half of the century. Upon leaving the post in the fall, each hunter was given by the company a quantity of goods which was paid for in furs the following spring. Com-pany traders recognized that it was in their interests to advance ammuni-tion and other necessaries to certain individuals who had had unsuccessful hunts the previous winter, otherwise these men and their families might perish or, more probably, spend most of the next season hunting game animals for food and clothing rather than fur-bearing animals. Also, the extension of credit was an inducement for Indians to trade at the bay rather than with the inland competition. According to Normandin, the French also gave credit, and experienced similar difficulties reclaiming it: "Les françois de ces endroits leur donnent à credit, et lorsqu'ils ont eu beaucoup à credit pendant plusieurs fois dans ces endroits là ils n'y retournent plus et reviennent à leur premier et véritable poste insolvables, et promettant beaucoup qu'ils n'iront plus" (1732, 117, in Collection Margry).

Not all hunters took debt every year and the amount granted each individual varied. Obviously the value of the previous season's hunt was the most important factor, since if a hunter had been successful, he would not need as much credit. Some postmasters were more opposed to trusting than others and consequently granted less credit. The most credit allowed at Eastmain House in this period seems to have been fifteen made beaver but most debtors received between ten and twelve made beaver, the price of a gun. Members of the homeguard were generally trusted for more than inlanders, since the homeguard, because of their proximity, were less liable to avoid debts by going to the French traders. The homeguard were given credit twice a year, once in the fall and again, in smaller amounts, in the winter when they visited the post with their fall hunts.

Initially the Hudson's Bay Company's official attitude to credit was that it was detrimental to the fur trade and should be abolished. "We are Informed that it has been a Custom of late years to Trust the Indians, which we apprehend is of great Prejudice to us, and ought never to have been introduced," the bayside postmasters were informed in 1739. "Therefore desire you by Degrees and with prudence to reform and put a stop as soon as you can to so evil a practice" (A.6/6: 34). The officials feared that the Indians would accumulate large debts with the company and, instead of repaying them, would begin taking their furs to the French (A.11/43: 16). Also, officials were convinced that credit acted as a disincentive, satisfying the Indians' basic needs and discouraging initiative. Another, less important, criticism was that when a hunter died, his debt was lost to the company (ibid.). Joseph Isbister of Eastmain House reported a conversation which briefly states the company's position and also explains why the hunters insisted trusting be continued:

Ye Hunters brought in 90 Geese. Allso ye Capt. of ye home Indians And wanted to be trusted So I Taulk'd with him ... and told him that it was a bad Custom and that it ye Reazon of All ye Southern Indians Goeing to ye French allso Mad them Carless in Catching goods They being soplied wth Necesereys upon Trust that it Mad Them Deilletery in Loking out for furs, He Answard and Sead iff they Culd

not be Soplied by trust that it Might bee a Means of Destroying them a
Sed formerly we traded Sumer furs So that there but Letle ocasion to tal
on Trust but we Traded Nothing but Winter Goods and Sead they Must be
Soplied with Neceserys to Catch them withall or Else Theire wold be but Letle
Trade, So I trusted ye Capt. and Some of his Gaurd a Small Matter as Much as I
thought they Culd well pay and no mor; for I Never trusted Much to Any mor
then Bear Neceserys for ye Winter. (B.59/a/4: 6d–7)

While the company complained about it and advanced as little as possible,
credit often proved an effective means of manipulating the Indians. For
example, Thomas Mitchell, master at Eastmain, recorded in 1743 that
"we had Severall Indians Come In and wanted Me to trust them But I
would Not Except they would stay and kill us Some Geese" (B.59/a/8: 8).
Nonetheless, the Hudson's Bay Company was never completely recon-
ciled to giving debt. As long as its competitors did so, the company followed suit, but in the next century when competition slackened, credit
was reduced or eliminated wherever possible.

All these practices – giving presents, applying double standards, and
advancing credit – were to one degree or another accommodations by the
European trading company to the culture of the Indian people (Ray
1975a). Traditionally Indian trade had involved the giving of presents
and the cementing of friendships, and so the fur trade incorporated this
noneconomic dimension. The Indians were not sympathetic to prices
which responded to supply and demand, and so a system of pricing was
elaborated in which the changes were negotiable, within limits, and meas-
ured in terms understood by them (Ray 1974, 63). Trusting was similarly
an accommodation to the Indians' life-style and to the fact that they experienced periodic scarcities of food and furs. This is not to suggest that any
of the practices ever or always worked to the advantage of the Indian.
But clearly the native people demanded and received a system of trade
which conformed in certain basic procedures to their way of life.

Most of the Indians trading at Eastmain House came from three general directions. The Hudson's Bay Company had decided that the Nottaway River was the boundary between the territory controlled by Moose
Fort and Eastmain House, and so the southerly Indians trading at Eastmain came primarily from the regions of Waswanipi and the modern Lac
au Goëland (or Gull Lake) (B.59/a/70: 18). Chamouchouane was the
most distant region mentioned in the records. Indians who hunted there
descended the Rupert River, and then made their way north along the
coast. Indians from the east came from as far as Lakes Neoskweskau and
Mistassini, travelling via the Eastmain and Rupert rivers, whereas the
northern Indians generally resided in the vicinity of the Big River,
though some moved north to Richmond Gulf in the summer (B.59/a/9: 4).

Before 1760 more than half of the inland trading canoes came from the north and very few from the southeast. While northern Indians continued to predominate throughout the century, the number of "southerners" increased dramatically in the 1770s, presumably as French competition slackened, and continued to be substantial until the proliferation of inland posts reduced in general the number of trading Indians patronizing Eastmain House. In terms of the value of their trade, the hunters to the east and southeast of James Bay were much more successful than either the coastal homeguard or the northerners. Those from the north exasperated company officers because of their preference for hunting caribou over furs, and Thomas Mitchell's comment in 1745 that "one Indian from ye Etward or mutch inLand Brings More furrs yn any too of these" remained true for the entire period (B.59/a/12: 25d). Exact population figures do not exist in the records, but from the Eastmain House journal it can be computed that in 1747–8 about 90 hunters traded at the post but by 1783–4 the number of hunters had increased to 177 (B.59/a/16; B.59/a/59).

Figures 2 and 3 indicate that the Indians trading at Eastmain House from 1730 to 1780 consistently brought in beaver pelts worth more than any other single animal fur. In fact, beaver usually accounted for more than fifty per cent of the value of the entire trade, though the beaver catch at times fell below fifty per cent. Between 1734 and 1744, for instance, the value of beaver pelts versus other furs declined to as low as forty-two per cent of the total (figure 3) or down to 700 made beaver from earlier highs of 2400 made beaver (figure 2). Beaver returns rallied to account for between sixty to eighty per cent of the total in the 1750s, a situation which lasted until the mid-1760s when once again the value of beaver pelts began to fluctuate around the fifty per cent mark. Generally when beaver made up a smaller percentage of the total value of furs traded, the value of marten traded showed an increase, except for the earliest years when the value of lynx represented a greater percentage of the total trade than did marten. As also seen in figures 2 and 3, the percentage of fox and bear traded vis-à-vis other furs was most consistent, though these furs were always of relatively minor importance in terms of the total trade. The variability in the makeup of the annual returns may be accounted for by a number of factors, besides the environmental factors which always affected the success of the hunt. If more than the usual number of hunters came in from the beaver-poor north, then the trade would show an increase in small furs. Periodically inland competitors became more energetic and drew off some of the beaver pelts destined for the bay. But invariably the beaver was in this period the most important fur-bearing animal in the economy of the James Bay people.

Figure 4 charts the annual value of the trade at Eastmain House in the fifty-year period from 1730 to 1780. Towards the end of the century the

Figure 2. Total returns in made beaver value of five furs, Eastmain House, 1730–1780

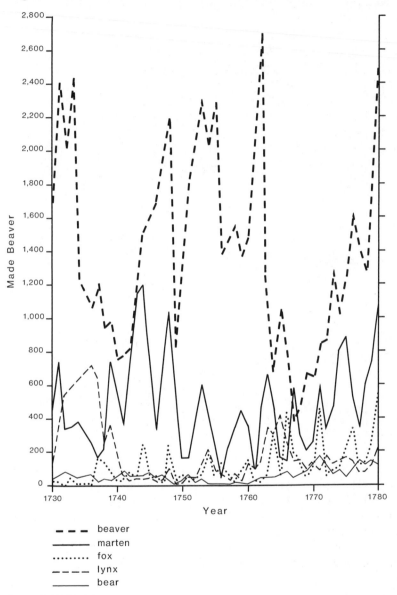

Source: B.3/d/38-88

Figure 3. Percentage of total value of trade accounted for by five furs, Eastmain House, 1730–1780

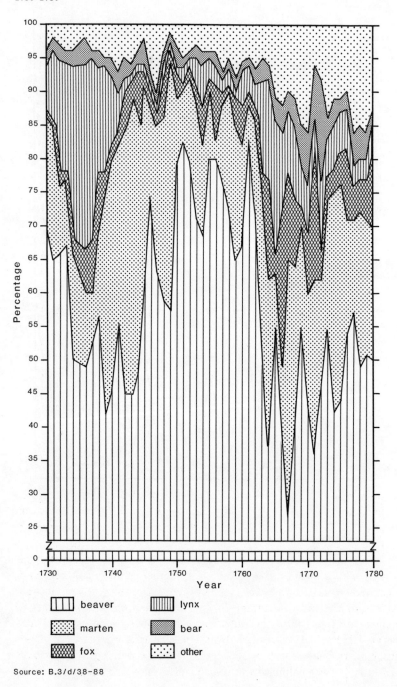

Source: B.3/d/38–88

Figure 4. Made beaver value of furs traded, Eastmain House, 1730–1780

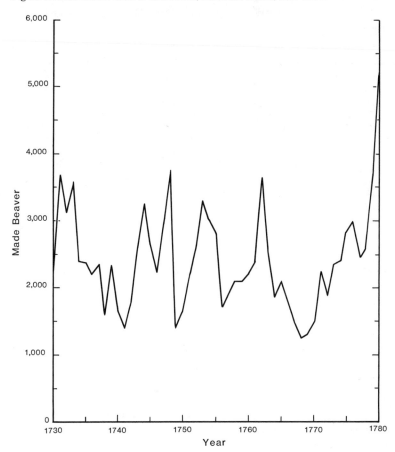

Source: B.3/d/38–88

situation was complicated by the proliferation of outposts and will be treated later. It would try the reader's patience to account for every variation in the trade, but a number of explanatory factors do emerge from the post journals, some unique, most recurring periodically.

The success of an Indian's fur hunt, indeed the success of his struggle for existence in general, depended on a number of environmental variables, both climatic and ecological. The quantity of snow, the mildness or severity of the fall, the timing of freeze-up, and the extent of spring flooding – all these factors could affect the availability of food and furs. George Gladman at Eastmain House described a particularly severe winter on the east coast in 1817, which clearly indicates the intimate connection between climate and Indian subsistence patterns:

but on the 5th November it began to thaw and continued until the 12th with very heavy Rain on that day, the Water rose in the River Rapidly, the River Ice was torn up, a heavy Gale and Change of Weather immediately following choaked the Creeks and River with rough Ice and Snow, filled the Marshes also and destroyed alike the fishery and hunting, and a winter of Hunger and Misery commenced that has been seldom equalled; before the end of the year Indians began to arrive with distressing accounts of want. The creeks by the sudden Change of Weather were filled with Ice to an uncommon thickness, made the taking Beaver Houses in some places impracticable, difficult in all, this was the universal account given by all the Indians who arrived, they also say that many young Beaver perished by the sudden inundation – the same scarcity continued all the Winter, neither Fox or Marten track were to be seen and few indeed were the Rabbits or Partridges procured and even fish did not afford much assistance, the snow was uncommonly shallow and hard, so that when a few Birds were found, the Snow shoes made so much noise in walking that no Hunter could approach them. (B.59/e/5: 1d)

As well as climatic changes, the Indians were also susceptible to seasonal fluctuations of the animal populations and in particular the tendency of certain of the smaller food animals to disappear at regular intervals. The "rabbit," that is, the hare, was a crucial source of food and clothing, as the anthropologist Alanson Skinner observed early in this century. Yet, every seven years (now believed to be ten years) the population was decimated by an epidemic, and it took at least two more years for the hare to recover (Skinner 1911, 25). Similarly Elton has shown that the mice and voles upon which the marten and fox feed disappeared approximately every four years, resulting in a drastic depletion of the populations of the two fur-bearing animals (1942, 276). Therefore the James Bay people regularly experienced winters of extreme privation during which starvation made it impossible for them to hunt or the threat of starvation kept them hunting food such as hare and ptarmigan, not furs. The Indians had their food preferences, of course, and Hudson's Bay Company men were known to complain that when caribou or fish or ptarmigan were plentiful, the hunters were less enthusiastic in the pursuit of furs (for example, B.59/a/14: 15, 19). As well, periods of sickness would keep the Indians from realizing large fur returns, as would a death in the family which often left close relatives disconsolate and unwilling to hunt.

The volume of trade at Eastmain House was affected also by the degree of competition provided by French, and later Canadian, opponents inland. The inland Indians, of course, profited from having alternative markets and often took no pains to hide the fact that they preferred to deal with the Hudson's Bay Company's opposition. Few, however, were as bold as Esquawino, whom the English named Snuff the Blanket, as an officer explained, 'from his delicate taste of holding his garment to his Nose when he enters ye Factory to avoid ye ill scent & from his refusing to eat any Victuals dressed in any Utensil of ours" (B.135/a/11: 67). (This Snuff is not to be confused with the man of the same name executed in 1755 by the Hudson's Bay Company for his part in the Henley House murders.) Esquawino was a leading Moose River Indian who infuriated the Hudson's Bay Company traders by establishing in the 1740s his own trading network, described by the Albany postmaster George Spence: "Our Indians who catch their Goods on this River trades nothing but ye worst of their Goods here and carries ye best of their Martins and Catts to him who takes them to ye French that live on your River [the Moose] and trades them for Cloth, Lace & Beads & sometimes for Tobacco" (B.3/b/2: 19). Esquawino continued to play English trader against French trader with great success for two decades. "This man," wrote James Duffield at Moose Fort, "is ye grand politician of all being a free Agent travelling about, sometimes to ye French, at others to Albany & this Fort, never drinks but has allways his scences about him & makes ye best of his Markett at all places" (B.135/a/11: 69). In 1759, however, Esquawino overplayed his hand. According to the Moose postmaster, in the spring of that year the Indian leader tried to rally the homeguard, and failing them the French traders inland, for an assault on the post. He was captured by the master and imprisoned in a small cell at the fort where after a number of attempts he succeeded in hanging himself (B.135/a/31: 29d).

Most of the hunters were not as flagrant about their dual loyalties as Esquawino, but the remarks of postmasters at Eastmain House confirm that the Indians were quite willing to patronize the trader who offered the best price, the best goods, or the best service. Competition was a constant factor throughout almost the entire eighteenth century but in years when it became unusually intense, the mid-1750s for instance, the returns at Eastmain House showed a corresponding decline.

By no means all Indians oscillated between French and English traders. Some regularly visited Eastmain House with their furs each year and others, called "French Indians" by the Hudson's Bay Company, regularly took their goods to the French. The degree to which the rivalries of white traders affected the relations between these Indian groups is impossible to estimate from the sources, but evidently some hostility developed because in the spring of 1756 there was a chorus of complaint among hunters arriving at Eastmain House about the depradations of the "French Indians." Typical was this entry in the post journal: "April 24 Sat. Came in Shametopano and his Two Sons but had but a fue skins ... He youst To Trade 300 beaver and now not above 50 beaver. He Complains of the french Indains Coming to his Ground and Takes his Beaver Houses So that he can gett no goods" (B.59/a/24: 12d). Shametopano's complaint was echoed by other Indians, many from up the Rupert River. It may be noted in figure 4 that the Eastmain House returns dropped off dramatically that season.

The volume of trade was affected as well by conditions at a particular post. As much as to the quality and price of the trade goods, the James Bay people reacted to the skill and benevolence of individual white traders. The temperament of the trader was crucial to maintaining a high level of returns. The examples of James Duffield, George Gunn, and George Atkinson are useful for emphasizing this point. Duffield was appointed master at Moose Fort in 1741 and immediately imposed a harsh regime of economy and hard labour on servant and Indian alike. He suspected everyone of laziness and dishonesty, whenever possible refused credit to the Indians, and punished his own men by flogging or by turning them out of the post for a few days without provisions (B.135/a/11). The quality of his generosity may be judged by the following entry in his journal: "Partridge, an Indian of our home guard came hither ... Complained he was almost Starved admonish'd him to be Industrious for ye future, but judging yt would not fill his belly at present, gave him some ... rotten bacon" (B.135/a/11: 21). Duffield's three-year tenure at Moose apparently drove some Indians from the post, as his successor claimed that "a great many of our Indians" were trading at Albany Fort because of "Mr. Duffields rough usage of them" (B.135/a/15: 3). George Gunn, postmaster at Eastmain House from 1732 to 1735, was similarly ill adapted for a position of authority, being recalled to England when Hudson's Bay Company officials discovered "he hath for the last two Years been very Sottish and hath given offence to the Indians at the Eastmain, to the disadvantage and lessening of the Companys Trade at that Place" (A.6/5: 105). Figure 4 shows how much damage Gunn did to the trade in the last two years of his tenure.

The success of George Atkinson's postmastership, on the other hand, suggests that the Indians would patronize an experienced and sympathetic trader. Atkinson began his long career in James Bay in 1768 as a crew member of the east coast sloop. After the establishment of Eastmain House as a year-round settlement, he became master of the Moose Fort sloop and in 1778 chief at Eastmain. He served as postmaster until his death in the bay in the fall of 1792. He married an Indian woman, Nucushin, and they had three children – Sneppy, later named George Jr, born 1777; Shesheep, later Jacob, born 1779; and a daughter, Jenny. The two sons became prominent Hudson's Bay Company traders in the next century (Rich 1954, 347–9). Even though his tenure coincided with a period of energetic Canadian opposition, Atkinson managed to increase the post's returns to double what they had been when he took charge. This feat was accomplished by attracting Indians from the north and east who previously had not traded at Eastmain House. From the fact that the overplus declined almost to zero (figure 1), we can presume Atkinson was encouraged by competition to give full measure and adhere closely to the standard.

As stated previously, the Indians were not naive consumers when it came to trading their furs for the white man's goods. Quite the contrary, they were quick to complain when merchandise was inferior or the price too high (see Ray 1980). In 1712, for example, a Hudson's Bay Company officer informed his superiors that the firesteels sent to the bay the previous year would have to be replaced because "I have offered some of them to some Indians that is come from Moose River and they do make a hooting and a laugh at them" (Davies 1965, 27). Similarly, in the late 1730s when the company attempted to interest the Indians in wearing brass collars, at four beaver skins each, the Indians simply refused unless the price was reduced (ibid., 302–3, 327). They often requested better goods or different goods from the postmasters and the requests were invariably answered. Figure 5 shows what portion of their furs the hunters at Eastmain House "spent" on various items. It must be remembered that the Indians may have traded some of their goods inland with traders from Quebec so that this graph cannot be assumed to show their total "income."

It has been the conventional wisdom that European trade items, especially metal goods, quickly replaced many traditional weapons and implements in the Indian material culture, rendering the native dependent on the white trader (for example, Rich 1960, 35). While it cannot be denied that kettles replaced bark containers, guns replaced bows and arrows, iron axes replaced stone ones, and twine replaced roots and leather thongs, to mention only a few examples, replacement did not occur with equal speed and thoroughness among all Indian groups. A distinction must be drawn between those Indians who lived close to a fur-trade post, may have been employed there for short periods, and spent most of the winter months hunting furs and those Indians who lived distant from the posts, visited infrequently, and may have engaged in traditional subsistence activities unconnected with the fur trade. The dispersion of guns will serve as an example. The homeguard Indians appear to have become reliant on this weapon to the exclusion of the bow and arrow sooner and more completely than the inland people did. Their participation in the goose hunt would have made them proficient in its use and the proximity of their hunting grounds to the post afforded relatively easy access to repairs and stocks of ammunition. On the other hand, inland Indians were probably slower to become reliant on the gun because a year's supply of ammunition was bulky to carry, and when the weapon was damaged, there was no armourer available to fix it. William Falconer observed this distinction at Severn in the 1760s. He noticed that whereas the home-

Figure 5. Percentage of total furs traded "spent" on selected trade goods, Eastmain House, 1730–1780

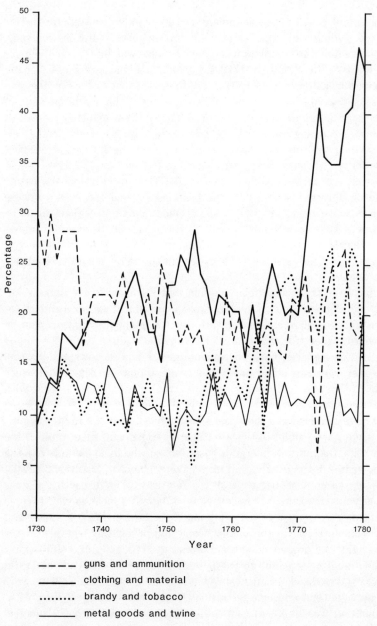

Source: B.3/d/38–88

guard at the post could no longer use the bow and arrow with any effectiveness, the inland people "can do very weel without us at present" (1769, 32). However, even the reliance of the homeguard on the gun should not be exaggerated. The following entry from the Eastmain House journal from May 1766 suggests traditional hunting techniques still complemented the newer weapon: "Few or no partridges for the Indians to get they not being able to afford Powder & Shot & the Scarcity of Partridges has been such they could not get any wth their Bows & Arrows" (B.59/a/35: 17d). Others (Ewers 1972, 12; Sharp 1977, 38) writing of the western fur trade also question the importance of the gun from the standpoint of its marginal superiority to traditional hunting weapons and the problem of supplies of ammunition. Furthermore, material for clothing was not accepted as quickly by the Indians who wintered northeast of Eastmain House and mainly hunted caribou as it was by the more southerly Indians who were primarily fur hunters. The southern Indians, who had formerly used fur for clothing, switched to cloth when furs became valuable. On the other hand, when the northern Indians came to the post, they brought few pelts to trade, and as Thomas Mitchell complained, "ye Best of there Dear Skins they dress wth ye hare on for winter Clothing" (B.59/a/12: 25d). Apparently factors such as the distance of the Indians' hunting grounds from the post, the extent of their contact with the white traders, and the nature of their traditional activities, all affected the speed with which European trade items were adopted and replaced aboriginal weapons and implements.

Neither was the flow of cultural influences all in one direction. Europeans arrived in the bay technologically ill-equipped to cope with its environment. In order to navigate the rivers and lakes they learned to paddle bark canoes. To traverse the country in winter they used snowshoes and sleds. Skin or bark tents sheltered them from the cold and the wet. All this technology was adopted from the Indian culture, along with less tangible survival skills. Clearly dependence, with its connotation of inferiority, is not a word which accurately describes the results of contact between Indian and European material cultures.

The Indians trading at Eastmain House asserted their independence in a variety of ways, some of which have already been noted. For example, they forced the Hudson's Bay Company to continue granting credit and they defied the English traders by taking their furs to the French. Furthermore, once they had gathered furs sufficient to satisfy their needs, which were not always extensive, the eastern James Bay people would not exert themselves to acquire a surplus. Normandin noted that the Indians near the height of land tended not to hunt furs so long as there was sufficient food to eat (1732, 96, in Collection Margry). In the spring of

1741 Thomas Mitchell observed a similar disposition among the coastal Indians:

I am very Mutch deciv'd wth our bordring Indians for as we had Plenty of Partridges I was in hopes they would ventor in Land & kill a Good Many beaver & Martains, but to ye Contrary I find it, for as I have often Mentioned, if They Can Cetch plenty of fish or Partridges or dear they will Never look out for any Martains or beaver; ... I Canot find that anything will in duse our Long Shore Indiens to Cetch Many furrs more then what will Trade them a kettel hatchit or Ice Chezel when they are in want of them, Som have the ambition to provide for Som brandy & Som of our clothing. (B.59/a/14: 19)

The James Bay people used the fur trade to obtain items of particular use to themselves. It would be absurd to claim that the trade had no impact on their material culture, but it would be equally absurd to claim that they became abject dependants on the Hudson's Bay Company stores. As we have noted in other contexts, the Indians had their own attitudes to trade and could not be induced to respect the conventional economic incentives.

CHAPTER SIX

A Decade on
Richmond Gulf

As the Hudson's Bay Company's early preference for coastal, as opposed to inland, settlements is well known, it is not
surprising that the first extension of the company's operations on the east
main beyond the single post at the Slude River was along the coast to the
north. The eastern shore of Hudson Bay had not been explored since
Henry Hudson's voyage of 1610 and the area was a vast blank in the
company's knowledge of its chartered territory. It was in the 1740s that
the first attempts were made to fill in that blank.

The year 1739 may be marked as the beginning of official company
interest in the coastline beyond Cape Jones. In that year Joseph Isbister,
the postmaster at Eastmain House, was told by some northern Indians of
"a large Lake near ye Latitude of 60° about 100 Leagues in Compass
which communicates with 2 other Lakes of a vast Circumference so that
the greatest part of the Labradore is occupied by these 3 Lakes" (A.11/2:
97d–8). The report continued that on the northern shores of these lakes
lived the "Usquimows" and, to the south, groups of Indians which traded
at Eastmain House. These two peoples were believed to be enemies, but
Albany postmaster Rowland Waggoner, transmitting the information to
London, argued: "We think if a Sloop was sent annually it might be a
means effectual to mediate a Peace between ye two People and in process
of Time a beneficial Trade may be commenced with those Savages"
(A.11/2: 98). While the details are exaggerated, the Indian report of three
lakes may well have referred to Richmond Gulf, Lake Clearwater (Lac
à l'Eau Claire), and Lower Seal Lake (Lac des Loups Marins) which did
form part of the traditional border between Indian and Inuit lands
(Davies 1963, xixn). At any rate, after a few years' delay London officials
responded positively to the suggestion of a northward voyage and sent a
new sloop out to the bay expressly for that purpose. French competition
to the south and east of James Bay had made the company particularly

anxious to make contact with native peoples who were as yet innocent of the fur trade or only indirectly involved in it.

The captain of the new vessel, the *Eastmain*, was Thomas Mitchell, also master at Eastmain House. He was guided by the captain of the Eastmain homeguard, Mustapacoss, and accompanied by John Longland in the *Phoenix* sloop. The party set sail for the north early in July 1744. They stopped first at Gilpin's Island where they were told by the local people that they would find the remains of an old building. Mitchell recorded that "there we found Like a pinnacle of Stones and Post set up in ye middle with this Inscription ...: In ye year 1692 wintered there Ships at this Island with 123 Men under ye Goverment of Capt. James Knight – then we Erected this Monument In Rememberance of it" (B.59/a/9: 3). This rubble was what remained of the winter camp of the Knight expedition which had captured Albany Fort from the French in the summer of 1693. Mitchell and Longland hurried on to "ye Great River" (subsequently called Big River and now known as La Grande Rivière or Fort George River), "a very fine River where our Northern Indians ketch all there winter furrs," and proceeded north to Great Whale River (B.59/a/9: 4). There they encountered "in 3 Tents 157 Indians and All Live Chiefly on what white whail they Kill in this River" (B.59/a/9: 7). Mitchell, interested in the mineral resources of the coast, was led at Little Whale River to a nearby deposit of lead ore by some local Indians. He was hopeful the lead might contain silver and he also collected "Saverral Christal Stones which May Be dimonds" (B.59/a/9: 9d). All of these samples Mitchell stowed away to be sent back to England to be assayed.

Leaving Little Whale River, the explorers sailed north into "ye Lake calld By ye Natives Winepeg," soon to be renamed Richmond Gulf by the English (though Mitchell suggested "Muskeetey Gulph for Such Nombers I never See nor No Body a Long with Me Before"). There the sloops remained about a week, charting the shoreline, determining the area's resources, and looking for a suitable harbour. Mitchell learned from the Indians that "in ye Summar they Com as farr as this Gulph or Lake to kill dear & as the winter Coms on thay Return towards ye Great River & all there abouts resorts all our Northen Indians in ye Winter season" (B.59/a/9: 12). Deciding not to venture any further, the two captains left Richmond Gulf and turned their vessels southward, arriving back at the bottom of the bay in mid-August.

Because England was at war with France, it was not until 1749 that the Hudson's Bay Company could conveniently resume the exploration of the coast. The company naturally remained eager to integrate the far northern natives into its trading system but now there were additional incentives to settle the north. Back in London the company was coming under criticism at a parliamentary inquiry for not exploiting its char-

tered territory with as much enthusiasm as it might, and other merchants, inspired by the extravagant description of "Labradore" in Arthur
Dobbs's polemical *Account of the Countries Adjoining to Hudson's Bay*
(1744), were hinting at their own plans for "improving" the region.
Alarmed at the possibility of competition, the company dispatched Capt
William Coats aboard the *Mary* and Mitchell in the sloop *Success* to sail
down the coast from Cape Digges to Richmond Gulf in search of a suitable location for a trading post (Davies 1963, xx). By the middle of
August the expedition reached the gulf, having found no preferable site
farther to the north. Coats wrote that "there is neither a river bay nor
creek to shelter a ship in (except at Sr Thomas Smiths sound) nor wood
nor bush nor brake nor hardly one liveing thing uppon that whole coast
down to this place" (A.11/57: 2). Sir Thomas Smith Sound, the modern
Mosquito Bay, provided a safe harbour but was surrounded by country
too barren to support a post. In Richmond Gulf fuel was plentiful and
"fine fishing and hunting is all around" (ibid.); consequently the post was
located on an island off the south shore to be inhabited the following summer by a contingent of men, including three miners, led by Mitchell.

Richmond Fort began inauspiciously. Mitchell and his men returned
from Eastmain House early in the summer of 1750 and constructed a
dwelling house. However, rumours that he had engaged in private trade
reached London, and in August John Potts arrived to succeed him as
postmaster. Potts found "a Lifeless, Spiritless, discontented crew" at the
new settlement (A.11/57: 7). The miners had been left unsupervised at
the mine site near Little Whale River and had accomplished almost
nothing, while at the post, far from giving vigorous leadership, Mitchell
believed "the Mine is a Chimera and the Settlement a Joke" (ibid.).
Initially Potts was optimistic about the future of the northern settlement.
He set the miners to work in earnest, reporting they had found copper as
well as lead, and on the strength of Indian reports he wrote that furs of
various kinds were plentiful (A.11/57: 7d). He engaged four Great Whale
River men – he called them Netap, the Old Fisherman, Friday, and
Robinson Crusoe (variously spelled) – to remain close to the fort during
the winter "to do anything I Desire Such as Fishing, Hunting partridge,
making Snow Shoes" (B.182/a/1: 10). For the next five years Robinson
Crusoe was of constant service to the company. As well, Potts brought
north an Indian woman from the Albany River to instruct him in the
dialect of the Richmond Gulf area. One can only speculate that this
woman might have been native to the area. At any rate she was sent back
to Albany in the fall of 1753 when the trader believed he had mastered
the language (B.182/a/6: 3).

Despite these brave beginnings, each of Potts's projects in time failed.
The next summer (1751) he reluctantly sent home the three miners,

"since for a Considerable time they have had no Success nor no prospect" (A.11/57: 10). The mining venture was succeeded by a whaling operation at Little Whale River, which continued for the life of the post but which never alone justified the continuance of the establishment. As for the fur trade, it did not develop either. The post failed to draw down the large number of Indians originally anticipated and those who did come were not primarily fur gatherers at all but instead preferred hunting caribou. And so, by 1756, Potts had to admit that "as to a good Trade at this place it can never be expected" (A.11/57: 37).

According to information gathered by Potts, Richmond Gulf at this time was ringed by four groups of Indians, each inhabiting its own territory and pursuing its own pattern of seasonal activity. To the northeast lived a small group of families Potts called the Nepis'cu'the'nues Indians (A.11/57: 37d). These people, most of whom had not seen a trading post before, inhabited a country poor in beaver and marten and subsisted primarily on caribou "wch is both Meat & Clothing to them" (B.182/a/1: 26). Potts encouraged them to trap furs but invariably they brought few when they visited the post, dealing instead in hides and venison. These people did not join the summer whaling at the Whale rivers, preferring to remain inland hunting caribou (B.182/a/11: 24d). To the south of Richmond Gulf was a group of people Potts called the Pis'he'poce. These Indians summered at Great Whale River where they hunted whales, but in the winter they moved southward or inland to trap furs. Before the establishment of Richmond Fort they had travelled annually to Eastmain House with their hunts and many continued to do so in this period (A.11/57: 37d). A group Potts named the Ear'ti'wi'ne'peck's lived to the southeast of the gulf and were the most important suppliers of furs to the new post. He described the role they had played in the trade before 1750:

All (or most) of the Indians who come here useing the Eastmain before this Settlement was built, where they Used annualy to carry their Furrs in the Spring under the direction of their Old Captain Caw'pa'chis'qua and who from thence came back to one or other of the Whale Rivers where they mett with the Ne'pis'cu'the'nues, those we call the Northward Indians: and there gott from them what Furrs they had (if any) and carried Them to Eastmain the Spring following. (A.11/57: 37–37d)

It is evident from Potts's remarks that Richmond Fort was attracting primarily Indians who already were involved in the company's trading system or else Indians who were not trappers at all. Table 6 shows that as a fur-trade post Richmond Fort proved to be unprofitable and unnecessary.

The fourth group of Indians inhabiting the area inland from Richmond Gulf was the Nashcoppees (Precisely who this group was is a mystery, as "Naskapi" [modern spelling] are recorded in the early historical records as occupying different widespread localities in the Quebec-Labrador peninsula and it is not likely they were all one and the same people. One very plausible explanation of this confusion has recently been offered by Mailhot (1981) whose linguistic analysis of the name suggests it refers to the people "at the other end." This territorial description accords well with the historical facts for they were always people inhabiting distant territories. Today this designation is applied only to the most northern group of Montagnais speakers who traditionally were barren ground dwellers and caribou hunters. This seems to be the same group referred to in the Richmond Fort records.) The Naskapi hunted caribou in the interior and seldom travelled to the coast. Since it had been learned that "ye said Nash, coppy Indians Never Comes to Trade wth ye English or French but Trafficks wth the Other Indians, wch Trade wth Both Nations," establishing a trade with these people was one of the company's highest priorities in the north (B.182/a/4: 41). Potts was ordered to send one of his servants inland to entice the Naskapi out to the coast to trade, but instead he attempted to engage local Indians to undertake the mission. In December 1754 he succeeded in convincing a man, on threat of cutting off his ears, to go inland:

I gave him some Brandy, Tabacco and Several Other Goods to present to Leeding Indians of ye Nashcoppe Clan to Encourage them to Come & trade wth us and if they had nothing to trade I Desired to See them and wou'd make them Wellcome at Richmond Fort and Trust them wth Some Goods to put them in a Way to procure Skins for Trade & provisions and inable them to Defend their Selves against Any Enimy that may Attackt them. (B.182/a/7: 16d)

The following summer the messenger returned with a party of twelve Naskapi. They had no furs – "they had Sent all their goods away to ye SEast to Trade wth Some Indians that Trades wth ye French" – but Potts gave them some presents and urged them to visit Richmond Fort in the future (B.182/a/7: 43d). The Naskapi told Potts that a post at Little Whale River would be more accessible to them. As well, they apparently feared encountering the Inuit in the vicinity of Richmond Gulf (B.182/a/7: 47). So in response to their request Richmond Fort was removed to the more southerly location in 1756–7. Nevertheless the number of Naskapi frequenting the post was never large and the amount of trade received from these people never equalled initial expectations.

While the fur trade stagnated, the company's whaling operation was also disappointingly slow to develop. The fishery, as the English called it,

TABLE 6
Richmond Fort Trade Returns, 1751–1759

	1751–2		1752–3		1753–4		1754–5		1755–6		1756–7		1757–8		1758–9	
	Qu	MB	Qu	MB	Qu	MB	Qu	MB	Qu	MB	Qu	MB	Qu	MB	Qu	MB
Beaver:																
whole	135	135	102	102	68	68	89	89	86	86	41	41	158	158	80	80
half	70	35	51	25	32	16	52	26	32	16	18	9	50	25	40	20
Bear:																
old	17	34	11	22	2	4	2	4	6	12	–	–	–	–	1	2
cub	–	–	–	–	–	–	2	2	1	1	–	–	–	–	–	–
Cats (lynx)	–	–	1	1	1	1	4	4	–	–	–	–	–	–	2	2
Fox:																
grizzled	4	8	5	10	13	26	10	20	9	18	4	8	1	2	4	8
red	9	9	8	8	18	18	20	20	52	52	16	16	1	1	22	22
black	–	–	1	3	–	–	–	–	–	–	–	–	–	–	–	–
white	74	37	18	9	5	2	–	–	26	13	2	1	1	½	17	8
blue	4	2	–	–	–	–	–	–	–	–	–	–	–	–	–	–
Feathers, partridge, lb	115	11	140	14	–	–	–	–	5	2	–	–	–	–	3	1
Marten	105	35	267	89	303	101	230	76	109	36	370	123	285	95	301	100
Otter	21	10	7	3	15	7	39	19	15	7	26	13	29	14	20	10
Wolf	6	12	1	2	–	–	2	4	1	2	–	–	–	–	–	–
Wolverine	5	7	3	4	–	–	2	3	55	7	–	–	–	–	2	3
Oil, hogshead/puncheon	40	243	32	192	–	–	–	–	–	–	/1	8	/30	240	/30	240

	1 Qu	1 MB	2 Qu	2 MB	3 Qu	3 MB	4 Qu	4 MB	5 Qu	5 MB	6 Qu	6 MB	7 Qu	7 MB	8 Qu	8 MB
Deerskin, buck/doe	–	–	4	4	3	3	10	8	8/54	8/27	–	–	–	–	–	–
Blubber, ton	–	–	–	–	12	288	6	144	6	144	–	–	–	–	–	–
Whale skins	–	–	–	–	–	–	8	8	30	30	–	–	43	43	25	25
Value in MB		579		489		535		522		462		219		579		522
Value of goods traded		528		454		529		509		391		208		579		522
Overplus		50		35		5		12		71		10		0		0

Source: B.182/d/1–9.
Note: Qu = Quantity; MB = Made Beaver. Fractions have been omitted.

Naskapi women at Fort Chimo in 1891. By this late period the Naskapi had been more fully drawn into the fur trade as shown by their use of European clothing.

began in the summer of 1752 when Potts had learned that Indian families traditionally gathered at the mouth of the Little Whale River in July to hunt the white beluga whales as they swam up the estuary in search of food. These animals, seldom exceeding eighteen feet, were valuable for their blubber, which was rendered into lighting oil, their meat, and their skins. Potts described how the whales were hunted:

I am to Acquaint your Honours that its Impossible to kill Whale Unless there is a great no. of Indians in Cannoes to stop ye mouth of the River when ye fish is come into it then Robinson Crouseo wth Some of the Most Expert Indians Strikes the Whales wch when Struck Darts Out of ye River; wth great swiftness they are then Joyned by those Indians that stops ye River's mouth; and ye fish Drags them Out to Sea Sometimes two or three miles before ye fish is dead & sometimes Over setts their Cannoes. (B.182/a/4: 3)

This technique produced anywhere from two to a dozen whales daily and required at least twenty canoes of Indians. At the height of the 1752 season at Little Whale River there were fifty men and their families whaling in twenty-five canoes. Potts planned simply to engage the Indians for the length of the season, usually until the end of August, paying them in brandy, tobacco, and standard trade items. To discourage them from hunting only long enough to acquire the items they needed, Potts paid the Indians in instalments. "I pay them one half when they kill a fish & the Remainder when ye fishing Season is Over So by that I keep my Selfe in there Dept So that I am Sure they Cannot go away till ye Season is Over" (B.182/a/4: 1d). This procedure kept the people at Little Whale River for the duration of the summer but it also resulted in their taking their half pay in "perishable goods." "So what they trade at Whale River for the Whales they kill is Mostly Brandy & Tabacco wth wch they Make themselves Merry Every Evening" (B.182/a/4: 2).

In 1752 the only building at Little Whale River was a log tent (B.182/a/3: 61). The next summer a small storehouse was constructed and the foundations of a dwelling house, to be called Whale River House, were laid (B.182/a/4: 51). Initially this house, located on the north shore of the river, was occupied only during the whaling season but in 1756, both to be closer to the fishery and to promote the Naskapi trade, Potts decided to dismantle Richmond Fort and move it to Little Whale River. Construction continued throughout that winter and the next, though the men not directly occupied remained at the original post. The new establishment was not completed and fully occupied until the spring of 1758 (B.182/a/10: 25).

Potts relied on Indian manpower for his whaling venture, but he hoped to improve on the Indian technique by employing a net. The experiment was made in the summer of 1755 (B.182/a/7: 45). A long net was strung across the mouth of the river, hemming in the whales so they could be harpooned more easily. As long as weather conditions remained good, the net proved successful but weather conditions were not often good. Two weeks after it had been put in place, heavy rainfall and high water levels in the river covered the net with mud and half of it had to be cut loose and abandoned (B.182/a/7: 48d). Unsettled weather plagued the whaling venture. High winds would whip up the water, making the chase too dangerous; rainstorms and the resulting high water muddied the river so that most whales refused to enter and those which did could not be seen; dense fog made it difficult to track the animals. When, for any of these reasons, the fishery had to be suspended for a number of days, the Indians naturally wanted to leave the river and engage in more productive activities elsewhere. To keep them on hand, Potts had to dispense presents of grain, liquor, and tobacco, all of which added to the expense of the fishery without really satisfying the Indians. The summer of 1757 was typical: "Most of ye Indians wants to go away from here to look for Deer, being allmost Starv'd wth living upon Oatmeal, there being no Whales to be got on account of ye great freshes in ye River, this Day I was Obliged to give ye Indians Flour, Brandy and Tabacco, ye wch I have been Oblig'd to give ym Several times to keep them here till please God to Send fine Weather" (B.182/a/9: 31).

To add to an already formidable list of difficulties facing the new post – an inhospitable climate, a population of Indians who would rather hunt caribou than trap beaver, a scarcity of fur-bearing animals – two incidents at Little Whale River disrupted the local inhabitants and dashed another of the Hudson's Bay Company's hopes, a profitable trade with the Inuit. Not much was known about the "Eusquamays" except that they lived north of Richmond Gulf and were the traditional enemies of their Indian neighbours. Company officials had expected that a settlement on the gulf might promote amicable relations between these two peoples, allowing a regular trade to commence. For the first few years no contact was made, but then in January 1754 a party of company servants encountered five Inuit a few miles north of the Little Whale River outpost. John Potts described the initial meeting: "When the Eusquamays got Near Our Men, they Lade Down their Bows and Arrows, Calling Chimo, Chimo, Claping Their Brests and Made all ye Signs of Friendship they Could, Our people then Lade Down their Guns, Call'd Out Chimo Chimo and made the Same Signs of friendship as the Eusquamays did, then Each party Advanced and Embraced each Other wth Great Signs of Joy" (B.182/a/6: 25d). A few days later Potts's second-in-command, Henry Pollexfen, accompanied two of the Inuit to Richmond Fort where the postmaster met them, explaining with sign language that he wished them to bring their furs in trade (B.182/a/6: 28). These two Inuit were part of a larger party of twenty-six men encamped on Knapp's Island off the coast. In the days that followed a number of the group visited the post and were given presents and encouraged to start trading. Though Potts readied his small arms and loaded the post's two cannon, it seemed the precautions were unwarranted.

On 9 February Henry Pollexfen and the small number of men who had returned with him to Whale River House quit the post to go hunting, leaving behind a boy named Matthew Warden. When the men returned later in the day, they found the house looted of iron implements and weapons and young Warden missing (B.182/a/6: 33). Immediately they retired to Richmond Fort which was secured against what Potts believed would be an imminent attack by the Inuit. Deciding against a rescue mission which would have divided his small force, the postmaster chose simply to wait and see what might develop. Two weeks later three Inuit men openly approached the post as if nothing unusual had happened. Feigning friendship, Potts welcomed them into the post, then immediately imprisoned two in irons, and sent the third back to his people with the warning that either they return Warden or the captives would be executed (B.182/a/6: 37d–40). The prisoners passed a quiet night in the guardroom while Potts tried to impress on them the size of the garrison by having his men repeatedly walk through the room, each time in different clothing. The next morning, however, the Inuit appeared agitated, and seizing two rifles which had been carelessly left within reach, they attempted to fight their way out of the post using the weapons as clubs. According to Potts, they

fought wth Great Resolution and Fury, the place being Narrow and low, that our people Could not knock them down, though Desperately Wounded, being fearful the Esquamays Guns Might go of and Shoot Some of Our People. Christopher Smith Shott one of them through ye Head, the other Esquamay Stud his Ground and fought wth great Rage and Fury. I gave Orders not to Shoot him but knock him down but he keeping his Garde So Well not Withstanding he was Wounded in Several places the Thumb of his Right Hand Cutt off but at last was Oblig'd to Shoot him Allso. (B.182/a/6: 42)

Fearing that young Warden would be killed in retaliation, Potts had some local Indians secretly dispose of the two corpses beneath the ice in a nearby river. From each body he took a single ear, which he sent "to ye Indian Captains of Moose & Albany Forts" (B.182/a/6: 45). The men remained on alert but no more Inuit approached the settlement and gradually normal activities were resumed. In May Matthew Warden's remains were found about two hundred yards from Whale River House (B.182/a/6: 59). This incident not only thwarted the Hudson's Bay Company's attempts to commence a trade with the Inuit, it also affected the trade already begun with the local Indians. Aware that their traditional enemies had been in the vicinity of Richmond Fort and had killed a European, these people became reluctant to visit the post. The next winter (1754–5) John Potts disappointedly wrote, "We have had very few Indians here this Winter they being fearfull of the Eusquemays so that we have had little or no Trade" (A.11/2: 162). Figures in table 6 indicate, however, that overall the trade suffered only minimally.

The following summer hostility between native groups was aggravated by the arrival at the whale fishery of fifteen Indians from James Bay who had come north by canoe to attack the Inuit. The first mention in the records of these "Esquimaux hunts," as the company servants called them, occurs in relation to de Troyes's expedition to James Bay in 1686. As de Troyes and his men were approaching Charles Fort, they met four Indians who told the French soldiers that "ils venoient de faire la guerre aux eskimos" (Collection Clairambault 1016: 439). This early encounter suggests that northern sorties may have predated the first European settlements in the bay, but whether this was the case, the Hudson's Bay Company records thereafter contained frequent references, though little detail. (See Francis 1979.) The initiators of the attacks were homeguard Indians from the Albany River area, often joined by warriors from Moose

River. For some reason more easterly Indians from the east coast did not participate. The usual practice was for half a dozen or more canoes of Indians to leave Albany Fort after the goose hunt in late May or early June and, after a brief visit to Moose to recruit from the homeguard there, to begin the five-hundred-mile voyage north. They sought the Inuit in the vicinity of Richmond Gulf. Hudson's Bay Company accounts suggest that encounters invariably favoured the southern Indians probably because early contact with the white man had provided these people with muskets before the Inuit. Generally the Indians were back at the bottom of the bay with scalps and sometimes child captives by early September to take part in the fall goose hunt. The fate of the captives is not known, though in at least two cases Hudson's Bay Company postmasters "purchased" them and put them to work for the company.

The explanation for the northern raids is unclear, though they seem to have satisfied some cultural need of the Albany and Moose Indians. They do not seem to have been an example of the kind of economically motivated warfare over territory or trade which so often led to the complete destruction of one side by the other (see Hadlock 1947). The Indians themselves accounted for their behaviour by attributing magical powers to the distant Inuit and blaming them for periods of disease or famine (B.3/a/16: 18; B.3/a/47: 37d). William Coats, in his *Geography of Hudson's Bay* (1852, 56), claimed that the Moose River people went "Usquemow hunting" because they were commanded to do so by the more southerly "Outawais" (or "Notawais") Indians, "a war-like people, and a terrour to all the neighboureing Indians." Coats wrote that these people frequently desired Inuit captives "for their annuall sacrifice" and that the Moose Indians "must provide them against such a moon, or be that sacrifice themselves." Dramatic as it is, Coats's account is also highly unlikely. Aside from being geographically confused, the captain's report is not supported by any other source from the period, improbable if the Moose people really were being terrorized in this manner. Whatever the rationale for the raids, the company began to look askance at them because of their detrimental effects on the fur trade. The situation at Little Whale River during the summer of 1755 was a case in point.

The fifteen marauders arrived at the river in mid-July. John Potts was having trouble enough persuading the local Indians to remain at the fishery, and he described the effect on them of the appearance of the James Bay people:

The Albany Indians, 10 men & 5 Women, Came Over ye river & tented Close by Our Whaleing Indians, wch frightened Our Indians extremely, So Much that they wanted to go away, I did all I could to persuad them to Stay, I gave them Some Brandy to give to ye Eusquamay hunters and got them to give me all their Guns

to keep wch made all things Easey, Our Indians tells me that its Common for ye
Albany and Moose River Indians when they cannot find the Eusquamays they kill
Our Indians, for their Scalps & Makes their country Men Believe their Scalps is
Eusquamays. Robinson Crouseo tells me that his Brother and 3 More was kill'd
by the Albany and Moose River Indians about 12 years ago & scalp'd. (B.182/a/7:
43)

After camping at Whale River House for three days, the "Eusquamay
hunters" continued on to Richmond Fort where they were given ammunition and then for three weeks were not heard from as they pursued their
bloody business. On 11 August Potts wrote in the Richmond Fort journal:
"Came here two of ye Eusquamay Hunters and informs me they had
found some of ye Eusquamays that kill'd Our Boy and plunder'd Whale
River House the Indians kill'd all they found and has got 4 childeren for
Slaves, they found Several of the things wch was Stole from Whale River
House" (B.182/a/7: 47d). Satisfied by their success, the Indians returned
south without further disrupting the whaling. Two years later nine
canoes of southern Indians reappeared at the gulf, once again killing several Inuit and once again "teryfying our Indians by telling ym that if they
did not See ye Eusquamays, they woud on their return kill and Scalp
them, wch filld them wth dread that they deserted ye fishery sooner then
they woud have done" (A.11/57: 46; B.182/a/9: 36d).

The Hudson's Bay Company's involvement in the "Esquimaux hunts"
was contradictory. On the one hand all the postmasters in James Bay
were ordered to discourage the sorties in whatever ways they could and
the masters claimed to be doing so. (See, for example, B.3/a/18: 18.) Yet
on the other hand it was common for the "hunters" to be outfitted at the
company posts with ammunition and other items they needed for the trip
north. Potts's actions exemplify this confusion, for while he complained
about the visits of the southern Indians, at the same time he encouraged
them by sending severed ear trophies to their leaders. It would appear
that by mid-century, however, all the company servants agreed that the
"Esquimaux hunts" were immoral and detrimental to the trade and were
doing their best to discourage them. Despite the opposition of the company the raids continued for the rest of the century (Francis 1979).

One by one the various enterprises at Richmond Fort had failed. The
lead and copper mine proved to be, as Thomas Mitchell had warned, a
chimera. The fur trade yielded disappointing returns, since the northern
Indians were resistant to concentrating more of their time on hunting for
furs. The Inuit trade was thwarted by traditional enmities the company
could not alter. The whaling operation was disrupted by bad weather, its
dependence on the local Indians, and the visits of the southern people.
Apart from the mine, the characteristic each of these failures shared was

that the company had tried to engage Indians in activities contrary to their traditional life-styles. Company servants had endeavoured to turn hunters into trappers, enemies into friends, itinerants into disciplined employees. But as Henry Pollexfen remarked, the Indians "are a People that can't nor won't be Commanded; will go when and where they please" (A.11/-/57: 38). The way the white trader wanted to exploit northern resources was not the way of the Indian and so to an important degree the native people simply did not cooperate.

In 1759 London officials informed Potts that "many years Experience having Convinced us that it is impracticable to procure any Trade either in Skins or other Commodity from Richmond in any Degree Adequate to the great Expence of Supporting that Factory, We have determined to withdraw the same this Year" (A.6/9: 109). That summer the postmaster and his men packed up all the stores and trade goods and sailed away from Richmond Gulf.

CHAPTER SEVEN

Daily Life At Eastmain House

While European settlement was failing to take hold in the north, life at Eastmain House had settled into a pattern which persisted until the close of the eighteenth century. The prospect of trade had brought Europeans to these shores but in fact the trading season lasted only a few weeks. For the rest of the year both white men and Indians engaged in activities largely dictated by the seasons. Each season had its specific employments, which for trader and hunter were different but complementary.

Before 1770 Eastmain House was abandoned each summer when the total complement of eight men, with all the surplus trade goods, made the trip across the bay to Albany Fort. Upon their return to the east coast in the fall the servants would fire guns to announce their arrival to the Indians, who would then come in for debt or ammunition to hunt geese. In 1770, however, in the hope that the inland Indians would come regularly if assured that a trader was in continuous residence, the complement was increased to twelve men, a few of whom stayed at the house while the sloop was absent (A.6/11: 81). Since the vessel often did not return to the east coast until October, this change allowed an earlier start to the fall goose hunt and enabled the inlanders who wintered relatively close to the coast to take debt and get away to their territory sooner in the fall. Near the end of the century the number of men at the post increased to twenty, eight of whom remained for the summer (B.59/a/62: 29).

Though not much trading took place in July and August, the summer residents were more than caretakers. They did some hunting and fishing themselves and traded provisions from the homeguard, principally ducks and fish. As well, hay for the post livestock was harvested from the marshes. The livestock consisted primarily of cattle, which were kept for butchering. The size of the herd, about twelve head in the 1780s (B.59/b/2: 11) and twenty-nine in 1796 (B.59/a/72: 29), necessitated a part-time cow-

Eastmain plantation, post-1802

Source: HBCA G.1/97. Undated–post 1802

1. Stockades around the gardens and houses
2. Masters house
3. Mens house
4. Warehouse
5. Boat builders shed
6. Still house
7. Old cattle shed
8. Hay shed
9. New cattle shed
10. Forge
11. Lime kiln
12. Belfry
13. Magazine
14. Old cook room
15. Stock shed
16. Stock shed garden
17. Turnip garden
18. Hay stadle
19. European burial ground
20. Mens garden
21. Pond
22. Half garden
23. Ridge path

keeper. During the winter the cattle were kept in a cow shed but the rest of the year they grazed about the post. Oxen were kept to haul firewood and logs in late winter, and goats were received from Moose Fort in 1796 (B.59/a/72: 18d). Mares were reported in use early in the 1800s at the later posts at Fort George and Great Whale River (B.77/a/3: 5, 9). A garden was begun at Eastmain as early as 1739. Turnips, collards, and potatoes were grown with most years yielding poor results. It was specifically mentioned that peas and beans were not sown because they would not grow (B.59/b/2: 2). A garden at Rupert House, the successor to Charles Fort, fared no better.

During the century construction at Eastmain House was going on almost continually, since the structure had a life span of only about twenty years. The original house was erected in 1719 and was fortified during the winter of 1723–4. In 1737 postmaster Joseph Isbister requested that the post be moved across the river and closer to the coast where the supply of wood was more accessible (A.6/6: 11). At first his superiors balked at the idea, pointing out that "the reasons that it was not placed lower down or at the mouth of the River was for fear of a Deluge which might sweep away Factory House, Goods, Servants and Indians" (A.6/6: 11d). But Isbister persisted and finally received permission to relocate on the south shore of the Eastmain River on George's Point. Like its predecessor, the new house was a log structure with a board roof coated in tar and with a brick stove and chimney. It was surrounded by a log stockade (B.59/a/4: 7ff). This post was succeeded in its turn by what Andrew Graham described as "a small square wooden building" erected on the same site in 1762 (1969, 256). Twenty years later this building deteriorated to the point where yet another Eastmain House had to be constructed (B.59/a/58: 18d ff). Regular rebuilding was the result of using unseasoned softwood logs to construct the posts. It was a complaint heard around the bay that the logs shrank as they aged and were quick to rot. In the summer, wrote Joseph Robson, a mason at York Fort, "the water beats between the logs, keeping the timber continually damp; and in the winter the white frost gets through, which being thawed by the heat of the stoves, has the same effect" (1752, 30). As well as the main dwelling house the post had a small number of rooms built into its flankers which were used as storage sheds, makeshift stables, or workshops for the tradesmen. These, too, deteriorated rapidly. In addition to the buildings, the sloop used to transport furs to and goods from Albany had to be maintained and made seaworthy each spring. The upshot was that carpenters, joiners, and masons were busy members of the Eastmain complement.

The main activity of the local Indians during the summer was fishing at lakes and rivers not far from the coast. Each family or group of families seemed to have a favourite fishing spot to which they dispersed after the

A View of Eastmain Factory, early 1800s, a watercolour by William Richards, native-born Hudson's Bay Company employee.

spring goose hunt. Trout, tikomeg (whitefish), methy (burbot), and jack (pike) were the most important fish caught. Some were consumed during the summer, some were traded to the men at Eastmain House and, later, at Rupert House for tobacco and brandy, and the remainder were dried for use during the winter. In the summer of 1775 John Thomas, a Hudson's Bay Company servant, explored about two hundred miles up the Nottaway River. On his return he encountered five families of Indians, among them Cobbage, captain of the Eastmain homeguard, encamped below a falls a short distance up the river from the coast. Thomas described how fish were being caught.

They use Netts but if they want a few fresh Fish and do not choose to go to their Netts they take a Small hand nett such as the Fishmongers use for taking the Fish out of their Cisterns and in the Space of about ½ an Hour I have seen them scoop out about 20 fine Tickomeg Up Ruperts River (Cobbage says) is a Fall where he never uses his Netts but Scoops them out many at a time by one of the small Hand Netts. (A.11/44: 17d–18)

The falls mentioned by Cobbage may have been the place where early in the next century James Clouston, company teacher, trader, and explorer, saw many Rupert House people gathering to fish. According to Clouston's description, the Indians used a large oval hoop net affixed to a pole, which when swept through the water, picked up as many as a dozen fish in a pass. Another technique involved building at the base of the falls a rock pool with a small outlet and sides as high as the water level. The turbulent water would throw the fish into the pool and they could be netted easily at the outlet (Davies 1963, 30). Larger fish, sturgeon for example, were speared.

Summer was also the season when the Indians travelled between James Bay posts, visiting friends and relatives and trading for goods among themselves. This trading activity increased on the east coast in the late 1770s when the people inhabiting the southern areas of the bay began to experience a shortage of leather as the caribou population declined. At Eastmain House people from as far north as Richmond Gulf came to trade and brought with them large quantities of leather, since caribou were still plentiful in that region. In order to acquire some of these skins, members of the Moose River homeguard began to pay summer visits to Eastmain, led by the captain of the guard, Chickahenish (B.59/a/57: 26). There was occasional intermarriage between the Eastmain and Moose homeguards – for example, Chickahenish's granddaughter was married to an Eastmain man – but relations between the Moose River people and the more northerly Indians were not friendly (B.59/b/4: 14). The visitors brought items to trade for the skins, including birch bark, but according to Hudson's Bay Company records the northern people were often bullied into trading and violence was not uncommon. In the 1790s a Moose leader named Pisso collected leather at Eastmain House, which he conveyed to the Indians at Abitibi. According to George Atkinson, Pisso also ran a protection racket: "He intimates to the Indians here that it is to prevent some (which he calls bad Indians) from coming to kill them and being naturally timid they are soon imposed upon; last year I'm told it was a he Martin Skin which he collected from each of our North'rd Indians ... this year it is a Deer Skin" (B.59/b/12: 14d). Another Eastmain postmaster complained that the Moose River Indians, by taking away all the skins they could, were "distressing East Main for leather," but more importantly it was feared that the northern Indians might begin to take their trade elsewhere (B.59/b/1: 12). At Moose, however, John Thomas refused to intercede, reasoning "twould be cruel for me to hinder their supplying themselves with so necessary articles as Deer Skins for Snow Shoes & Shoe Leather" (B.59/b/5: 3d).

In the fall the number of inland people visiting Eastmain House was small, generally about twelve to fifteen. These were men whose hunting grounds were close enough to the coast that they could come to the house and still reach their winter quarters before the rivers froze over in November. The purpose of their visit was to get more credit to help outfit themselves until the following spring. They did not remain at the house for more than a couple of days and took no part in the main activity of the season, the fall goose hunt.

The goose hunt was carried out by the homeguard, who left off fishing and gathered at the post in late August and early September in anticipation of the birds' arrival. Customarily the hunters, between ten and twenty of them, were given a quantity of brandy or strong beer to celebrate the beginning of the hunt. They then received measures of powder and shot and, along with their families, went out to hunt in the marshes along the coast. In the early years one or two company servants accompanied the people to the goose camp to distribute ammunition as it was needed. Later it became usual for the hunters themselves, or members of their family, to go to the post with geese and return with the ammunition. The women and children plucked the dead birds and the feathers were traded to the company separately. At the post the geese were salted in casks for consumption during the winter. By mid-October the geese had usually left the bay and most of the homeguard had taken debt and left the post. A very good hunt was considered to be between two and three thousand geese but this total was seldom achieved, the fall season more characteristically producing between five hundred and a thousand birds. Salt geese constituted a large part of the diet of the men at Eastmain House, though the Indians themselves preferred them dried. Rupert House was established in 1776 at least in part to procure geese for the parent post (B.3/k/1: 9d). In its early years Rupert House had a smaller homeguard but salted as many geese as Eastmain did and by the 1790s it was producing over two thousand geese in the fall hunt (B.186/a/9: 2d ff).

The homeguard captain was given the responsibility by the Hudson's Bay Company to ensure that the goose hunters appeared at the right time in sufficient numbers. Like the trading captain, the homeguard captain was selected for his influence over the coastal Indians and his principal role was to act as intermediary between the white man and the Indian. At times he may have performed other more traditional leadership roles, such as deciding a winter's hunting strategy or seeking supernatural guidance through divination, but it is probable the Indians recognized other leaders among themselves as well. Whereas a total of about thirty-five trading captains were recognized at Eastmain House over the years, there were just five homeguard captains and only one at a time. While the recognition of trading captains was a practice which lasted well into the nineteenth century, the homeguard captain as an institution began to die out in the 1780s. In 1785 Cobbage, captain of the goose hunters, died and the postmaster did not appoint a successor. The final homeguard leader was named in 1803; he was Mistigoosh and he was recognized as leader of a group of northern goose hunters only. In fact, his appointment was part of an effort to solidify Indian support in the face of a North West Company challenge in the bay and had little to do with goose hunting. He lost his distinction in 1813, though he continued to be known as one of the best hunters at the post and continued to manage the northern goose hunt (B.59/e/3: 4d). Homeguard captains did not receive as many gifts as did the inland trading captains, nor did they enjoy the same degree of influence with the Hudson's Bay Company. While servants were reliant on geese as a staple food, so too were the Indians and they in turn relied on the post for ammunition. Furthermore, the coastal people were only part-time fur hunters, relying on the Hudson's Bay Company stores in times of starvation. Unlike the inlanders, they did not have the opportunity to trade with Canadian competitors, and consequently they did not have the opportunity to manipulate their relationship with the white trader to their advantage.

In return for supplying the posts with geese the homeguard people received the traditional gifts of brandy at the beginning, the end, and sometimes the middle of the hunt; as much ammunition as they could use for as long as the geese were in the area; a quantity of geese for their own use; and, as well, a variety of trade items including cloth, knives, tobacco, guns, and vermilion (B.59/d/1: 14). The amount of ammunition taken by an individual hunter was recorded and he was expected to produce a given number of geese in return. Those who were successful hunters were rewarded with ample credit for the winter; credit was decreased or withheld for those Indians who produced few geese. This excerpt from the Eastmain House journal of 1749 illustrates how credit was used to encourage the homeguard:

The Capt. and his Gard ... came and Told me thair was no geas to keel and thay wanted Soum Troust to go to thair winter's Quarters. I was willing to have as Many geas keeld as posebell. I Told tham Who Ever ould Stay a Week Longer to See if any Moar Geas was to be goat I ould lett tham Nesscarys have for to go and tham that ould not Stay I ould Trost Tham Nothing so Thay ingaged again to Stay. (B.59/a/17: 4d)

After leaving the post, members of the homeguard either travelled to their hunting grounds to begin gathering furs or returned to favoured fishing spots. Fall fishing, by both Indian and company servant, continued into December, and after the rivers and lakes froze over, nets were set beneath the ice. In the final three months of the year it was not uncommon for homeguard fishermen to bring more than a thousand pounds of fish to Eastmain House. In return they received primarily brandy and tobacco and sometimes cloth. The Indians usually were paid for food provisions with luxury items. This policy was intended to encourage the hunting of fur animals, since only furs could be exchanged for necessities such as guns, knives, and kettles. By the 1760s a few families of Indians were remaining at or near the house for at least a month longer than the others in order to knit snowshoes and fish nets and hunt provisions for the servants (B.59/a/32: 3d). The Indians were given twine for the nets and were paid in trade goods. It was in this capacity that the first hunters were employed by the company. During the next century one of the important changes in the Indian way of life would be the tendency for more and more of the homeguard to become seasonal employees at the post, thereby supplementing their trapping and subsistence hunting and fishing activities with wage labour.

With the Indians gone to their hunting grounds, the men at Eastmain House settled into their winter routine. The requirements of trade and survival in the bay demanded a variety of skills; therefore the complement of men at the post was drawn from across the spectrum of the British labouring classes. In its first decades the complement at Eastmain House consisted largely of the sailors who manned the sloop on its voyages to and from Albany Fort. During the winter they worked as general labourers. This situation lasted until the house became permanently occupied in 1770 at which time tradesmen began to be added to the complement. The first was a tailor, whose responsibility it was to keep the servants outfitted in warm clothing and to produce the elaborate uniforms presented in the spring to the principal Indian hunters (B.59/a/40: 33d). By 1775 a gunsmith, or armourer, had been added, largely at the insistence of the Indians. "He Greatly wants to have En Armerer Sent to this place," wrote Thomas Moore, master at Eastmain, of a principal captain, "so that the Indians might have there Guns Mended and Kettles Repeared" (B.59/a/40: 42d). The muzzle-loading weapons needed frequent attention and it was suspected that because repairs were not available at Eastmain House, many Indians were going to the French. As well as attending to the guns, the armourer produced and repaired a variety of metal goods for the trade. By 1780 a bricklayer had joined the complement. He, along with the shipwright and later a carpenter, was responsible for keeping the buildings inhabitable. And finally, a cooper was added, to fashion the casks for the salt geese and the containers used to ship goods upriver to the new inland posts. Rounding out the list of servants were a surgeon, a writer to prepare the journals and correspondence, and, of course, the postmaster. These men were officers, who inhabited separate quarters and took their meals at a separate table. Table 7 documents the growth of the Eastmain complement. Wages remained fairly constant during the century, the large increase in the master's wage being accounted for by increased responsibilities. Two men doing identical jobs could receive different wages because of seniority; wages usually increased with each

TABLE 7
Servants and Wages, Eastmain House, 1744, 1770, and 1790

	1744		1770			1790 (incl. Rupert House)		
Name	Position	Wages (in pounds sterling)	Name	Position	Wages	Name	Position	Wages
Thos. Mitchell	sloopmaster	40	Thos. Moore	master	50	Geo. Atkinson	master	100
Chris. Rowberry	sailor	20	Geo. Atkinson	sailor	25	Geo. Gladman	writer	25
Chris. Hardy	sailor	18	Matt Colling	shipwright	36	John Clark	writer	15
Wm. Shepheard	sailor	24	Chas. Maculock	sailor	15	Jas. Foggett	carpenter	25
Robt. Whorlton	sailor	18	Wm. Gee	sailor	15	Magnus Flett	cooper	18
Wm. Lamb	sailor	20	John Emerson	sailor	15	Geo. Loutit	tailor	8
Chas. Cromarthee	apprentice	10	John Mason	sailor	15	Wm. Robinson	sloopmaster	25
Jack Eskemay	Inuit boy	not paid	John Irving	labourer	6	Thos. Halcrow	labourer	8
			Wm. Davis	sailor	15	Peter Sabaston	labourer	6
			John Kay	labourer	10	Thom. Johnston	labourer	6
			Hugh Sclater	sailor	15	John Flett	labourer	6
			Jas. Robertson	labourer	6	And. Moar	labourer	6
			James Forker	labourer	6	Magnus Norn	labourer	6
						Nicol Spence	carpenter	25
						Alex. Mitchel	armourer	25
						Thos. Johnstone	labourer	6
						Thos. Loutit	labourer	6
						Barth. Nelson	surgeon	40

Sources: A.16/3; A.16/4; A.16/13.

year spent in the country. A servant's wage was supplemented by free board and lodging at the post and a percentage of the proceeds from any furs he managed to trap during his stay in the bay, though this was usually minimal.

Aside from the tasks associated with each trade there were myriad jobs about the post to be performed – chopping and hauling firewood, cutting logs and sawing boards for construction, picking oakum for caulking the wall of the house, tending the livestock. To supplement their European provisions company servants were sent out for a few days or a week at a time to fish and hunt at log tents not far from the post. While tenting out, the men also trapped fur-bearing animals for their own profit. Here is George Atkinson recording the returns from one of these hunting expeditions in 1784:

Dec. 7, Tues. the whole of the Tenters return'd Home – receivd from Mr. Paulson's Tent at Canniapascatch, Martins 10, Rabbits 23, Fish Trout 48 lb., Partridges 3, Porcupines 3. From Mr. Watson, at the Trout Creek, and his Men, Martins 9, Fish Trout 450 lb. From the Writer and Man, at the Fall Tent, Martins 2, Rabbits 75 – From the fishing Creek, Fish Tickomeg 137, Martin 1, Mink 1 is the whole of your Honors' Servants Trappings, and likewise Victuals. (B.59/a/60: 8)

If the men at Eastmain House had had to subsist on hunts as meagre as this, they would have starved. Earlier in the century London officials had instructed their bayside officers 'to Inure some of the most Expert of your Men to Hunting and Fishing, until they become good Artists therein," hoping to reduce the posts' reliance on the Indians (B.135/c/1: 14). With the exception of servants who remained in the country long enough to become proficient with the gun and snare, the necessary skills were never developed and Atkinson had to admit of his men that "they are entirely at a Loss how to hunt Provisions" (B.59/a/60: 7d). Table 8 indicates clearly that most of the country food consumed at Eastmain House was provided by the Indians.

Complaints about the sobriety, ability, and discipline of the servants were a recurring theme running through the correspondence from the James Bay posts, especially in the early years. In 1703 John Fullartine described the new batch of recruits as "poor, sorry, helpless souls and no ways fitting for the country at this juncture," and twenty-four years later Joseph Myatt complained, "There is not one labouring man that came over the last year but what are sots to a man" (Davies 1965, 6, 123). Company records do not allow a voice to the servants themselves; therefore we cannot know if they were as ineffectual and debauched as their superiors often claimed. We can conclude that given the discomfort and

TABLE 8
Country Provisions Hunted by
Hudson's Bay Company Men and Indians at
Eastmain House, 1 October 1784 to 1 August 1785

Provision	Hudson's Bay Company	Indian
Fish, lb	612	4272
Rabbit	111	1205
Geese	–	1725
Partridge	190	–
Beaver	–	26
Porcupine	3	18
Seal	–	10
Venison:		
whole caribou	–	1
hearts	–	22
tongues	–	6
shoulders	–	28
rumps	–	10
sides	–	32
briskets	–	8
dried, lb	–	440

Sources: B.59/a/60; B.59/d/2.

isolation of the life and the sometimes cruel discipline imposed by the postmasters, it is not surprising to encounter outbursts of drunkenness and disobedience among the men. One of the few public defenders of the servants was Joseph Robson, who had served at York Fort and Churchill River in the 1740s and in 1752 wrote a book entitled *An Account of Six Years Residence in Hudson's Bay*. Criticizing what he called "the oppressive and cruel behaviour of the governors and captains towards the inferior servants," Robson described the postmasters this way: "These men have generally sea-officers principles and exert the same arbitrary command, and expect the same slavish obedience here, as is done on board a ship" (1752, 38). Though the officers had dictatorial power over their men, not all used it with equal severity. A reading of the daily journals, admittedly kept by the postmasters, suggests that life at the posts was neither as vice-ridden nor as fear-ridden as Robson and the more censorious officers claimed.

Clearly, however, men suitable to the rigours of life in James Bay would have been hard to find among the labouring classes of England, especially since European wars were using up the available manpower. In recognition of this shortage an apprenticeship system had been introduced by 1684. Young boys, sometimes in their early teens and often from welfare institutions, were bound to the company's service for up to seven years. During this time they learned the skills of the trade, and when their term expired, they invariably signed on as servants, providing the company with a pool of experienced, disciplined men from which to choose its officers. Almost half of the Eastmain sloopmasters between 1700 and 1736 were "graduates" of the apprenticeship system. Another policy intended to improve the quality of company servants was to favour their recruitment from the Orkney Islands. Whereas Londoners were "so well acquainted with the ways and debaucheries of the town," as Joseph Myatt complained, Orkneymen, bred to the hard life of the crofter and fisherman and innocent of the depravities of the city, were considered ideal for work in James Bay (Davies 1965, 123). And so it became usual for the supply ship on its way to the bay to pause at the islands and take on a complement of men hired by a local recruiter commissioned by the company.

Servants were strictly forbidden to fraternize with the local Indian population. There was to be no social intercourse, outside of the ceremonies associated with the trading, and business dealings were the sole responsibility of the postmaster or a designated officer. The English traders felt very uncertain about the intentions of the Indians, did not trust them, and feared that some might be in league with the French. As a precaution against sudden attack, servants were trained in the use of firearms and forbidden to leave the post without permission (ibid., 17). The men were expected to be celibate and to have no liaisons with Indian women but predictably enough this rule was regularly violated, especially by the postmasters, who invariably took a local woman "to bed and board." Joseph Isbister, Eastmain postmaster in the 1730s, took as his wife the daughter of Bullshead, a prominent east coast hunter, and by her had a number of children. Similarly, John Thomas, master at Moose Fort from 1782 to 1813, took a wife named Meenish, and George Atkinson, the energetic master of Eastmain House, was married to Nucushin. The children of both marriages had successful careers in the James Bay fur trade. These are examples of successful Indian-white relations. A markedly different case involved James Hester, Eastmain master during the 1760s, who had to be returned to England after suffering a mental breakdown and attempting to castrate himself with a knife "for fornication that he had committed" with an Indian woman (B.59/a/36: 21).

The official injunction against sexual relations with local women was no doubt an attempt to maintain discipline at the posts but, further than that, Indian women were suspected of being thieves and spies, potential fifth columns who might in the middle of the night open the fort to an attack by their jealous menfolk. Resentment among Indian men at having their women stolen by whites was one of the factors believed responsible for the Henley House murders of 1754, described in the next chapter, prompting an officer to inform London: "Women has been the distruction of your People, your Goods and Trade" (A.11/2: 174d).

Another consideration which explains the attempted separation of Indian and European was the reluctance of company officials to "civilize" the Indian. Theirs was a business concern and they were content to have the Indians remain untutored as long as they continued to bring in their furs and did not question the practices of the trade. This policy was enunciated forcibly in 1724 when Richard Staunton, then master at Albany, was scolded by his superiors for attempting to teach a young Indian lad to read and write. "The Company are very much displeas'd," he was told, "to hear that any Indian is taught to Write & Read or admitted into ye Trading Room to prye into ye Secrets of their affairs in any nature whatsover without our order & charge you strickly not to continue that nor suffer any such Practices for ye future" (A.6/4: 86d). When it came to Europeanizing the Indians, benign neglect would remain company policy until the next century.

As much as fear, suspicion, and prudery influenced the official attitude to the Indians, profit, more precisely the threat posed to profit by private trade, was perhaps the most important factor in the relations between officers and men at the post. "To converse with an Indian is a great crime," wrote Joseph Robson, "but to trade with him for a skin is capital, and punished by a forfeiture of all wages" (1752, 17). Servants were permitted, indeed encouraged, to trap furs in the vicinity of the posts, but these furs had to be delivered into the company storehouse from where they were shipped to England and sold, half the value going to their owner (A.6/3: 47d). Instead the men often concealed their trappings and used them to barter with the crew and captains of the annual supply ship, usually for liquor. Seamen were not permitted to bring home furs privately but smuggling was common. Another form of private trade involved using trade goods smuggled into the bay aboard the supply ships to barter for furs with the Indians. Since intercourse between servant and Indian was banned, meetings had to be arranged when the servants were in the woods trapping, hunting, or gathering wood. In 1715 it was decided that the men might be dissuaded from concealing their furs if they had an opportunity to sell them on the spot; therefore masters were given authority to purchase the servants' half share in their trappings "by giving them a Bottle of Brandy & half a pound of Sugar for each Martin Skin" (A.6/3: 133). While the offer was frequently taken advantage of, officials continued to complain of private trade throughout the century and it was this continuing concern which caused most dissension between officers and men.

Since it was difficult to surprise the men in the act of trading, the master periodically searched their personal effects for furs and private stocks of trade items, a practice bound to cause ill-feeling at the post. In 1738, for example, Joseph Isbister wrote: "Having an infirmation of pouder and Martins being among our people, in ye for Noone Mad a Sarch for ye pouder and Martins that I was informd of, beginning with John Turnbulle I found 1 Martin and three pounds of pouder" (B.59/a/2: 19d). Six years later Thomas Mitchell made one of his frequent searches and found in a servant's chest ten pounds of gunpowder and eight knives which had been smuggled in from England (B.59/a/12: 9). Mitchell's tenure as master (1743–50) seems to have been especially troubled, as more than once his servants disobeyed his orders, on one occasion beating him, and he responded with the whip and the irons (B.59/a/12: 20; B.59/a/13: 18; B.59/a/15: 39d). The reasons for these incidents are not apparent, since the only accounts are provided by Mitchell himself. Even if he was a tyrant, he must have enjoyed the confidence of his superiors because he was not recalled and in 1750 was given responsibility for establishing the company's new post in Richmond Gulf. However, he was dismissed that same year, ironically enough because he was suspected of carrying on a private trade himself. The problem did not end, of course, with Mitchell's departure. In 1769 officials were concerned enough about it to stiffen the penalty and warn their servants that "all Persons that shall be found Guilty of such fraudulent Practices will be immediately put in Irons, & so kept untill the arrival of the Ship, when they will be sent to England there to be punished, as Purloiners of the Company's Property" (B.3/b/7: 5d).

Despite the restraints on movement and privacy which resulted from the war on private trade, relations between officers and men at Eastmain House appear to have improved in the last half of the century. More and more servants were experienced, long-term employees who felt comfortable in the country and many were mixed bloods (Indian mother, British father) who had been raised in a fur-trade environment. Furthermore, as relations between Indian and servant became more confident, it was possible to relax the discipline imposed to keep them separate. The post thus lost its resemblance to a jail. Still, the postmasters had supreme authority, and when challenged, they reacted with harsh punishments. Witness the following entry by George Atkinson dating from 1791: "Punished

Wm. Duffle with a Dozen lashes, for breaking open a Liquor Case, getting drunk & making use of the most abusive Language" (B.59/a/67: 17d).

By about mid-October all the Indians had left Eastmain House for their winter quarters, but towards the end of November members of the homeguard began coming from their coastal territories with the first furs. The men came either by themselves or in company with another man or their sons. Only rarely did they bring their wives, who were left at the camp with the young children. On these visits to the house the hunters remained only a day or two before returning to their tents, and throughout the winter there were men coming in every few days. As well as furs, they brought fish, rabbit, and caribou meat.

We have seen in chapter 5 that starvation was a common occurrence in eastern James Bay. When hunters and their families arrived at the post in a starved condition, they were given oatmeal by the master and sometimes a quantity of ammunition to allow them to resume the hunt, if there were animals to hunt. In bad winters the homeguard often came into the post in March and camped there, as many as one hundred people in some years, awaiting the commencement of the spring goose hunt. During this time the Indians were supported when necessary by rations of oatmeal from the post. The provision of food by the company during periods of scarcity was not an act of charity. For one thing, it was in the traders' interest to keep the hunters alive and healthy and able to continue gathering furs. But more importantly, it may have been an act of compensation, since starvation among the homeguard was exacerbated by the company itself in its desire to have them present at the spring goose hunt. This need to attend the hunt made it impossible for the people to travel very far inland where furs were more plentiful because the goose season began before breakup and the hunters had to come in by foot. The fact that the homeguard inhabited the coast also denied them regular supplies of venison, usually an important part of their diet, since Eastmain House records state that by the mid-1760s "Deer is not to be got in 100 Miles of this Place but Seldom wch makes it very bad for the Home-Guard Indians" (B.59/a/35: 17d). The homeguard people were not completely confined to the coast, and when in the early winter their hunts were poor, they often journeyed a short distance inland. As Thomas Mitchell made explicit in 1745, they could not go very far if they were to attend the spring hunt and, recognizing this, the company was obliged to provide oatmeal. "Servd ot to 36 Indians small & Great 6 lbs of damidgd flower. These Indians if thay where a 100 mile in Land they might find Supply a Nough But yt we Should want them to kill Geese" (B.59/a/12: 19d).

E.E. Rich has wondered why, given the threat of starvation, Indians never traded for oatmeal but preferred to rely on the goodwill of the white trader. Rich believed this attitude was explained by Indian "improvidence" and the fact that "the Indian did not react to the ordinary European notions of property nor to the normal European economic motives" (1960, 46). But these explanations ignore the understanding between Indian and trader that each would supply the other with provisions. This understanding removed food from the ranks of the trade commodities and made it part of a reciprocal gift exchange. An Indian need not "spend" his furs on oatmeal when he could claim it freely at the post. Neither should the periodic necessity of the Indians to rely on the post for food during the winter obscure the fact that when the year as a whole is considered, the Indians provided the post with much more food than the company provided the Indians. That the homeguard were dependent on the company for short periods of time was a situation created by the fur trade, and a more accurate characterization of this aspect of the relationship between Indian and company would be a state of mutual reliance or interdependence. A company servant who recognized this was James Isham who wrote at mid-century from York Fort: "It's to be observ'd that those Indians that hunts at Seasons for the forts, can not do without the assistance of the English, any more than the English without them, for the Cheif of our Living is this Country's product" (1949, 78).

In good years, when the Indians were not forced to the post early because of starvation, they began assembling for the goose hunt early in April. The entire family arrived and camped outside the post. The homeguard population at Eastmain House remained constant until the 1780s at about one hundred men, women, and children, of which about twenty were goose hunters. This number increased during the 1780s until by 1790 there were thirty hunters (B.59/a/65: 28d). Most of these additional people were Indians from the northward between Eastmain and Big River who previously had been trading Indians but became goose hunters when the master established a northern goose tent at this time. By 1800 there were eighteen canoes of northern goose hunters alone (B.59/a/77: 27d). This goose tent was supplied by boat from Eastmain House and the hunters were considered part of the homeguard. While waiting for the birds to arrive, the goose hunters socialized and performed odd jobs for the company, such as hauling firewood, picking oakum, or dislodging the sloop from the ice. Every 23 April, St. George's Day, was celebrated with a target-shooting competition and an extra ration of brandy. The hunt began towards the end of April or early in May (the earliest recorded date was 7 April in 1738 but that was most unusual) and continued until late May, early June. As soon as it was over, the Indians departed for their summer fishing grounds.

Company servants at this time were occupied salting the geese and preparing trade goods for the arrival of the inland hunters. The ice on the rivers broke up towards the end of May and generally the first few days of June saw the arrival of the first inlanders and the commencement of the trading season. Life at Eastmain House had come full circle.

The inland Indians were not involved in the round of activities at the post, except for the few days in June when they came in with their furs. Their round of activities centred wholly on traditional pursuits, but their participation in the fur trade emphasized their hunting of fur animals and preparing the pelts for trade. Subsistence was of course the most important activity, as it was with the homeguard, but hunting for food was not necessarily incompatible with fur hunting unless all animal resources were scarce. The seasonal round of activities of the inlanders depended on the species of game available. An abundance of caribou in one year meant a different hunting schedule than in a year when there was a scarcity. In good years the hunters could decide which of several hunting strategies they wished to follow.

The social organization of the Indians is more easily compiled from nineteenth-century records and appears in chapter 10. There is no indication that in the eighteenth century Indians, when it came to organizing themselves for carrying out their daily activities, would have grouped themselves very differently. There were tendencies in organization that had been evolving in the seventeenth century and were becoming more developed in the eighteenth, leading to a very discernible pattern by the early decades of the next century. One such likely development was in the size of the winter hunting group, the coresidential unit. In 1754 postmaster John Longland recounted that an Indian had told him too many people together hindered their hunting for furs at which Longland remarked, "I find that to be True for where there is 3 or 4 famileys in one Tent they Do nothing but Contrive for there Belley and not Look out for furrs" (B.59/a/23: 3d). This remark suggests the possibility that before the emphasis on hunting fur animals the James Bay people tended to remain in larger groups during the winter, conditions permitting. If this was so, then as involvement in the fur trade progressed, a slight reduction in the size of such cooperating groups occurred. By the 1830s, as is shown in chapter 10, often two family households were the norm for the winter season.

Another eighteenth-century development was the land tenure system. Anthropologists writing in the last twenty years have denied the existence of individual family-owned hunting territories until late in the nineteenth century and even well into the present one. Only Bishop has attributed the emergence of such a system to the middle of the nineteenth century (1970, 3). The reasons given for not entertaining an earlier development of individual family-owned hunting territories are several. Rogers suggested a correlation between the existence of individual "rights to certain resources ... with the highly evolved fur trade of the late nineteenth century," meaning the Indians became greatly involved in the fur trade rather recently (1963, 84). This would suggest the Indians produced fewer furs in early years, but a comparison of the per capita fur returns at Eastmain in 1753 and 1828 showed no dramatic increase (Morantz 1978, 231). In fact there were striking similarities, indicating that at least by the mid-eighteenth century the James Bay people were as deeply involved in the fur trade as they would be nearly a century later.

Similarly Leacock argued that subsistence needs predominated over fur hunting to the extent that individualistic tendencies, so necessary to the development of family-owned territories, could not have developed very early and communal patterns prevailed (1954, 6). Leacock ignored the fact that fur animals, particularly beaver, provided a considerable amount of food – an average of 1770 pounds per hunter or approximately 354 pounds per person in 1753 (Morantz 1978, 232). Moreover, the nature of the game used by the people did not require large communal hunting groups. Although Rogers conceded that the extension of credit was a practice promoting individualism, he ascribes its appearance and thus its impact to the late nineteenth century (1963, 84). However, as seen in chapter 5, debt, or trust, was a well-developed institution already in the 1730s and was extended by the Hudson's Bay Company to individuals, not groups.

Since Leacock emphasized the dichotomy between food and furs, she concluded that it was "impractical" for the Indians to have held the notion of trespass (1954, 7). Bishop (1970, 6) and Rogers (1963, 85) join Leacock in viewing the notion of trespass as a central issue in the discussion of the land tenure system. As Bishop says, "There can be no trespass without boundaries and no resentment if ideas concerning rights are not present" (1970, 6). What is missing in the various discussions in the anthropological literature on the subject of trespass is, however, consideration that this notion could have existed in the mid-eighteenth century. Yet in 1745 there is the following clearly worded comment by postmaster Thomas Mitchell:

Ever Indian hath a River or Part where ya Resorts to ye winter Season & in Som are More fish yn others. But ya Count it a Trespas to kill anything in one anothers Leiberty for Last winter one of our Indians did not kill one Martain & I asked him ye Rason. He sade another Indian Tould him all ye martains Be Longd to him so he sade he lived on dear & Som Rabbits. (B.59/a/12: 17d)

Here is evidence of Leacock's dualism between food and furs but it is manifested in a way that she denied could have existed in the 1700s. The notion of trespass here is extended only to animals involved in trade, not to animals of interest primarily for food. This quotation also establishes the correct perspective on the whole question. It is the fur resources which are of paramount interest, whereas the land serves as the "unit of management" (Tanner 1973, 112). Other references from throughout the eighteenth century indicate the Mitchell quotation was not a chance, accidental remark.

In 1814 three different postmasters discussed individual grounds in the context that encroachments could not be controlled. By 1823 comments such as this one appeared regularly in the records: "It appears to me that the Coast Indians and the majority of the Inland Indians who visit Ruperts House are tenacious of their Property in their Lands and are not pleased when other Indians encroach on them" (B.186/e/5: 9d). The fact that the James Bay people practised conservation, as discussed in chapter 10, is more conclusive evidence for individual territories, as there would have been no point sparing beaver if someone else could take them. Furthermore, in 1842 several Rupert House Indians were complaining that Indians from other posts were "working lands" they had "left in reserve" for three years (B.186/b/43: 14).

Since the reporting of Indian life in the nineteenth-century records is much more detailed than that in the previous century, it is tempting to say the earlier evidence indicates only a development towards the family-owned hunting territories of the mid-1800s. However, this may well be understating the situation. What is important to note is that the necessary elements of such a system – individualization, the correlation of food and fur animals, full involvement in the fur trade, and the notion of trespass – had all developed and thus the existence of the whole, of family-owned hunting territories, must be seriously considered. As expected, there is much evidence that it was a flexible system allowing families to join others on their lands when resources failed or to hunt for food on anyone's land in times of need. Fishing grounds are described as "neutral grounds" (B.186/e/6: 8). As seen above, both the homeguard and inland Indians had family hunting territories. There were no discernible differences in the functioning of the hunting territories of these two groups.

The fur trade in the seventeenth and eighteenth centuries probably underscored the development of smaller social groups and more individualized ownership of resources among the Indians. Smaller hunting groups based on two families were better suited to fur hunting, since they required less food resources in a given area and provided a higher per capita yield of furs. Family-owned hunting territories may have arisen or become better defined as a result of the European trading system providing individuals with trade goods for which they had to produce furs in exchange. Consequently the individual hunting territories developed as a means of managing these resources.

CHAPTER EIGHT

Penetrating the Hinterland, 1770–1820

From its inception Eastmain House shared the fur resources of the up-country with French "woodrunners" trading inland on the rivers draining into James Bay. The Hudson's Bay Company post became the trading centre primarily for the Indians living north of the Rupert River as far as Richmond Gulf and inland from this stretch of coast, depending of course on where the mobile French established themselves from year to year. As we have seen in chapter 4, those living generally southeast of the Rupert River traded with the French. Even the establishment of Moose Fort in 1730 failed to alter this balance of trade. Yet the Eastmain House journals do not betray undue concern over the French presence inland in the early years, and there was by no means as much active competition at the eastern settlement as there was at Moose and Albany forts.

In the 1750s, however, competition increased as French traders were reported much closer to the coast than usual. More and more "French Indians" (that is, Indians outfitted by the French) began appearing at Eastmain House. The master, John Yarrow, encouraged them with liberal presents of brandy and tobacco, but the local Indians began to complain their hunting grounds were being looted of beaver by the "strangers" (B.59/a/24: 12d, 15, 16). By the spring of 1755 French traders themselves had descended the Eastmain River to within a day's paddle of the coast and were intercepting uplanders on their way to the Hudson's Bay Company post (B.59/a/23: 15ff). As always, the presence of "woodrunners" in the neighbourhood made the Hudson's Bay Company men expectant of an armed attack and the new master, John Longland, informed headquarters: "I have Imploy'd a Indian to Go up to ye falls to Catch Jack and Give him Two netts with him. It is To furr to Send any of my men for the french is all Round us – the Indians Says they are with in a Days Journy of us So that I Keep all my men a Hoam and Keep a Good Look out"

(B.59/a/23: 14d). Longland's precautions proved unnecessary as there was no attack on the post, either by French traders or by their Indian allies, but his fears were understandable given the events of the previous winter on the west main.

Early in March 1755 three Indians had arrived at Albany Fort with a report that Henley House, a Hudson's Bay Company outpost erected twelve years earlier at the juncture of the Albany and Kenogami rivers, had been broken into, looted, and abandoned (B.3/a/47: 21d ff). The Albany postmaster, Joseph Isbister, a former master of Eastmain House, assumed the ransacking had been carried out by inland Indians encouraged by French traders. Nothing more was learned until June when a woman, originally from Richmond Gulf, told Isbister that the previous December a group of Indians led by a man named Wappisis (also known as Woudby) had been allowed to stay overnight in Henley House and the next day had murdered the five Englishmen employed there, traded provisions with other Indians for a few days, and when these ran out, plundered the post and departed (B.3/a/47: 36d–37). After hearing this story, Isbister lured Wappisis, a regular visitor to Albany, and his sons, Shanap and a man the English called Snuff the Blanket, into the post and arrested them, whereupon they confessed. In short order the three were condemned for murder and, on 21 June, hanged (B.3/a/47: 42). Three other men, Annssoet, Assittaham, and Pethessis, were also implicated by Indian informants but were not captured. George Rushworth, the surgeon at Albany, recorded three possible reasons for the murderous events at Henley House. First, when Isbister had become chief at Albany in 1753, he had antagonized Wappisis by restricting his accustomed access to the post, and Rushworth speculated that Wappisis had been plotting against the company since that time (A.11/2: 173). Secondly, Rushworth divulged that the Henley House master, William Lamb, had been keeping two Indian women at "bed and board," both of them married to men involved in the murders. Their motive, he thought, was revenge. Thirdly, the surgeon asked Wappisis shortly before his execution why he had committed murder. "He tould Me he was hungry; I tould him Mr. Lamb had no Victuals, only for ye Englishmen, he tould me I Lyed ye victuals was for them as Well as Englishmen, as they keeped there Women; they had a Right to there Victuals" (A.11/2: 173d). Wappisis's response indicates that the Indians may have believed they had an understanding with Lamb regarding the reciprocal exchange of services, sexual and subsistence, and Lamb's violation of this understanding was followed by unfortunate results. An analysis of this event and a discussion of balanced reciprocity is to be found in Bishop (1976).

The troubles at Henley House did not end with the execution of Wappisis and his two sons. The post was re-established in the summer of 1759, but that September it was attacked by a party of forty Indians. One Hudson's Bay Company servant was killed and the post once again abandoned (A.11/3: 32, 41). Robert Temple, the new Albany postmaster, believed the Indians had been encouraged by French traders, and when this report was coupled with rumours that inland Indians were planning an assault at Eastmain House, the master of that post understandably was alarmed. In the summer of 1760 he removed his trade goods to the sloop to facilitate a hasty retreat (B.59/a/29: 7d, 17). By that time, however, the threat, if it had ever existed, passed. The French and Indian War (1754–63) had embroiled New France in a struggle for its survival and the coureurs de bois had withdrawn from the northern woods. For a brief period the Quebec trade was dislocated, and for the first time in the century there were no competitors opposing the Hudson's Bay Company in James Bay.

The Hudson's Bay Company was not long allowed to enjoy unopposed the fruits of the northern fur trade. Once the war in New France was over, traders from Quebec again began to penetrate into the country back of James Bay. They are referred to in the records as the "pedlars from Quebec." Many of them were French coureurs de bois who previously had been active in the north country and were permitted to resume trading under the British regime; others were Englishmen new to the trade. The first mention in the Eastmain House records of these new English-financed opponents was in the spring of 1765 when an inland trading captain told of "a Log Tent formerly with French, but now English" (B.59/a/34: 29d). Rather vague, this report was followed a year later by the news that a post had been erected at the mouth of Big River, and by 1769 postmaster Thomas Moore at Eastmain House complained, "There are Several french and English Small hutts Very Near us Which is of great hindrance to our Tread at this Place" (B.59/a/35: 20d; B.59/a/38: 38d). At least three of these "hutts" were southeast of Eastmain House up both the Rupert and Nottaway rivers, as Moore reported the next year: "One of the Peple Belonging to the Setlements up Nodeway River was at the Mouth of the Same this Summer and Brought Brandy and Tobacco to Treat the Indians Belonging to Moose fort and this place in order for them to Come to there Tents and Trade there goods in the Winter as they have 3 Logg Tents up Nodeway and Ruports Rivers, the Person was a French Man" (B.59/a/40: 22). Moore had cause to be concerned at the activities of his competitors. While in the first years of the 1760s the fur returns at Eastmain House had increased to a value of 3640 made beaver (as in 1762), this trend was reversed in the last half of the decade and returns sunk to a low of 1242½ made beaver for 1768 (B.3/d/70: 12d; B.3/d/76: 19). Clearly the Hudson's Bay Company would have to respond to its newest challengers.

At Eastmain House, as at the other posts around the bay, the company reacted to the pedlars initially by modifying its trading practices in three ways. First, postmasters were told to increase the presents they sent out each year to lure the inlanders down to the posts. In the fall of 1767 Moore was instructed: "You are by Presents of Brandy, Tobacco, Knives, Beads, etc. & by kind usage to draw the natives to trade with You. Be carefull the presents You send to Uplanders are sent by Indians You can trust" (B.3/b/5: 2). Secondly, it was decided that many of the Indians at Eastmain House were taking their furs to the opposition because they had accumulated debts at the post which they could not repay, and so Moore sent word that "I will forgive them the Whole of thir Debt if they Will Come in and Tread there goods as usual" (B.59/a/37: 30d). But perhaps most importantly, the company increased the price paid for a variety of furs. The new standard was issued from London in May 1769 and raised the value of prime marten, bear, otter, grey fox, wolf, and wolverine pelts and caribou hides (B.135/c/1: 79).

The result of these policies was that the Eastmain trade rallied during the 1770s. However, at the same time as the returns were increasing, the overplus was declining and inland competition was intensifying; therefore the company decided that after a century of waiting at bayside for the furs to come down to the posts, it was necessary to carry the trade to the Indians by establishing inland outposts and opposing the pedlars on their own ground. This significant change in the prosecution of the trade was explained by the company's London committee in a letter to the Moose Fort postmaster in 1777:

As We find the Canadians carry on their Trade Inland by going up the great Rivers & Lakes on the Back of Our Factories & thereby intercept the Natives who used to come down to them to Trade We Apprehend the only Method to regain that Trade will be to send proper Persons from each Factory with Goods & Brandy to proper Stations upon their Track & thereby underselling them & using every other means of ingratiating themselves with the Natives Endeavor to make it not worth while of the Canadians to come there anymore. (Rich 1954, 338)

At Eastmain House Moore had received similar instructions directing him "to forward with your utmost diligence all inland discoveries" (A.5/1: 165). But the first outpost to be settled from Eastmain House was not inland at all but along the coast at the mouth of the Rupert River. Indians who descended that river to the coast, especially newcomers to the post, had expressed their unhappiness at having to paddle along the exposed and often ice-choked shore to the Eastmain River (B.59/a/50: 7). In the summer of 1776 Moore travelled to the Rupert and decided that the best location for a post was near the site of the old Charles Fort:

View of Rupert House, 1867, from upriver. Originally established as an outpost in 1776, it had become the major trading post in eastern James Bay by the mid-nineteenth century.

This is the Only Place whear I think a Settlement Can be built there being good Water for the Sloop to Lay a float all the Wintor and the Beatch is Steep so that She May be Layed a Ground. Naither Wind Ice or Sea Can hurt her. there is Tolarable good Woods for to Build a Settlement if Required, and Capt. Cobbage informed Me that there is Plenty of Gees to be got both spring and fall hear. (B.59/a/50: 40d)

This last point was important since initially the post, called Rupert House, was planned primarily as a goose tent; its role in the trade was as a provisioning station for the people bringing their furs down the Rupert and Nottaway rivers to Eastmain House (B.3/k/1: 9d). It would be fifty years before the log tent built by a complement of three men in the fall of 1776 became the most important fur-trade post on the east coast.

The first expedition actually intended to frustrate the activities of the Canadian pedlars consisted of Thomas Buchan, a company servant, and two coastal Indians, George Gun and Jack Spires. This small party left Eastmain House early in June 1776 "in order to Explor the Contry and

Rivers Lakes in Land as far as they can" (B.59/a/50: 30). The trio's major objective was "the Great Lake Mistsinna," but they returned at the end of the month without having found it (B.59/a/50: 32d). This brief foray was followed up two years later when James Robertson and two Indian guides were dispatched from Eastmain House "to Lake Mistasinia and to Exploar the Rivers and Leaks boath a Going and a Comming back down Ruports River and to see what Settlements he shall Meet with in his Journay" (B.59/a/52: 25). The records do not divulge where Robertson went but he returned later that summer. In January 1779 postmaster George Atkinson wrote to Albany: "I should have sent James Robinson [Robertson] inland to Mistassin with the Uplanders last fall. But their Canoes being small and so many of themselves had not Room. But have sent an Indian Leader to that place with presents, and he promis to do great things" (B.3/b/16: 9d). The following summer (1779) Robertson, along with Matthew Tate and five canoes of Indians, did return inland "to Mistosink Lake to Build a Log Tent till More hands Can be Shaired To build a house" (B.59/a/53: 22). It is not known exactly where they erected their tent or if in fact they reached Lake Mistassini, but Robertson and Tate were back at Eastmain House in June 1780 with a disappointing trade of only 355½ made beaver, all from Indians already trading at the coast (B.59/a/54: 25). That summer Robertson became postmaster at Rupert House and the position of inland trader fell once again to Buchan, who in the fall set off for Mistassini (B.59/a/56: 4d). The next May Atkinson announced in his journal: "The Indian Captn. with whom Thomas Buchan went Inland Oct. 1780 came down the river with 2 Canoes he brings me the melancholy account of the said Thomas Buchans Death in Jany. last, who died from real want of Victuals in crossing a Lake" (B.59/a/56: 28–28d).

Buchan's was the last inland expedition to leave Eastmain House for the next decade. Atkinson explained this inactivity:

I am sorry To inform you that the Upland Settlement is not going forward, nor is it likely as to answer the purpose, I find At this time the Uplanders are not agreeable to assist up with any part of the goods nor even to bring the furrs down Without being largely paid for it, which would be heavily expensive further More all the Indians inform me the Roads is so bad that it is past travelling with any heavy load, as no Englishmen have ever been up any rivers about East Main I cannot Contradict them, Neither have I experienced Officers or Men capable to do anything for the purpose. (A.11/57: 78)

While the company's thrust inland was temporarily halted, officers were continually reminded of the presence of opposition by the frequent arrival at Eastmain and Rupert houses of Indians from Canadian settlements at

Abitibi, Mistassini, and "Showapamshon." This last was presumably the lake (Chamouchouane) mentioned by Normandin as being the site of a French post in the 1730s. In the late 1770s, according to Indian reports, it was deserted briefly, but in 1781 John Long, a trader in the employ of some Canadian merchants, settled there (B.59/a/53: 22; Long 1791, 158–9). As well as these settlements to the southeast, Atkinson reported "Strange Indians" arriving from Canadian posts inland from Richmond Gulf, most probably a reference to a post on Lake Manicouagan (B.59/a/65: 26d). None of these posts were at this time necessarily occupied continuously, as the Canadian trade was shared by a number of merchant groups each financing parties of traders which might establish posts for a winter or simply pass through the country in the summer collecting furs.

The Hudson's Bay Company renewed its attempts to reach Mistassini in 1790 after Atkinson had learned that a party of six Canadians had "made a Settlement last Fall upon the very spot where James Robinson & Mathew Tate stayed one winter" (A.11/57: 101). John Clarke, a writer at Eastmain House, left the post in May with a group of eight Indian men and women and returned 20 June after having become possibly the first company servant to reach Lake Mistassini (B.59/a/66: 31, 35d). His efforts, however, did not meet with Atkinson's approval:

Mr. Clarke has made a Journey to the Canadian Settlement at Mistacinne Lake but unfortunately the master with the rest of the settlers had left the place about forty eight hours before his arrival and were gon down with seven Canoes in which they had a very good Trade. I am extremely sorry that Mr. C. should be so unthinking as not to follow them which if he had there is not a doubt but what we should have got them down here with their Trade they being a set of Men unconnected with any other Company whatever. (A.11/57: 128)

Inland activities were delayed once again, this time by Atkinson's departure for England for reasons of ill health and his subsequent death at Eastmain House in 1792. The new postmaster, Bartholomew Nelson, was critical of his predecessor for not pushing more ambitiously into the interior, especially towards the east, "as it is from Mistacinne and the Country adjacent to Cheasquacheston that E.M. got its principal Trade" (B.59/a/69: 62). Nelson wrote to Moose Fort that "Eastmain from what I can learn is now compleately surrounded with Canadians," and to meet this challenge in the spring of 1793 he launched two expeditions inland (B.59/b/12: 6).

Once again John Clarke travelled towards Mistassini, but this time it was intended that he should establish a post. Accompanied by a party of seven Hudson's Bay Company servants and sixteen Indians (B.59/a/69: 62), he arrived at Neoskweskau Lake, about three days short of Mistas-

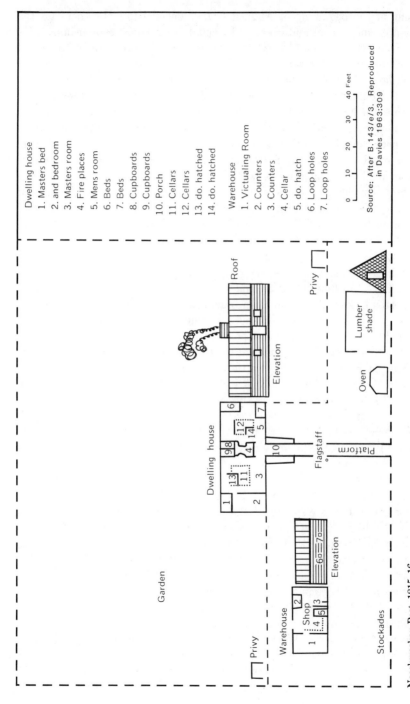

Dwelling house
1. Masters bed
2. and bedroom
3. Masters room
4. Fire places
5. Mens room
6. Beds
7. Beds
8. Cupboards
9. Cupboards
10. Porch
11. Cellars
12. Cellars
13. do. hatched
14. do. hatched

Warehouse
1. Victualing Room
2. Counters
3. Counters
4. Cellar
5. do. hatch
6. Loop holes
7. Loop holes

Source: After B.143/e/3. Reproduced in Davies 1963:309

0 10 20 30 40 Feet

Roof

Elevation

Privy

Lumber shade

Oven

Garden

Dwelling house

Flagstaff

Platform

Warehouse

Shop

Elevation

Privy

Stockades

Neoskweskau Post, 1815–16

sini, at the beginning of August. Clarke decided to settle there for the winter and a month later erected a small trading-post establishment. He was told by Indian informants that he should not continue on to Mistassini because provisions were scarce and for that reason the Canadians never wintered there (B.143/a/1: 1). As it turned out, a Hudson's Bay Company post would not be established on Lake Mistassini for another twenty years, the company being content to remain at Neoskweskau.

That same summer, in 1793, with four Rupert House people as guides, George Jackman, the surgeon at Eastmain, led a second expedition up Rupert River and overland towards Cheashquacheston Lake, the modern Lac au Goëland, at the headwaters of the Nottaway River. Eleven days above Rupert House, Jackman reported encountering a hunter named Wawpatch, "who Inform'd me that a French trader and 3 Indians had visited him only 4 Days before my arrival and after having forcibly oblig'd him and his Gang to trade the whole of their Furs return'd to the Southd, such is the General Character that I have received of this man that he travels about the Country plundering the Indians" (B.186/a/10: 5). Early in June Jackman and his companions arrived at Cheashquacheston Lake and the tent of an Indian named Shenap. There the surgeon met the master of the Canadian settlement at "Swapmouson," who told him he intended establishing a post at Cheashquacheston that winter. The Canadian also told Jackman that the Frenchman who had taken furs from Wawpatch also planned to settle at the lake that winter "so great had been his success during his last visit at that place as to carry away with him 7 Large Bundles of Furs supposed to contain nearly 2000 Beaver the greatest part of which were traded with those Indians belonging to the Factory" (B.186/a/10: 6–7). Having gathered valuable information about travel routes and the activities of the competition, Jackman descended the Nottaway River to Rupert House.

Upon receiving his surgeon's report, Nelson almost immediately dispatched a party to establish a post at Cheashquacheston Lake, but it did not get as far as Nemiscau Lake before the Indian guides deserted and the Hudson's Bay Company men had to return (B.59/a/70: 2d). The following summer a second attempt to reach Cheashquacheston was thwarted when the canoes built for the trip proved so badly made the party could not advance beyond Nemiscau (B.59/a/70: 37d). For the next five seasons the company maintained a post at Lake Nemiscau (Nemiskau Post). In the summer of 1799 it was removed, as first intended, to Cheashquacheston but in 1802, according to an agreement with the company's opponents at Waswanipi, the post was relocated at Nemiscau. A North West Company post was also built on Lake Nemiscau, in 1804, but it was closed in 1806. In 1809 the Hudson's Bay Company followed suit and closed its post, reasoning that the Indians in the vicinity would agree

to trade at Rupert House (B.59/b/28: 3). Temporarily at least, Neoskweskau was the only Hudson's Bay Company post inland from the east main.

From the turn of the century it became clear that traders associated
with the Montreal-based North West Company were providing the major
competition for the Hudson's Bay Company in eastern James Bay, as
they were active right across the continent. The North West Company
had been formed in 1779 as a partnership of eight Canadian merchant
concerns trading above and beyond Lake Superior. This union dissolved
soon after and the company was reorganized in 1783 minus some of the
original, smaller partners (Wallace 1934, 6–8). Through the next few
years the North West Company successfully competed with and absorbed
a number of Canadian fur merchants, the last, the XY Company, being
driven into partnership in 1804. "The decade that followed ... saw the
North West Company's greatest period of expansion and success" (ibid.,
21). Relations between the Hudson's Bay Company and its Canadian
competitor were initially friendly enough, but as competition increased,
the North West Company proved to be a bold rival and relations between
neighbouring traders were often marked by threats and violence.

Based at Abitibi, Waswanipi, and Mistassini lakes, the North West
Company operated in eastern James Bay by intercepting Indians on their
way to the coast, thus closing the back door to the Hudson's Bay Company posts. But in 1803 Simon McTavish, the company's principal part-
ner, decided to extend the competition right into the bay itself and
dispatched to Charlton Island the 350-ton *Eddystone* under command of
John Richards, a former Hudson's Bay Company captain, and manned by
forty Orkneymen (Wallace 1947, 33). Two overland parties, one of fourteen men led by Angus Shaw and another smaller one led by a "Mr
Frazer," joined the *Eddystone* crew in James Bay in August and a post,
Fort St Andrews, was erected on Charlton Island. Using this fort as a
supply depot, the Nor'westers fanned out around the bottom of the bay,
building outposts on Hayes Island at the mouth of the Moose River, at
Hannah Bay, at Rupert River, at Big River, and the next summer at Old
Factory River. The major handicap experienced by the North West Company in its rivalry with the Hudson's Bay Company in the Canadian
northwest was the high cost of transporting goods from Montreal overland across the continent. If the Canadian company could gain access to
the northwest through Hudson Bay, then it could compete on more equal
terms. McTavish intended to use these newly established James Bay
posts as leverage to negotiate a right of passage for his company through
the bay (Campbell 1957, 141).

The Nor'westers arrived in James Bay prepared to back up with force
their right to trade there. John George McTavish, one of the leaders of
the expedition, wrote to his brother: "You'll no doubt be surprised to hear

that we are armed to force our ways but I can assure you that now in this country we are almost obliged to fight for every skin we get from an Indian with the other Traders" (Wallace 1947, 33). The newcomers were permitted to settle peaceably into their hastily constructed posts, however, and it was not until the spring of 1804, when the inland hunters began to arrive, that the pattern of competition was established. As the Indians approached the coast, parties from both companies sent out men to intercept them and secure their furs. These escorts were armed and occasionally shots were fired, but the strategy was to outflank the opposition, not to overpower it. The situation demanded constant vigilance, as this entry from the Rupert House journal of May 1804 illustrates: "May 17 ... Saw a canoe from the Canadian House crossing to the Indians tent; immediately man'd the Boat, and it blowing a fresh breeze was inabled to get there before them, and secured the Geese, and a Bundle of Furrs from an uplander who had followed the Ice down with an intent of trading with our opponents" (B.186/a/20: 13d).

The degree of competition varied from post to post. At Moose River eleven Nor'westers had installed themselves on Hayes Island, and by the fall of 1805 the Hudson's Bay Company postmaster, John Thomas, was asking for reinforcements, claiming his opponents were beating up Indians who accepted employment with the company (B.135/a/93: 6d). At Rupert House, on the other hand, where the Canadians had settled two miles upriver from the Hudson's Bay Company post, Thomas Alder complained of the Indians being lured to his opponents with large presents of brandy but he reported no incidents of violent confrontations (B.186/a/20). Similarly at Hannah Bay and Old Factory River the rivalry was peaceful. It was at Big or "Great" River that traders came to blows and Indians were repeatedly molested.

After the Canadians had settled on Charlton Island in the summer of 1803, they had hired Jack Hester, a mixed blood hunter trading at Eastmain House, to accompany a party north to establish a North West Company post at "Keeshay or Great River" (B.59/a/81: 1d). Alarmed that northern hunters might be intercepted on their way to Eastmain House, William Bolland immediately sent George Atkinson Jr and his brother Jacob to oppose the Nor'westers. The brothers' settlement, at that time called Big River Post, was the original Fort George. For the first two seasons the Atkinsons successfully, and peaceably, neutralized their opponents, but in 1805–6 the Hudson's Bay Company supply boat did not arrive at Big River Post until late in October by which time many of the Indians had taken debt from the Canadians and had left for their hunting grounds (B.77/a/1: 1). Because of this setback, George Atkinson agreed to deal with the North West Company trader, Duncan McDougall, by sharing the year's fur returns, two-thirds for the Hudson's Bay Company and the remainder for the opposition (B.59/b/24: 17). Atkinson had no authority to arrive at an agreement of this kind and no doubt would have been reprimanded for doing so, but as it turned out, the arrangement dissolved in a series of violent clashes that spring.

Early in March of 1806 McDougall seized the furs of two Indian captains a short distance from the Hudson's Bay Company post at Big River. Thomas Alder, then in charge, went out to the Indians and despite the threats of McDougall managed to secure the furs that McDougall had seized (B.77/a/1: 4). Two days later, according to Alder, whose account of these events is the only one surviving, McDougall sent a letter challenging him to a duel (B.77/a/1: 5). Alder dismissed the challenge as the idea of a "madman," but later in the month McDougall and his men captured Alder and George Atkinson and locked them in the Canadian post. Alder claimed that first one of the Nor'westers attempted to shave his head, then McDougall beat him. The company servants were released amid threats of further violence (B.77/a/1: 6). Attacks on Indians continued and in mid-April Alder summarized the situation this way:

Unless men are sent to protect what Trade we have in the Warehouse, 'tis more than probable we shall be robbed of that likewise, it has been long threatened, and we ... expect hourly an attack, many of the Indians also who have given offence to this formidable gang of Ruffians are threatened with sever chastisement; where the business will end, God knows, but if the Spring should pass without bloodshed 'twill be a miracle. (B.59/b/24: 34)

According to Alder, the local hunters were preparing to take up arms against McDougall but we cannot know with any certainty that the Indians were as unhappy with the Canadians as Alder claimed (B.77/a/1: 15). Regardless, relations were strained to the flash point when, conveniently, the North West Company decided to withdraw from the bay.

The Nor'westers did not seem to have any difficulty importing supplies into the bay. The second summer, 1804, no ship arrived, but John Thomas at Moose reported that "three large canoes mann'd by Iroquois chiefly came down the Abbitibbi River and arrived at our Opponents Settlement on Hazey [Hayes] Island the 13th July" (B.135/a/92: 27d). In the summer of 1805 Captain Richards returned to Charlton, this time in the *Beaver*, and as well three more canoes "manned by 18 Iroquois" made the overland trip (B.135/a/92: 50; B.135/a/93: 15d). In the fall of that year Thomas wrote, "Our opponents muster much stronger than last year and I believe are well supplied" (B.135/a/93: 4). As can be judged from the evidence of fur returns, the Hudson's Bay Company posts were affected in different degrees by Canadian competition. Moose Fort, for example, was receiving as many furs in the years before the *Eddystone*'s arrival as came in during the season of 1805–6. At Eastmain, however, and to a lesser extent at Rupert House, competition did divert a sizeable quantity of furs from the Hudson's Bay Company warehouse.

Yet, despite how successful or unsuccessful the North West Company was in prosecuting the trade, its presence in James Bay did not depend on the fur returns of its posts. McTavish, and after his death in 1804 William McGillivray, had hoped to use the posts to negotiate transportation rights from the Hudson's Bay Company (Rich 1959, 259–63). In 1806, when negotiations failed, the Canadians destroyed their posts and withdrew from the bay. Thomas reported that three of the Nor'westers came to him and "informed us that they had abandoned all the East main Coast and that they would these posts at Moose if we would abandon some of ours up the River" (B.135/a/94: 1d). Thomas recognized that the three were grasping at straws to gain some advantage from their James Bay adventure. He refused to entertain the idea and the Hayes Island post was soon after evacuated with all the others. (See Mitchell 1977, 64–79.)

The North West Company may not have achieved its immediate objective, but in general it was posing a considerable threat to the future of the Hudson's Bay Company. This was as true in eastern James Bay as elsewhere, and in 1812 the inland extension of settlements in opposition to the Canadians was resumed. Previously, Neoskweskau Post was the farthest east any Hudson's Bay Company servants had settled, three prior attempts to establish an outpost on Mistassini Lake having failed, but in the summer of 1812 a party of three men, led by John Isbister, travelled to Mistassini and erected some kind of dwelling there. This post was in existence for only four seasons before it was withdrawn in favour of another which was established in 1815 on Rush Lake, the modern Lake Chevrillon, southwest of Mistassini (B.143/e/3: 2d). The company resettled Mistassini, this time permanently, in the summer of 1818 at a different location from the original post (B.19/e/1: 1d). (See figure 6.)

At the same time as the trade was being extended south of Neoskweskau, Hudson's Bay Company servants were penetrating the territory to the north. In 1816 John and Thomas Isbister, guided by six Indians, established a post at Lake Nichicun, about two hundred miles from Neoskweskau (Davies 1963, 313). This post, called "Nitchequon" House, later rendered as "Nichikun," remained in operation until 1822.

The Hudson's Bay Company's expansion eastward to Mistassini and the height of land was accomplished with just one mishap, the death of Thomas Buchan. Unfortunately, the extension of trade southward towards Waswanipi Lake was attended by one of the worst tragedies to result from inland exploration in eastern James Bay. In September 1817 a party of five Hudson's Bay Company servants, accompanied by Indian guides and led by John Pitt Greeley, left Rupert House to establish a post at

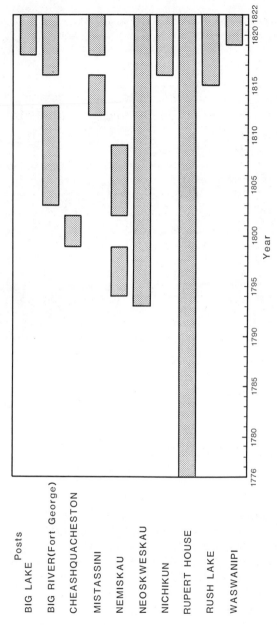

Source: Hudson's Bay Company Post Journals, 1737-1822

Figure 6. Hudson's Bay Company inland expansion before 1822: posts in operation

Mistassini Post hunters and employees, 1884. Although it took the Hudson's Bay Company until 1812 to establish an inland post at Mistassini, its successful fur trade ensured its continuous operation.

Waswanipi to oppose the Nor'westers there (B.135/b/37: 22). Unable to reach their destination before winter made travel impossible, the men decided to settle at a place they called Big Lake, the modern Lake Evans, between the Rupert and Nottaway rivers (B.135/b/37: 48). Alexander Christie, the postmaster at Rupert House, sent Stacemow, son of a prominent coastal Indian, in February with supplies to relieve the party, but when Stacemow arrived at Big Lake, he found three of the men dead of starvation and exposure, the two others missing, and a lone survivor, the Indian wife of one of the dead servants. Christie wrote that Stacemow believed the woman was insane. "She would not taste any of the Victuals he offered her and made several attempts to take his life and that in self-defense he put an end to her sufferings" (B.135/b/37: 64–5). Christie did not wholly believe Stacemow; he attributed the man's actions to the fact the woman had survived by eating the corpses of her companions: "With respect to her insanity, it appears very improbable. But it is common amongst Indians to put to death, even their nighest relations, when they know of their having been reduced to the dreadful necessity of eating human Flesh" (B.186/e/1: 3d). It turned out that William Laughton, one of the missing members of the party, had left Big Lake and passed the winter at the tent of Amoshish and Camitchisit, two local hunters. Christie learned that early in the spring Laughton had returned to the lake and found the bodies of his companions. Christie continued, "Early in April Amoshish went to the House and there he found Laughton by himself and dreadful to relate he put a period to his existance – the reason Amoshish assigns for committing this barbarous act is, that finding Laughton alone and observing that he had been subsisting on human flesh, led him to suppose that he had murdered the others" (B.135/b/37: 88–9). The body of the fifth company servant was found in a tent not far from Big Lake. Four years later Andrew Moar, then the Rupert House master, gave a fuller account of the Indian attitude to cannibalism:

The Indians have a notion that either Man or Woman (Indian or European) who has once tasted Human flesh imbibes a predilection for it and will not hesitate earlier than otherwise to resort to the Same dreadful means of satisfying his Hunger which he had on a former occasion resorted to from dire Necessity; and viewing the matter in this light, without taking into consideration any superstitious motives by which they might be actuated, they may perhaps, as a means of prevention merely, under the idea that he might kill their women or children while they themselves were about endeavouring to find some sort of Provisions, take his life. (B.186/e/5: 8)

The unhappy fate of the five servants did not discourage Hudson's Bay Company officials from attempting to settle Waswanipi Lake. In the summer of 1818 another expedition reached Big Lake and constructed two dwelling houses and a warehouse on a site thirty miles from where Greeley's party had halted (B.19/e/1: 7). The next summer a post was finally erected at Waswanipi Lake, though Big Lake Post remained in operation until 1822.

All this activity in eastern James Bay between 1770 and 1820 would not have been possible without the assistance of the Indian people. The Hudson's Bay Company did not have men proficient in the hunting and travelling skills necessary to accomplish long voyages on their own. Because company servants had only a rudimentary knowledge of the inland territory, Indian guides were required to lead all the expeditions. Once the inland posts were in operation, the Indians became even more indispensable, since they were required to man the supply canoes each summer. Because competition involved the Indians directly in the fur trade to an unprecedented degree, it changed the terms of the trade, intensifying the effects it had on the traditional Indian way of life. On the

Repairing a birchbark canoe of the type used by the Nemiskau brigades, Rupert House, 1867. The company relied on Indian know-how and labour.

one hand the Indians benefited from declining prices, bribes, and easier access to trading posts. On the other hand competition altered their seasonal pattern of activity, providing alternate sources of income but exacting a price in terms of self-reliance. Traditionally the Indian passed the summer months fishing, socializing, and hunting. With the proliferation of inland posts a greater number of Indians were engaged by the Hudson's Bay Company, first as guides, then as voyageurs. For example, in 1778 two men were given forty made beaver each to guide James Robertson towards Lake Mistassini (B.59/a/52: 25). By 1820 one-third of the Rupert House homeguard alone were employed in supply canoes travelling inland (B.186/b/3: 31d). The inland business required a large number of canoes annually and the manufacture of these became another source of income for certain Indians. Increasingly, then, work for the company, at least in the summer months, was replacing subsistence activities among the Indians.

In 1821 the Nor'westers and the Hudson's Bay Company admitted they could no longer bear the costs of a continent-wide competition and agreed to merge. By this date the Hudson's Bay Company had penetrated the hinterland of eastern James Bay as far as the height of land and administered an arc of trading posts extending from Nichikun in the northeast to Waswanipi in the south. Before considering the changes amalgamation brought to this vast area, we must venture again into the north where the company had been equally energetic, with less success.

CHAPTER NINE

Big River Post
and Beyond, 1784–1824

With the abandonment of Richmond Fort in 1759, the Hudson's Bay Company also abandoned further plans to identify and exploit the resources of the east coast of the bay. The climate had proven inhospitable, the Indians intransigent, and the dreams of diamond and lead mines chimerical. However, northern exploration began to gain favour once again in 1784 when John Thomas became intrigued by Indian stories of a water passage "a great way to the Nwd of Richmond" connecting Hudson Bay to "another Sea" to the east (A.11/44: 183). The following year Thomas elaborated on this "very considerable River," reporting that his informants "mention'd the Names of three different Nations of Indians which they learnt from the Natives about Richmond & Whale River, viz. the Moo, sha, pis, co, Mus, ca, tway & Ne, pis, kee Indians" (A.11/45: 21d). Interested in extending their trade, and alarmed at reports reaching Eastmain House that an opposition post had been erected "back of Richmond," company officials approved Thomas's plans to send a sloop north in the summer of 1786.

Late in July the *Moose* sloop left the bottom of the bay. George Donald, an interpreter, kept a journal of the voyage. He described passing Great and Little Whale rivers where Indians had gathered to hunt white whales. "I counted 27 men in one tent where they were assembled (after greasing & painting themselves) to welcome us on shore, besides many young lads in the other tents. The women (of which there are a very great number) were employed in drying the flesh of the Whales and rendering the blubber into oil" (A.11/45: 55). The expedition sailed past the entrance to Richmond Gulf and just south of Cape Smith discovered an opening in the coastline which appeared to be the sought-for passage. The sloop made its way inland, trading with a group of Inuit as it went, but on 18 August Donald unhappily wrote: "2 P.M. to our great mortification, saw the end of the supposed streights which proves to be nothing more than a Bay 14 or 15 miles deep" (A.11/45: 56d). The expedition had entered the modern Mosquito Bay. Disappointed, the men returned south, "being satisfied there is no opening or passage between Cape Jones & Cape Smith" (A.11/45: 57).

The negligible results of the slooping voyage did not discourage Thomas who continued to recommend that a northern post be established, but his advice was contradicted by George Atkinson at Eastmain House who told his superiors "that to form any settlement in those parts would not produce Any benefit, as all the Furs those Indians get are brot to East Main" (A.11/57: 72). Even the suggestion that the company begin a summer whale fishery at one of the Whale rivers was greeted negatively by Atkinson: "The Expence of Boats, Sloop and Men would amount to a great Sum, besides white Whales are killed soon in the Year before the Ice is gone off the Coast ... and we apprehend our Sloop would not get to Whale River one Year in three time enough to kill The whale" (A.11/57: 81). However, company officials were determined to commence a trade in whale oil; therefore in 1791, and annually thereafter, a sloop sailed from Eastmain House to Great Whale River where oil was obtained from the Indians who customarily gathered there in the summer (A.11/57: 134d).

Indian reports that Canadian traders had sailed into Richmond Gulf and erected a post encouraged the company to overrule Atkinson's objections to a northern settlement, and in September 1793 a party of six men, led by George Jackman, recently returned from his trip to Cheashquacheston, set sail from Eastmain House (B.59/b/13: 1). Later that month Jackman wrote that he was building a house a short distance up the Little Whale River on the ruins of the original Whale River House: "The whole aspect of the Country is really dismal beyond conception, nothing presents itself to view but a heap of barren rocks without either Wood or Vegitation of any kind; I live however in hopes that this Winter may produce something if not from the Indians, most probably from the Esquemauxs" (B.59/b/13: 2d). This was the last his employers heard from Jackman. The next summer a northern Indian informed Bartholomew Nelson at Eastmain House that "Mr. Jackman and all his people have been cut off by the Esquemauxs sometime last Winter ... He says that he saw but one of their Corpse, everything was broken up and riffled" (B.59/b/13: 14). Company servants remained suspicious that Indians had committed these murders until 1840 when among a large party of Inuit arriving at what was then Fort George an elderly woman was discovered who had been in the vicinity when the murders had occurred. The woman told postmaster Thomas Corcoran that "the deed was perpetrated by a party of about twenty Esquimaux men, all of whom are dead, and that the only reason they had for doing it was plunder" (B.77/a/14: 53).

The activities of the North West Company did not allow Hudson's Bay Company officials to be dispirited at the fate of Jackman and his companions. As we have seen, in 1803 the Nor'westers invaded James Bay, forcing the older company to meet their challenge by establishing a post near the mouth of Big River. After the withdrawal of Duncan McDougall and his men three years later, this post continued in operation, despite the complaints of Eastmain House officers who argued that the new house was simply collecting furs which in the event would have reached their warehouse (B.59/b/26: 2). This objection, however, plus a desire to involve the Inuit in the fur trade, led the company in 1813 to relocate Big River Post at Great Whale River, the site of the summer whale fishery. The new establishment, situated on the north side of the river on a point about one mile from the bay, consisted of two log buildings, one a dwelling house for officers with a trading room in the loft, the other a dwelling house for the men (B.372/e/2: 1d). It became the trading centre for three groups of Indians, identified by postmaster Thomas Alder. One he called the "Whale River Tribe" which numbered about eighty hunters and their families and provided most of the summer whalers. Another group wintered to the south between Great Whale River and Big River, both along the coast and inland. The third wintered to the northeast about whom Alder complained that they "are principally Deerhunters, who seldom give themselves any concern about furs" (B.372/e/1: 5).

Alder's attempts to commence a trade with the Inuit were unsuccessful in the face of continued conflict between those people and the northern Indians. As we have seen in chapter 6, during the eighteenth century homeguard Indians from the Albany and Moose rivers frequently made excursions north to the Richmond Gulf area to attack the Inuit. It is possible the Inuit believed white traders were allies of the Indians, a belief which might account for the incidents at Little Whale River in 1754 and 1793. Because they were disruptive to company activities, the northern raids were discouraged at the James Bay posts, but nevertheless they continued until the end of the century when employment as inland voyageurs left no time in the summer for the southern Indians to persist in their northern sorties (Francis 1979). The last incident in the Hudson's Bay Company records dates from 1794. North of Cape Jones, however, hostility continued. For example, in the summer of 1815 Alder reported that a family of Inuit had been "barbarously destroyed by three of the most worthless Indians here" (B.372/e/2: 7). The postmaster realized that as long as this enmity between Indian and Inuit continued, the Hudson's Bay Company would receive no trade from the Inuit.

The country around the mouth of Great Whale River was not receptive to a fur-trade settlement. Food resources were slight, the rocky coastline made shipping hazardous, and wood for fuel and building was scarce.

After three years Alder and his men abandoned the post and retreated south. They hoped to settle just below Cape Jones but could not find an "eligible situation" and so, in 1816, Big River Post was reopened (B.372/e/3: 1d).

While the company found it impossible to maintain a permanent post north of Cape Jones, officials were anxious to have the interior of the peninsula explored, especially when reports were received of Canadian activity inland. The first of these exploratory expeditions was carried out by George Atkinson Jr who in 1816 journeyed up Great Whale River to its source and in 1818 reached the height of land near Upper Seal Lake, returning down Little Whale River. Atkinson's travels were followed up by James Clouston, former Neoskweskau postmaster, who in 1819–20 explored the territory between Lake Nichicun and Richmond Gulf. (The details of these expeditions can be found in Davies 1963.)

The Hudson's Bay Company was interested in establishing its summer whaling operation on an economic footing, and in 1818 Alexander Christie, Rupert House chief trader, sailed to the Whale rivers to witness the fishery in action. In his report Christie explained that whaling techniques differed at the two rivers. Because the width of Great Whale River made the placing of a net impractical, the beluga "must be killed by the Indians harpooning them in their Canoes, without the bar in the open Sea, a tedious process and from which very little benefit can ever be derived" (B.186/e/2: 2d). At Little Whale River, on the other hand, a net was placed in the shallow part of the river and the whales driven towards it. "The whales are forced beyond the shoal that lies in the middle of the River ... by a number of Indians with shouting and throwing Stones into the River from their Canoes, that affright some of the fish towards this Nett and into shoal water where they are more certain of harpooning them" (B.77/e/2a: 1d). Christie counted forty-two Indian families attending the hunt at the two rivers. Towards the end of August they abandoned the fishery and returned inland to hunt caribou. Christie recommended that the company continue to send a sloop north each summer to trade oil from the Indians but on no account to re-establish a post on Great Whale River: "I will venture to affirm, that the advantages arising from the Oil Trade will never be so productive as to justify the Establishing a Settlement at Whale River solely with the view of Procuring Oil, and it would be for nothing else, as I am certain not one skin more Furs will be got" (B.186/e/2: 3d).

Until 1824, then, Big River Post was the only Hudson's Bay Company settlement on the coast north of Eastmain House. It was the trading centre for a homeguard of about forty Indian families whose wintering grounds were spread along the coast from south of the Big River north to Cape Jones and inland (B.77/e/4: 3). About the Whale rivers there were from fifty to sixty more Indians who traded with the Hudson's Bay Company sloop which sailed north each summer. Many of these people passed the winter inland on the barren grounds hunting caribou, and as James Clouston, then postmaster at Big River, explained, "When the Indians winter in the Barren Ground they procure but little Furs, not because their hunting Grounds are narrowly limited, but because the grounds contain few Fur animals" (B.77/e/5: 7d).

Following the absorption of the North West Company by the Hudson's Bay Company in 1821, officials cast about for posts which could be considered expendable. It was decided that Indians trading at Big River could just as easily bring their furs to Eastmain House or to the summer whale fishery at Great Whale River. In fact, Big River Post was not only failing to add anything to the fur returns from the bay; its existence was considered an impediment to the trade, since so many of its Indians, when they went inland in the fall, veered north to hunt caribou. Erland Erlandson, postmaster at Eastmain House, speculated that the evacuation of Big River "will be the means of drawing the Indians to the Southward and consequently towards the fur Country" (B.59/e/11: 1d). And so, in 1824, the post was closed, and Hudson's Bay Company activities to the north were confined once more to the summer voyage of the whaling sloop.

CHAPTER TEN

A New Relationship

The absorption by the Hudson's Bay Company of its Canadian rival touched off a flurry of post closures and openings in eastern James Bay. Big River Post was actually the fourth Hudson's Bay Company establishment to be closed in the immediate post-amalgamation period. Confident that Mistassini and Waswanipi were adequate for drawing in the Indians along the height of land, the company abandoned three inland settlements – Neoskweskau, Nichikun, and Rush Lake. Neoskweskau, the first inland post established, had proven difficult to provision, its master recommending as early as 1818 that it cease operation (B.143/e/5: 5). Nichikun and Rush Lake were closed on the assumption that the company would succeed the North West Company as the lessee of the King's Posts, those posts situated across the height of land in the territory drained by rivers flowing south into the St Lawrence. When this assumption proved false and a private trader was awarded the lease, the Hudson's Bay Company opened new posts along its eastern frontier almost as quickly as it had closed the old ones. In 1825 Temiskimay Post was established on the lake of the same name about one hundred and forty miles northeast of Mistassini. The next year Pike Lake Post was built, about fifteen miles west of Lake Nicabau, followed two years later by Migiskan on Lake Pascagama south of Waswanipi. (The latter lake is not represented on the Zone Two map, falling south of the area represented. Its coordinates are 48°34′N 75°36′W.) This second phase of expansion to the east was completed in 1834 when Nichikun was reopened and a small outpost called Kaniapiskau was established on Lake Caniapiscau linking the James Bay posts to Ungava Bay on the Labrador coast. (See figure 7.)

The proliferation of Hudson's Bay Company posts which took place during the period of competition and after must have been welcomed by the inland Indians. For many of them trade goods became more accessible

Figure 7. Hudson's Bay Company posts, 1822–1870

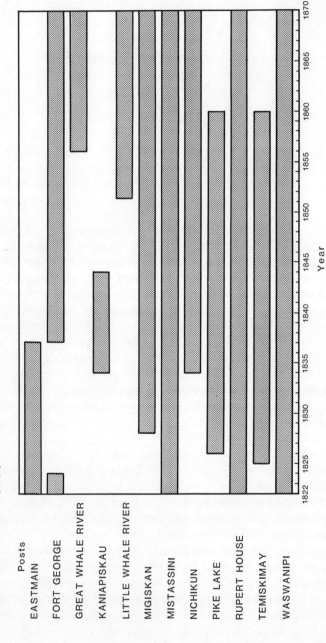

Source: Hudson's Bay Company Post Journals, 1822–1870

and the annual trip to the coast with their furs unnecessary. As well, these Indians were adept at exploiting the existence of alternate markets. Fur values and the price of trade goods were supposed to be uniform at the different posts – the company was adamant that there be no competition among their own traders – but the Indians were able to manipulate the granting of debt to their advantage. After taking credit at one post, instead of returning to repay it they simply took their furs to a different post where more credit was obtained. Referring specifically to the hunters who wintered at the headwaters of the Great Whale River, Rupert House chief Alexander Christie wrote in 1819: "In this manner these North East Indians keep going from one Post to the other and when entrusted with Debt, it is never more thought of till such time as they have visited all the Posts within their reach" (B.186/e/2: 6d). However, this practice was curtailed as the Hudson's Bay Company elaborated a more exact accounting system, and in the longer term the most important result of the extension of the inland posts was the increased regularization of the Indian way of life. Each family was assigned by the company to a particular post where that family was expected to bring its trade and when necessary obtain credit. If a hunter brought his furs to a different post, they naturally were accepted but were credited to his "home" post where he was encouraged to return as usual the next season. Indians who "wandered" were mistrusted by the company officers for being suspicious characters. The company intended this arrangement to enable a more accurate evaluation of the trade at each post and also to ensure that one trader did not increase his returns at the expense of his neighbour. Whatever the bureaucratic benefits to the company, the effect on the Indians was to restrict their traditional freedom of movement. Their identification with a particular post was accentuated by the men's participation in the canoe brigades which supplied the inland posts each summer. While the men were away, the families, who maintained themselves by fishing, often settled close to the posts to await their return and in this way the posts acquired a permanent summertime population of Indians. The settlement of the people should not be exaggerated, of course. A small number became seasonal employees of the company but most still pursued their traditional hunting and trapping activities during the winter. As well, the possibility of a large number of Indians living year round near a post was firmly opposed by the company for economic reasons.

After its merger with the North West Company the Hudson's Bay Company made certain changes in its trading procedures aimed at cutting back on what were considered excess expenditures. The two changes which most affected the Indians were reductions in the amount of credit and in the quantity of presents. Credit had always been viewed by Hudson's Bay Company officials as a necessary evil and amalgamation seemed

Indian summer encampment at Fort George, 1899. As the nineteenth century progressed, the number of summer residents at the posts increased, drawn there by summer employment and missionary activity.

to provide an ideal opportunity to abolish it, at least at posts not bothered by competition from the King's Posts. Officers found, however, that the Indians were opposed to any change and so trusting was continued, though in smaller amounts (B.135/k/1: 20). Significantly, when trading contact was first made with the Inuit to the north, it was decided from the beginning not to allow them any credit (B.186/b/40: 31).

The company was more successful when it came to reducing the quantity of presents given to the Indians. In competitive circumstances masters lavishly, and unsystematically, presented trading Indians, especially captains, with gifts of liquor, tobacco, clothing, and assorted trade items in order to secure and retain their loyalties. The number of recognized captains and lieutenants at Eastmain House had increased to about twelve during the last quarter of the eighteenth century. This increase was partly due to the increased numbers of Indians in general trading at the post, but it may also be attributable to the existence of competition and the need to attract inland Indians away from the Canadians. Whatever their number, at the turn of the century captains were receiving in presents as much as one-half the value of their gang's winter hunt. As inland posts were established, however, it was no longer necessary to entice the Indians into making long journeys with their furs, and especially in areas where the Nor'westers posed no challenge, the practice of creating trading captains died out. The company's point of view was expressed succinctly in 1814 by a retiring official referring to the Whale River trade:

The Custom of distinguishing particular Indians by large expensive Presents of fine Cloth, Orris Lace etc. is now considered by Persons acquainted with the Natives of the other Parts of Hudson's Bay as not only unnecessary but absurd and extravagant and I really do not see any Impropriety in abolishing it at Whale River and treating every Indian according to his real Merit, but I would strongly recommend the holding out proper Rewards to the Indians as an Incitement to Diligence. (B.3/b/50a: 12)

All around the bay the term "captain" was gradually replaced simply by leader or principal Indian. The last man to be called a captain on the east coast was Patashuanoo, who visited Big River Post in 1818 (B.77/a/4: 32d).

Unlike trading captains, principal Indians were not appointed by the Hudson's Bay Company, nor were they cultivated by the postmasters with large presents. They seem to have been recognized as leaders primarily by their own people, though company officers occasionally may have shown them preferential treatment. The principal Indian achieved his position by being a competent hunter, perhaps by evidencing certain spiritual powers and, very importantly, by having a number of sons. Sons automatically provided an Indian with a following to which, if he was a successful provider, others would attach themselves. The following observation was made by the Mistassini master in 1840: "Cawosawisit a principal Man among the Indians, and when all his Sons were alive had great influence amongst them but now has not so much ... In former days he was an excellent fur Hunter but now he is getting old and failing fast" (B.133/e/16: 4). Unlike the trading captains, the principal Indians did not enjoy their position for life.

Because more detailed records exist, it is possible to describe, at least in outline, James Bay Indian social organization in the nineteenth century. (See Morantz 1980.) Each principal Indian was the head of an aggregation of from six to nine hunters and their families, called here a local group. The hunting grounds of each member were located in the same general area and the group seems to have had a patrilateral bias, though others were not excluded. Some examples of the composition of local groups are: Neoshaihao, four sons, brother, brother's dependant, brother's son-in-law (adapted from B.186/e/5: 4d, 6d); Nosepetan, son-in-law, brother, brother's son, brother's brother-in-law, latter's son-in-law; Cheemooshominaban, son, half-brother, latter's three nephews, a man, latter's brother, another man (adapted from B.133/e/9: 4). The average family size of the James Bay people was five individuals; therefore a local group consisted of anywhere from thirty to fifty men, women, and children, the upper limits being too many to inhabit successfully the same tract of land and carry out fur-trapping or fur-hunting activities. This is indicated in the quotation given in chapter 7 stating that three to four families camping together hindered their procuring furs. Furthermore, this assumption is supported by the fact that all the members of the larger local groups did not camp together in the winter, a subject discussed later. An analysis of local groups trading at Rupert House between 1820 and 1840 indicates that they were stable in terms of membership and that changes in composition resulted mainly from death and attainment of adulthood (Morantz 1976). There is also evidence in the archival records of macro-groups, that is, loosely structured, noneconomic socio-religious groupings of sixteen or so families distinguishable by their common deference to a leader, sometimes referred to as a patriarch (Morantz 1980, 220–30).

Each local group was made up of a number of coresidential groups, what Dunning has defined as the largest unit of society in which there is a continual degree of economic cooperation (1959, 57). Periodically several of these coresidential groups met for specialized hunts or to socialize but they passed the winter on separate hunting grounds. The Mistassini postmaster provides an example: "Meewoppaish. This man is a principal Indian of a small party of Indians some of whom go to Swobmooshwan and others to Swan Lake with their Furs; they all meet together a short distance to the eastward of Little Mistasinny every summer and sometimes in the Winter" (B.133/e/9: 5d). The sources are unclear as to the exact composition of these small winter groups likely because this level of social organization was most affected by the state of the animal resources that year and the membership of coresidential groups changed accordingly. Single family households (generally a father and adolescent sons) did winter alone particularly when food was scarce, but more often there is mention of other groups of two and occasionally three adult hunters (fathers, sons, sons-in-law, brothers, brothers-in-law, older men, and dependants) and their families tenting together during the winter. The head or leader of the coresidential group was the senior hunter and most often the "owner" of the hunting territory.

Others (Ray 1975b, 61; Bishop 1974, 210) have attributed the development of family hunting territories, in part, to a policy initiated by the company after the merger in 1821. A report submitted by Hudson's Bay Company Governor George Simpson to his superiors in London in 1828 advises them that "we are endeavouring to confine the natives throughout the country now by families to separate and distinct hunting grounds, this system seems to take among them by degrees and in a few years I hope it will become general but it is a very difficult matter to change the habits of Indians" (D.4/92: 5d). This company initiative may account for such a development in other areas. In James Bay, however, this does not explain the formation of individually owned hunting territories. As was discussed at the end of chapter 7, the roots of such a land tenure system seem to go back at least to the early 1700s and the presence in the records of clearly worded references to such a system already in existence predate the company's stated intentions.

The nuclear family composition is clearly set out in the records in several lists (for example, B.186/e/5: 13; B.133/e/3: 7), though this does not necessarily mean they always functioned as nuclear families. Such reporting could well be due to the Englishmen's bias. Most of the families were monogamous, but in five of forty-nine cases at Rupert House in 1823 and five of twenty-nine at Mistassini a man had two wives. In the majority of cases the principal Indians or their sons had polygamous unions. The records also provide some information on extended families, showing one to two dependants were involved, most often the man's mother.

For all Indians, leaders or not, the flow of presents was curtailed following amalgamation. The new policy was embodied in the following instructions received by the master at Rupert House:

The irregular and indiscriminate manner in which (from a certain degree of necessity now no longer existing) the usual Presents of Coats, Shirts, Handkerchiefs, Tobacco, Spiritous Liquors, etc. have hitherto been made may under present Circumstances I think be abandoned without giving offence or Disgust to the Natives and a more regular and systematic method adopted by bestowing the Presents in proportion to the Furs and Geese brought and Services rendered. (B.186/b/6: 31)

According to the system which was implemented, each Indian was given a pint of rum and six inches of tobacco as a premium for every five made beaver worth of furs he brought to the post. Next, each "hunting Indian" was given an assortment of trade items including a knife, needles and thread, an awl, and a firesteel. As well, a hunter's wife might be given some cloth, some gartering, and some lace to make clothing. Depending on the number of skins he brought in, the hunter might be awarded a coat and a cotton shirt and a handkerchief. Lastly, again depending on the size of the previous season's hunt, he was given quantities of rum and tobacco as he took debt for the ensuing winter (B.186/b/31: 43). This system remained in operation for the rest of the period for which research has been done, that is, 1870. Presents associated with the goose hunt were also reduced and were given in proportion to the number of geese killed (B.135/b/43: 2). Furthermore, oatmeal, which had long been given freely to the James Bay people in times of distress, was made a trade item, costing at Rupert House one made beaver for ten pounds (B.186/b/36: 10d).

Liquor, first brandy and then rum, had been widely used as a present and as a trade item since the fur trade had begun. Following the amalgamation the Hudson's Bay Company gradually introduced prohibition in eastern James Bay. First, in 1827, the postmasters resolved that "the use of spiritous Liquors be gradually discontinued" (B.135/k/1: 34). This rather vague intention was given force a decade later when the postmasters decided liquor was no longer to be an item of trade and finally, in 1851, the company declared that no liquor at all for any purpose was to be allowed in eastern James Bay (B.135/k/1: 84d, 144d). There can be no question that while it was available, liquor was consumed in quantity by the Indians but its effects should not be exaggerated. Indians were social drinkers; they drank in the company of other hunters when they met for brief periods at the trading post. They seldom took away any liquor to their hunting territories except when requested by the company to present some to inland Indians whose trade was desired. Liquor was too bulky an article to transport. An injury received in a brawl, a drowning, a violent death – these were the very occasional results of the trade in liquor in eastern James Bay, and as often as not they involved inebriated white men as well as Indians. There is no evidence that drinking impaired health or was socially disruptive in a permanent way. The company banned liquor at the urging of reformers, especially missionaries, and the records from eastern James Bay suggest the Indians raised few objections.

Beaver conservation was another policy company officials began to implement more strictly following amalgamation. Fearing that the animal was on the verge of extinction, they took various measures to modify the Indians' trapping patterns. Immediately after the merger a decision was made by the James Bay postmasters that "the Natives be discouraged from killing Cub Beaver and that ever practicable measure be adopted to carry this Resolve into effect – and that all Steel Traps be immediately abolished, excepting in Fox Countries – and that no Furs be taken from the Natives, killed in the Summer Season" (B.135/k/1: 6d). The motives for these restrictions were as much economic as conservationist. The pelts of young beaver and beaver killed in the summer simply were not very valuable. Nevertheless the preservation of the species was of obvious importance to the Hudson's Bay Company.

There is evidence to suggest that the James Bay people may have practised beaver conservation before the company initiatives. One method,
described in the Rupert House correspondence of 1842, was to leave a
portion of their lands untrapped: "They alternate years work different
sections of their lands, leaving such to recruit two or even three years, or
otherwise long ago their lands (particularly the Coast Indians whose
Beaver grounds are so limited) would have been exhausted" (B.186/b/43:
15). Furthermore Joseph Beioley, chief of the Rupert House district,
hinted in 1824 that the Rupert House people had refrained from killing
summer beaver before the company began to encourage it: "It was
recommended to them all ... not to kill Summer Beaver or Beaver out of
Season and also as much as possible to spare the Beaver in Winter, particularly the Cub Beaver, an Injunction which they always promise to
comply with and which they represent as perfectly accordant with their
own Ideas on the subject and their Desires of not impoverishing their
Lands" (B.186/e/6: 8). Clearly the Indians were willing enough to abide
by the Hudson's Bay Company regulations to help preserve the species
but unlike the company their prime consideration was not economic. Next
to caribou meat beaver was the most preferred food, and they could not be
persuaded to go to unnecessary extremes to preserve it. In an attempt to
discourage the hunting of summer beaver even for food the company in
1827 reduced the price of its fishing tackle, ammunition, and provisions by
one-third (B.135/k/1: 38). The exception to the policy of conservation was
along the height of land where opposition traders continued to be active.
The postmasters decided that in these areas it would be best to hunt the
beaver to extinction, thereby creating a barrier of territory where no
competitor could successfully establish a trade (ibid.).

A second conservation policy was the creation of beaver preserves. The
idea had been broached as early as 1806 by company officials, but it was
not until thirty years later that the first preserve was established on
Charlton Island (A.6/17: 76d). Live beaver were placed on the island
which was declared off-limits to all trappers and which as much as possible was kept free of natural predators such as otter and lynx. Two
James Bay families wintered on Charlton to guard against poachers and
to report on the progress of the experiment (B.186/b/46: 27). When the
population reached a certain point, restricted trapping was allowed. At
Rupert House Robert Miles reported that initially it proved difficult to
collect the live beaver from the Indians because, he said, they "imagine
the Beaver would leave their lands altogether were they to bring them
here alive" (B.186/b/36: 12). Eventually, however, the preserve was
established and the beaver flourished. In the summer of 1842 the island of
Ministikawatin, situated off the west coast of the peninsula of the same
name, was stocked with animals and became James Bay's second preserve (B.186/b/50: 11).

Figure 8. Beaver and marten returns, Rupert River district, 1825–1869

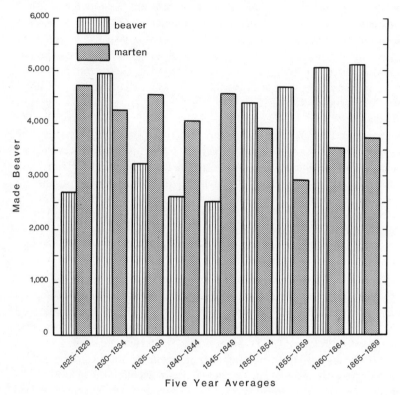

Source. B.135/h/1

By the late 1830s Governor Simpson decided that more effective measures were needed to preserve the beaver across the continent. At Rupert
House figures indicated that beaver returns had declined during the
decade by one-third (see figure 8), though Miles believed that "various
causes may nevertheless be assigned for this large diminution without
feeling the least apprehension that the country is becoming exhausted in
this the most valuable Fur" (B.186/e/23: 3d). At any rate, in 1841 Simpson implemented a three-year plan according to which the Indians were
allowed to trade annually no more than half the number of beaver pelts
they had brought in during the 1838–9 season (B.186/b/43: 68). To offset
this restriction the Indians were offered premiums for trapping marten
instead of beaver. The new regulations presented certain difficulties for
the Indians. First, as Miles explained, many inland Indians trading at the
coast had hunting territories interwoven with the territories of people
who traded at inland posts where the restrictions were not in force. When

Figure 9. Pounds sterling value of furs traded, Rupert River district, 1834–1869

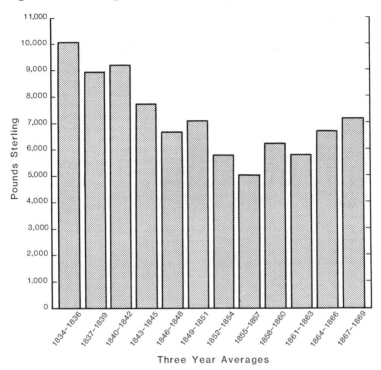

Source: B.135/z/2

the former left a section of their land for two or three years to repopulate with beaver, the latter sometimes trespassed on the land and trapped it out (B.186/b/43: 14). Secondly, Miles was convinced that what the hunters lost from not being able to trap as many beaver far exceeded what they could recoup through the premium system and he anticipated some might starve (B.186/b/45: 17). Before the regulations could be altered, however, Simpson decided that they had served their purpose, and in 1844 the Indians were once again permitted to kill as many beaver, in season, as they wished (B.186/b/50: 34). Figure 8 indicates that despite company policy beaver returns increased in the 1850s and 1860s, whereas marten returns generally declined.

By that time, however, beaver had declined in value and was more difficult to sell in Europe and the trade from Fort George (the former Big River Post), where beaver formed a small percentage of the returns, became more profitable (B.186/b/58: 14) than that from Rupert House which until mid-century had been the most productive of the eastern James Bay posts. Figure 9 charts the decline in the value of the Rupert

River district trade. The period ends with what appears to be a moderate recovery in the value of the returns, though not anywhere near the value of the trade earlier in the century.

The company responded to this decline in the worth of its former staple by discouraging the killing of beaver and by offering premiums for marten pelts, which had replaced beaver as the most lucrative fur (B.186/b/60: 14d). But figure 8 shows that marten returns too were on the decline at Rupert House. The geographical source of the trade remained similar to what it had been in the previous century, the majority of the furs coming from the inland Indians wintering around the headwaters of the various major rivers. In 1840, for example, inlanders accounted for over 70 per cent of the total trade at Rupert House and this was usual (B.186/e/23: 7).

Even though the North West Company was no longer a rival, the eastern James Bay posts continued to experience competition throughout the nineteenth century, expecially along the height of land. The lessees of the King's Posts during the 1820s operated a series of small posts which rivalled the Hudson's Bay Company establishments at Mistassini and Waswanipi and caused the company to erect three outposts to protect its trade. In 1831 the company acquired possession of the King's Posts but even so private traders from Canada, some of them Abenaki Indians who came via the St Maurice River, continued to cross the height of land into company territory. Referring to these traders, the Mistassini postmaster complained in 1834 that "these fellows are ruining the Country belonging to these poor Indians, they have such a number of Traps with them in general that no beaver escapes from them" (B.186/b/30: 5). Orders were issued from Rupert House to the inland posts to evict the interlopers, forcibly if necessary, but their incursions continued all during the rest of the 1830s and the 1840s. Neither did it matter that the Hudson's Bay Company operated the posts in the neighbouring St Maurice district, since the traders there did not attempt to stop the privateers from crossing the height of land and in fact themselves tried to draw down the Waswanipi hunters.

Opposition along the height of land decreased during the 1850s, but early in the next decade hunters who customarily traded at Mistassini began to visit Lake St Jean after discovering that traders and lumbermen there offered higher prices for their furs than did the Hudson's Bay Company. Word spread among the Indians until in the summer of 1862 Joseph Gladman at Rupert House complained that a "universal discontent prevails as to our system of dealing with the Indians" (B.186/b/70: 17d). By the middle of the sixties frontier Indians were also descending to Bersimis (on the north shore of the St Lawrence River across from Rimouski) where traders were outbidding the Hudson's Bay Company for marten and otter (B.186/b/69: 69d).

The company responded vigorously to this renewed challenge from the east. The outpost on Lake Temiskamay had been closed in 1860 as an economy measure, but now company servants were sent each winter in that direction to meet the Indians and persuade them to bring their furs as usual to the post at Mistassini. To the southwest Migiskan Post was maintained and generally, whenever it was learned that "intruders" from Canada had crossed the height of land, company servants were dispatched to counteract their influence. Friendly persuasion, however, was not nearly as efficient as price changes when it came to retaining the loyalties of the Indians. The company began by increasing the amount of ammunition and other presents it gave to the hunters and allowing the presents to be given irrespective of outstanding debts as long as the Indian in question traded his furs at a Hudson's Bay Company post (B.186/b/70: 47d). Later in the decade a new tariff was approved which increased the price given for the most important furs (B.186/b/70: 57d). In the 1860s, then, we find white traders opposing one another at the back of the bay just as they had done almost continuously for two centuries. The competition, however, was confined to the frontier regions. At the posts along the coast of James Bay the Hudson's Bay Company continued to enjoy the monopoly which had been secured by union with the Nor'-westers fifty years before.

From its establishment in 1776 as a three-man log tent, Rupert House was used primarily as a halfway house for Indians on their way to trade at Eastmain House. As Hudson's Bay Company posts proliferated in the up-country, however, it was discovered that the Rupert River was better suited to inland transport than was the Eastmain. Accordingly, in 1818 the post at its mouth was enlarged, the complement of men increased, and Rupert House became the supply depot and pre-eminent trading centre of the eastern region (B.135/b/37: 12). The brigades of canoes from Waswanipi, Mistassini, and Nichikun were expected to arrive at the coast with their cargoes of fur packs by the end of June, allowing time for the pelts to be forwarded by sloop to Moose Fort where they were received aboard the ship for England. After a stay of a few days the inland canoes, laden with trade goods for the Indians and provisions for the company servants, set off on the month-long return trip upriver, arriving at the main posts with time to spare to tranship a part of the cargo on to the tiny outposts before the onset of winter.

Preparation for the summer voyaging actually began early in the spring when the Rupert House blacksmith set to work forging the chisels, axe heads, knives, and traps so necessary to the Indian trade, while beside him the cooper fashioned wooden kegs, barrels, and rundlets to hold the stores during shipment. As many as ten canoes were required, each capable of carrying four or five men and a cargo of over two thousand

Birchbark transport canoe, c. 1870, built to Hudson's Bay Company specifications and bearing its markings and flag. Exact location is unknown; designated simply as eastern Hudson Bay.

pounds. The rivers were treacherous and accidents common and each season two or three canoes had to be replaced. At first they were made by Indians at the various posts, but by 1840 the company had decided it was cheaper for one of the mixed blood servants to do this work (B.186/b/37: 17). A total of about forty men were required for inland voyaging in the summer, and since the company had not servants enough to spare, it relied on the Indians, both coastal and inland, to supply the bulk of this manpower. Every Indian was paid between twenty-five and thirty-five made beaver for a return trip, depending on the distance involved, and received this wage either directly in trade goods or indirectly as a deduction from an outstanding debt. Though the amount paid to the Indians corresponded to one-half of the value of an average year's fur hunt, masters constantly complained that the men were reluctant to sign on, and when they did, often deserted along the route (B.186/b/2: 9d). One reason the Indians gave for not engaging as voyageurs was that they could not afford to give up any part of their fishing season, the produce of which sustained them during the winter (B.186/a/37: 3). Another consideration may well have been the arduous nature of the work. It took approximately fifty days to complete a round trip between Rupert House and any of the three major inland posts. During this time members of the brigade paddled from dawn to dusk, risked their lives in rapids (it was common for at least one voyageur to drown each season), and packed up to five hundred pounds of goods across lengthy portages, of which, as an example, there were seventy-one between Rupert House and Lake Nichi-cun (B.186/b/28: 43d). Despite the back-breaking work, enough Indians were always found willing to join the brigades each season.

Competition had allowed the James Bay Indians to influence the poli-cies and practices of the white traders. Where it continued, along the height of land, this influence could still be exerted but generally the end of competition between the Hudson's Bay Company and the North West Company changed the relationship between company and Indian. With no possibility that trade might be lost to a competitor the company was free to manipulate the Indians, using credit as a form of blackmail and taking policy decisions, such as the beaver quota, which adversely affected them. A case in point was the Ungava Bay adventure undertaken by the Hud-son's Bay Company in the 1830s. A trading post, Fort Chimo, was estab-lished at the mouth of the Koksoak River, and it was thought a good idea to induce some of the northern fur gatherers from the Fort George and Whale rivers to cross the peninsula and take up residence near the new settlement. As well as providing returns for Fort Chimo, the newcomers, reasoned Governor Simpson, "would rouse to habits of industry the indo-lent Creatures by whom the Country is now occupied" (B.186/b/28: 58d). Five Indian families agreed in 1835 to move to Ungava but all others refused, even when offered bribes of trade goods, until in 1841 Robert Miles suggested that Indians not agreeing to resettlement be forbidden to trade beaver pelts at the company posts (B.186/b/42: 36). This combina-tion of bribes and threats resulted in sixteen families moving across the peninsula (B.77/a/17: 4). The matter ended two years later after Fort Chimo closed and all the Indians returned to their original hunting grounds in debt and in bad humour. This incident illustrates that while the James Bay people were not necessarily defenceless – they could still oppose and obstruct company policy – in a monopolistic trading situation their economic independence vis-à-vis the company decreased.

CHAPTER ELEVEN

The Inuit and the North, 1837–1870

Only a decade after Big River Post had been closed, the Hudson's Bay Company began to contemplate the re-establishment of a post in the north. Since 1824 the company's activities along the coast towards Richmond Gulf had been confined to annual whaling voyages to the Great Whale River. The vessel left Eastmain House in July, remained in the north trading oil and furs with Indians who came to the river to hunt the belugas, and returned south in September when the Indians dispersed inland for another year. Hudson's Bay Company officers were dissatisfied with the results of the summer whale business, complaining that the Indians kept too many whales for their own purposes and did not pursue the hunt far enough into the autumn (B.186/b/28: 31d). Whaling had been a traditional summer activity for the northern Indians, who used the meat for feasting and the oil for winter fuel, and these uses came before the economic needs of the company. It was argued that a northern post not only would improve the efficiency of the whale fishery, but also would attract trade from the Indians who as yet remained outside the company's influence. "There are many Indians in that quarter," wrote Eastmain postmaster Thomas Corcoran, "who, though they should have furs and leather in their possession, do not think it worth while to come this far for the value they get for them, particularly as their country abounds with deer, which not only affords them the means of subsistence in great abundance, but also the means of clothing themselves & their families very comfortably in all seasons" (B.59/e/18: 7d). Furthermore, there was the consideration which time after time had drawn the Hudson's Bay Company into the north, the possibility of beginning a trade with the "Esquimaux." Of course, since most of the Eastmain House trade now came from the Big River area, the establishment of a northern post made the maintenance of Eastmain House unnecessary. And so in the summer of 1837, after 118 years of continuous operation, the post at the

A partial view of Fort George, 1867, from the hay field where two men are playing cricket. At the time of this photograph it was a thriving post at which 57 hunters traded.

mouth of the Eastmain River was abandoned, and its stores removed to a new location at Big River, christened Fort George Post (A.11/46: 24).

The new post became the trading centre for close to ninety hunters and a total Indian population of four hundred, the largest number of Indians frequenting any Hudson's Bay Company post in eastern James Bay (B.186/b/36: 2d). The coastal people, at least in the fall and early winter, inhabited the James Bay shore on either side of the Fort George River, as it was now called. Their lands were not rich in beaver and they trapped primarily fox and marten. Because these animals were susceptible to periodic reductions in population, the Fort George people regularly experienced winters of extreme privation. Depending on the success of their autumn hunt along the coast, these Indians would sometimes move inland in January in search of more productive grounds. Twice a year, just as at Eastmain House, they participated in the goose hunt. The number of hunters varied but, as an example, in the fall of 1842 about twenty men and their families took part (B.77/a/17: 12–14d). The hunt took place along the coast from Cape Jones in the north to Moar Bay in the south. Families hunting close to Fort George brought in their own geese but at the more distant tents the birds were salted in barrels on the spot and collected by boat. Late in the 1840s a "salmon" fishery was established at the mouth of the Seal River. At this outpost in the fall Indians netted fish, salted them, and transported them by boat back to Fort George. Between goose hunts, the coasters passed the summer fishing or hunting whales at

Coastal transportation, Fort George, 1896. In the early 1800s the Hudson's Bay Company began providing transportation between Fort George, the goose-hunting tents, and the whale fishery.

Great Whale River. Each August a small number were employed cutting hay for the company's livestock. After the fall goose season the coastal people dispersed to their hunting grounds.

The inlanders appeared at Fort George each June with their furs and settled on Horse Island, a place postmaster Thomas Corcoran called "the grand rendezvous of Big River Indians at this season" (B.77/a/12: 2). In mid-July, after a month of fishing, hunting, and socializing, the inlanders moved north to Great Whale River to join in the beluga hunt. The company continued to send a vessel to that river to trade each summer, and when the weather permitted, it also visited Little Whale River. In 1844 a man named Weestaky became the first Indian to command the whale boat (B.77/a/18: 37). The Indians received one made beaver worth of trade items for eight gallons of oil or ten gallons of blubber, plus a premium of rum and tobacco for every six made beaver worth of oil they produced. Extremely successful hunters were given cloth coats (B.77/b/2: 5). As well as whale products, there were furs and leather to be traded from

Indians from the interior barren grounds who never visited Fort George. At the beginning of September the inlanders dispersed, either to favourite fishing spots or to the barren grounds to hunt caribou. Later in the autumn they returned to their hunting grounds for the winter.

As we have seen, the Indian trade was only one attraction the north held for the Hudson's Bay Company. Ever since the establishment of Richmond Fort in 1750 the company had endeavoured to make trade contacts with the Inuit. To date, each attempt had failed, tragically in some cases. Company officials believed that the main obstacle to friendly relations with the Inuit was the traditional animosity which existed between these people and northern Indians. By this time the southern James Bay people had ceased their northern "Esquimaux hunts," but the Indians north of the Fort George River and the Inuit were still hostile to one another. As long as they were enemies of the Indians, the Hudson's Bay Company men concluded, the Inuit would not come into a company post so postmaster Corcoran took steps to establish a peace. First, he offered a reward to any Indian who would guide an Inuit to Fort George. And secondly, he dispatched into the north an Inuit man named Moses, a former employee of the company at Churchill River, who had been assigned to Fort George as an interpreter, to make contact with the Inuit.

In April 1839 Corcoran's initiatives met with their first success. An Indian named Katsaytaysit, hunting near Cape Jones, encountered a family of six Inuit and convinced them to accompany him to Fort George. The head of the family traded his furs, leather, and sealskin for a gun, an ice chisel, harpoon, axe, knives, a file, and ammunition (B.77/a/12: 60). He managed to make Corcoran understand – Moses the interpreter was absent – that he came from the islands off Richmond Gulf and would return to the post with more of his people. This was the first recorded instance of any of the Inuit coming in to a post as far south as the Fort George River.

Shortly before the arrival of this single family Moses had left Fort George for the north, equipped with light trade items to distribute as presents among any Inuit he might find. During the next year the interpreter travelled as far as Cape Smith, across the peninsula to Ungava Bay, and then back to the Richmond Gulf area where he passed the winter. In March 1840 Moses reappeared at Fort George, followed closely by about thirty families of Inuit which he had led south to trade. Greeting Corcoran, the newcomers presented him with a pair of boots and "several of them girded me with some sealskin line, which Moses interpreted as a token of friendship" (B.77/a/14: 51). The following day the Inuit brought their trade – twenty-one fox skins, an otter, three wolverine, and four wolf skins, a barrel and a half of seal blubber, some caribou skin coats, fifty large caribou skins, and 1300 fathoms of sealskin line. "They were

Inuit summer camp at Great Whale River, 1896. The drawing in of the Inuit to regular trade in the mid-1800s accorded the Hudson's Bay Company trader responsible a great deal of satisfaction. The richness of the furs worn in this illustration makes this readily understandable.

paid," wrote Corcoran, "with articles of no great value, except some tin kettles that did not answer well at this place for the Indian trade" (ibid.). The master learned that these people were residents of the Cape Smith area and what came to be called the Belcher Islands and that "we are the first party of Europeans, and this is the first Trading establishment that they have ever seen" (B.77/a/14: 52). He found that occasional trade with the northern Indians had given the Inuit a familiarity with the company's trade items, a fact which suggests the imperatives of trade had already improved relations between the two native groups. According to the Hudson's Bay Company sources, contact between Indian and Inuit at Fort George was amicable, and the 1840s might be marked as the end of violent hostilities between the two peoples.

Relations between the white man and the Inuit were also friendly. With one exception, there was no repetition of the deadly encounters which had characterized early meetings between them. The exception occurred in the early 1860s and an account of it survives in the company records. In the spring of 1861 James Anderson, postmaster at Little Whale River, employed a man named Noma to undertake an exploratory expedition north of Richmond Gulf. A year later Noma returned to the post. According to Anderson's relation of Noma's account, in the fall of 1858 or 1859 a ship was wrecked in the vicinity of Mosquito Bay and thirteen or fourteen members of the crew escaped by boat to shore. (This may refer to the wreck of the *Kitty* in 1859, five crew members of which were found dead on the coast north of Mosquito Bay the next spring [B.372/b/1: 29d].) The survivors encountered an Inuit family with whom they lived peaceably for some time. However, another party of Inuit who had never seen white men arrived from the north, and "either through fear of the Whites or from a desire of possessing their Property," murdered them all (B.373/a/3: 39d). Noma added: "All the Men and Women Engaged in the murder are said to have a line Tatooed across their nose extending down on either cheek – this was done in honor of, and to commemorate the exploit" (B.373/a/3: 93d). This incident was unique in the period under discussion. To the south, where the Inuit regularly visited the Hudson's Bay Company posts to trade, company records divulge only peaceful relations.

After the success of Moses's diplomatic mission in 1839–40, Fort George played host each spring to large parties of Inuit from the area north of Little Whale River and from the offshore islands. As they did in the case of the Indians, Hudson's Bay Company officers distinguished between two groups of Inuit – mainlanders, who wintered on the coast, and islanders, who inhabited the Belcher Islands. Initially the islanders did not visit the post, preferring to trade with mainlanders who travelled across to the islands when the ice had formed. The success of the "Esquimaux" trade at Fort George often depended on whether ice conditions were such that this trip could be made; if it could not, few Inuit trade goods were brought to the post. Later in the 1840s some of the islanders began making the trip to Fort George themselves. The Inuit, or "Huskies" as the Englishmen called them, arrived at the post on their dogsleds in March and April with a year's collection of fox furs, seal blubber, and caribou skins. They traded for a variety of items, the most important being metal goods, especially seal harpoons and fox traps. During their stay at the post, sometimes lasting several weeks, they lived in ice houses at a number of spots along the coast and hunted seal, white bear, and fox. According to the records two of the most popular camping spots were on the Loon Islands, off the mouth of Fort George River, and on "Wasteckon" (now Wastikun Point on the maps). However, sealing went on as far south as the Paint Hills. In May most of the Inuit returned north, either to prepare for the white whale hunt at Little Whale River or to seek the caribou in the barren lands. A small number remained behind and by the middle of the 1840s an Inuit homeguard had developed at Fort George. These people tended to remain quite close to the post all during the year, camping on the offshore islands and pursuing a number of activities, including sealing, fishing, and trapping fox.

Company officers were interested in establishing direct contact with the Inuit living on the Belcher Islands, as they believed these people to be the source of the most valuable fox furs. In the first half of the 1840s

Inuit whaling at Little Whale River, 1865. A hunter is preparing to skin, flense, and butcher a whale. Note the hunting equipment in use: a kayak, float made of a sealskin and harpoon.

Moses twice attempted to cross from the mainland to meet the Belcher Inuit and encourage them to bring their trade to Fort George. Both times bad weather forced him back. In the winter of 1845–6, however, the elderly interpreter reached the islands, finding them rich in fox and seals (B.186/b/53: 9d–10). Encouraged by his report, John Spencer, the Fort George postmaster, sent the mixed blood Thomas Wiegand across the ice with two Inuit companions in March 1847 to make contact with the islands' inhabitants and to discover a suitable harbour for a trading vessel. The results of this expedition were disappointing, Spencer reporting that Wiegand "saw but 5 Esquimaux at the Island he went to, as the rest had some time previously taken their departure to the Northward with the view of hunting the Seahorse, at the Sea Horse Islands" (B.186/b/53: 38). Nevertheless, the postmaster was not discouraged and in the summer of 1848 Wiegand returned to the islands, this time by boat. Once again few inhabitants were encountered and very little trade collected, the vessel returning with only two barrels of seal oil and a single coat of white fox skin (B.186/b/56: 10d).

A difference of opinion now arose between officers over whether any more visits to the Belchers should be made by company servants. Spencer argued that Wiegand should return to the islands, both to assist what

Little Whale River Post c. 1870s. Originally built in 1851 to exploit the whale fishery, which was discontinued in 1870, the post was abandoned in 1890.

Spencer now believed to be the poverty-stricken population of thirty-five families and also to establish a regular pattern of visits which he predicted would eventually result in a profitable trade (B.186/b/56: 27ff). However, Spencer's superior, Joseph Gladman, maintained that the Belcher Inuit should be encouraged to come in to Fort George themselves and he vetoed further voyages to the islands (B.186/b/56: 8d). Over the next few years a compromise solution was found, and in the summer of 1851 the company opened a small, three-man post at the mouth of the Little Whale River. It was intended that a whale fishery would be started at the river but primarily the new post was expected to become the centre of an expanded Inuit trade, attracting both islanders and mainlanders. This was the third attempt by the company to operate a trading post at Little Whale River. Two earlier attempts failed, at least in part because of Inuit hostility. The new post, however, was established with the blessing of the northern people and remained in operation for forty years until the increasing shallowness at the river's mouth made provisioning by schooner impossible and forced its closure (B.372/e/5: 4).

Coincident with the establishment of Little Whale River Post, Hudson's Bay Company Governor George Simpson began to plan an extensive whaling operation, or porpoise fishery as he called it, somewhere on the east coast of the bay. Encouraged by the success of a similar enterprise in the St Lawrence River, Simpson in the spring of 1852 dispatched to Moose Fort a small expedition led by a Quebec whaler named Belanger to identify the best whaling sites in the north. For a century the company had traded whale oil from Indians at the two Whale rivers but Simpson had in mind a more ambitious prosecution of the hunt, employing company servants and company techniques. (See Francis 1977.) After exploring the coast from Moose Fort to the Little Whale River, Belanger decided the latter offered the best prospects of success. Simpson was so encouraged by the French Canadian's report that he wrote to his superiors in London: "You may fancy me over-sanguine, perhaps, but I have no hesitation in stating my opinion that, for some years to come, the porpoise fisheries of the Bay will be more valuable than the present beaver trade of the whole country" (A.12/6: 152d).

During the winter of 1852–3 Simpson and Belanger conferred at Lachine and agreed on the details of the first summer's operation. The Quebecer was to be assisted by Robert Hamilton, postmaster at Abitibi, and was given a gang of twelve company servants. Additional manpower would be provided on the spot by hiring local natives as needed. Another dwelling house would have to be built at Little Whale River, as well as an oil house in which to boil the blubber. It was agreed that six furnaces would be built, for which bricks and iron work had to be imported. Fuel and building materials were a special problem so far north, where the wood supply consisted chiefly of stunted spruce and driftwood. It was planned to obtain lumber for building from the Fort George area but Simpson recognized the need to import coal from England to fuel the furnaces. Lastly, large numbers of barrels were required in which to store and ship the oil. Once again scarce resources made it impossible to obtain locally the wood for staves and so these too had to be imported and a cooperage established at the river (A.12/6: 307d).

This expensive undertaking was slow to produce the anticipated returns. The first season was spoiled by poor weather and the whalers' late arrival at the river so that no animals were caught. Furthermore, Belanger and Hamilton took a strong disliking to one another, Hamilton claiming Belanger was dishonest and ineffective, Belanger claiming Hamilton was interfering and incompetent (A.12/7: 50d). Despite this false and acrimonious start, Simpson refused to be discouraged, arguing that once it got established the operation would prove profitable. Then, in October, the fishery was dealt another blow by the sudden death of Belanger. He and another man were returning by boat to the post during a storm when the vessel capsized at the river's mouth. Belanger's battered corpse was found two days later washed up on the coast (A.12/7: 43–43d). Simpson had placed a great deal of faith in the Quebecer's expertise and his death was a major setback. Yet it was out of the question to abandon the fishery; a competent successor had to be found to take charge. Therefore, in the spring of 1854, the governor appointed James Anderson, a postmaster at one of the King's Posts (A.12/7: 90). Under Anderson's management the enterprise began to enjoy a moderate success. New buildings were constructed; in 1857 a separate fishery was begun at a new post at Great Whale River; and, most importantly, the number of whales killed began to increase, from 423 in 1854 to 743 in 1856, and at Great Whale River 1043 in 1857.

The Reverend John Horden, then an Anglican missionary based at Moose Factory (formerly Moose Fort), visited the north in the summer of 1858 and left the best description on record of how whaling was carried out by the Hudson's Bay Company at the mouths of the Whale rivers (Church Missionary Society [CMS], Horden Correspondence 1858). The most important piece of equipment was the barrier net, a long net strung across the mouth of the river where it was attached by ropes to anchors and allowed to sink. The beluga entered the river over the barrier on a high tide, and when it was determined that a large number were above the net, it was raised, buoyed up with kegs, and the whales were trapped. Now a second net, called a pond net, was brought into play. This was a small circular trap, a part of which was sunken to allow the animals to enter freely. Once it had been placed in the river, the drive began. Horden took part in one of these drives and described it this way: "Thirty-seven canoes and five boats were engaged in it. Some canoes were first sent a little way up the river to drive the whales down; we then gradually hemmed them in and drove a large number into the 'pond net,' the mouth of which was instantly raised and 300 were confined within; these were at once shot and drawn ashore" (ibid.). Once ashore the skin and blubber were removed with sharp flensing knives and carried to the oil house. Any meat on the carcass was taken by the Indian employees for their families and for feasting. At the oil house the blubber was removed from the skin, cut up into small pieces, and put in kettles to be boiled down into oil. When ready the oil was pumped from the kettles into barrels in which it was shipped to England for use primarily as a lighting fuel. The whale skins were cleaned and salted. Some were used to package furs at other company posts, but the rest were sent to Europe where whale skin was used as a leather substitute.

At Little Whale River about twenty to twenty-five Indians participated in the whaling each summer. This was practically the total number of Indians who visited the post during the year. Some were directly employed by the company for the season; others helped out when needed. Jobs included setting the nets, participating in drives, shooting the whales, cutting up the blubber, and cleaning the skins.

Most of the trade at the post came from close to five hundred Inuit who customarily came in between March and May with their season's collection of fox furs and seal blubber (CMS, Horden Correspondence 1858). The Inuit arrived by dogsled from the Belchers and from the coast north of Richmond Gulf and remained at the post for several days, living in ice houses built on their arrival. While at the post they were employed cutting up the blubber for boiling, stretching fox skins, and hauling wood with their sleighs. Afterwards they went to hunt caribou, one or two remaining at the post for the summer to hunt for the company.

The post at Great Whale River was constructed during the summer of 1856 (A.11/26: 24). Three years later Fort George ceased to be a trading establishment, and the Indians attached to it were told by the company to take their furs to the new post. Fort George remained in operation, but now primarily as a source of geese and timber. Most of the Indians arrived at Great Whale River in June after the ice had left the river and the coast and stayed to work for the company at the whaling. Others were hired at ten to twelve made beaver a season to work at Fort George gathering hay and cutting logs. As well, Indians from the Fort George River region were employed, as usual, spring and fall in the goose hunt. Following the whale season the Indians departed for their hunting territories. Two or three men and their families stayed close to the post and spent the winter hunting for the company. An Indian man tented at Cape Jones and regularly supplied Great Whale River Post with venison and fish. Country provisions at the post were almost totally supplied by these Indians.

The system of trade at the northern posts had changed somewhat since the early years of the century. As well as receiving the worth of his year's hunt, each trapper was given a variety of presents, the amount of which depended on the size of the hunt. The presents included awls, cloth, ammunition, knives, needles and thread, clothing, tobacco, sugar, and tea. Credit was advanced to Indians, but not to Inuit, again according to the quantity of furs brought in and what the postmaster judged to be the reliability of the trapper. Plugs of tobacco were given along with the credit. When he arrived at the post, each native trapper was given a quantity of grain, according to the size of his family, some tobacco, and a pipe and on departure these gifts were repeated. Evidently the provision of food by the company was no longer confined just to years of starvation. Anyone who brought in less than ten made beaver worth of furs was not eligible for any presents (B.77/z/1: 101). Table 9 indicates the variety and quantity of trade goods produced by the Indians and Inuit. It can be seen that beaver was a less important resource in the north than were marten, fox, and whale and seal products. Marten and fox experienced periodic population declines, but when they were plentiful, as in 1854 for example, they accounted for a much larger percentage of the hunt than did the beaver.

The Hudson's Bay Company's northern whale fishery failed to live up to Governor Simpson's prediction that it would prove more valuable than the beaver trade. Actually, the year the governor died, 1860, was the best season in the enterprise's short history. That summer at Little Whale River over fifteen hundred whales were killed and at Great Whale River another eight hundred (A.11/26: 40). But this success did not continue. Throughout the subsequent decade the number of animals taken declined sharply until by 1870 whaling had ceased at both rivers.

Any attempt to explain the failure of the east coast "porpoise fishery" must take into account its northerly geographic location. Aside from the additional expense this incurred in the form of shipping costs and imported fuel, the inhospitable climate of the Whale rivers presented a series of difficulties to the actual whaling operation. When spring came late and the ice was slow to leave the coast, the arrival of the whales was delayed. Heavy winds blowing in off the bay and frequent storms of rain, sometimes even summer snow, made the placing of nets dangerous when not impossible. Furthermore, rainstorms tended to stir up the rivers, filling them with mud which drove the whales back out into the bay. Thick fogs were not an unusual summer occurrence, which made it difficult to know if any whales were in the river, or if they were, to drive them into the nets. Lastly, it was only at high tide that the animals swam up the river, and when this happened at night, watchers could not see whether the whales were above the net. The whaling season was brief and to be successful had to be exploited intensively. Yet any one of the above conditions would keep the whalers idle for days at a time.

If the climate made it difficult to prosecute the fishery, the whales made it impossible. Quite simply, they stopped entering the rivers. It is possible their numbers may have been depleted but more probably, as the whalers themselves complained, the animals had become shy and conscious of the danger. Quite often they did not venture beyond the barrier during the whaling season, but no sooner had the company's equipment been stowed away for the winter than the animals were as numerous as ever in the rivers. Anyway, for whatever reason the whales began to avoid the Whale rivers. This was fatal to the company's interest. Unlike Indian whaling, which was a chase, the company's operation was stationary and land-based. It depended upon the regular arrival of the whales. When the animals' habits changed, the company was powerless to react.

In 1869 George McTavish, then postmaster at Little Whale River, wrote his employers that "I have decided upon giving Great Whale River a thorough rest for a few years as the Porpoise seem to be getting more shy every season" (A.11/26: 70d). Because of this decision the Great

TABLE 9

Returns, in Quantities, for the East Main District (Fort George, Little Whale River, Great Whale River), 1854–1868

	1854	1855	1856	1857	1858	1859	1860	1861	1862	1863	1864	1865	1866	1867	1868
Badger	2	3					1								
Bear, black:															
prime	21	12	13	12	47	24	10	26	23	12	8	12	13	11	8
common	7	1						2		1	2				
Bear, white	4	9	7	4	5	11	13	11	7	13	13	9	16	16	19
Beaver:															
prime	970	690	1176	627	1686	937	696	1155	792	856	914	541	1031	656	409
common			28	21	5	6		13			13				5
coating	1	1													
Castoreum, lb	56	40	75	38	97	52	36	45	38	38	33	30	55	33	12
Feathers, lb:															
goose and partridge	2016	1108	560	560	1723	900	1008	448	2688	896	1008	2240	1232	1512	784
Fox, cross:															
prime	147	201	82	55	73	159	39	64	57	37	86	37	104	113	110
common	16	5	7	1	4	15	2	4	6	3	3	1	2	10	5
kit					1										
Fox, red:															
prime	396	328	191	147	170	334	81	132	176	135	238	119	279	328	311
common	41	2	2	8	5	43	2	15	31	10	17	2	6	20	10
Fox, silver:															
prime	89	21	44	36	32	98	16	30	20	15	49	26	45	76	56
common	11		2	3	1	9		3	3		2		2	3	2
Fox, white and blue	4795	1700	548	435	1330	941	503	273	2685	2789	1980	376	728	4646	1854
Hare, arctic	14		3		12	4	8	3	12	20	12	16	14		2
Ivory, lb					45		61				79				53

	25	18	9	1	2	3	1	5	2	3	9	3	8	6	20
Lynx	1508	1579	867	314	1853	1778	1192	537	1765	2398	2092	1573	1382	1618	1648
Lead ore, tons								4							
Loon skin								37		31	38	18	17	10	
Marten: prime	71	54	28	52	170	39	19	30	99	166	164	40	118	172	58
common	31	21	8	22	46	12	40	43	70	104	35	17	50	55	25
Mink															
Muskrat	311	233	110	593	1355	777	716	1771	1400	972	485	564	1654	902	827
Oil, tons: whale	40	61	77	130	114	72	158	15	34	92	10	7	36	12	13
seal	5					13		26	6	5	4	4	9	17	12
Otter: prime	136	106	146	162	251	154	240	292	292	268	236	178	275	186	134
common	17	19	31	45	30	23	18	29	18	17	23	11	30	30	22
Quills, thousands	26	25	17	8	28	15	21		48		21	45	26	38	10
Rabbit skin, doz					17	14			3	21	99	39	175	175	
Sealskin	37	29	1	366	624	760			1178	783	438	699	853	1529	1354
Swan skin		12	6	5	1		1		9	2	2		2	7	7
Skunk		4													
Weenusk (groundhog)									6						
Wolf: prime	67	59	6	5	22	14	18	5	6	8	15	5	19	10	13
common					6			3		2	3		8	7	3
Wolverine	13	14	4	4	3	8	4	3	14	8	12	14	5	5	4
Whale skin, half	387	1006	1148	2097	1673	1204	1929	412	455	1397	241	230	664	234	346

Source: B.373/d/10: 2ff.

Note: Figures have been rounded off to the nearest whole number.

Whale River Post was almost completely closed and the trading establishment removed back to Fort George. McTavish explained:

In order that Great Whale River may not be disturbed by Craft entering it, I shall send the trading goods to Fort George for all the Indians who hunt in that quarter, and those who hunt inland and North of this will be dealt with here, which is quite as convenient for them as GWR. The establishment at GWR is now in charge of a careful man who will look after the buildings and keep the place in order until such time as it is thought advisable to resume the fishery. (B.373/b/1: 36)

The following summer whaling was suspended also at the Little Whale River, though it continued to be a trading centre for another twenty years. In 1870, therefore, the northern trade was once again centred at Fort George and Little Whale River.

CHAPTER TWELVE

Rupert House in the Nineteenth Century

During its early years the Hudson's Bay Company had attempted to keep the Indians of James Bay at arm's length, discouraging contact between them and the white servants and prohibiting the Indians access to the posts. Segregation, however, proved not only impossible but undesirable as well, and there developed between Indian and servant the mutual reliance described earlier. In the nineteenth century this relationship was transformed once again. More than ever before Indians and mixed bloods were employed by the company both seasonally and full-time to such a degree in fact that the operation, and often the supervision, of the fur-trade post was left in native hands. And more than ever before natives were using the Hudson's Bay Company, either calculatedly or out of necessity, as an alternate food resource when game animals failed or hunting conditions were not right. This increased involvement with the company resulted in certain important changes in the economic, social, and spiritual life of the James Bay people.

Indians had always been hired by postmasters to perform specific tasks but formerly these tasks had been accomplished away from the post. Examples are canoe and snowshoe making, hunting, and carrying the mail packet. The difference in the nineteenth century was that members of the homeguard now worked at the post, in the case of summer haymaking, or at least alongside company servants, in the case of inland voyaging. No longer were Indians employed solely to perform jobs suited to their traditional skills. Instead the homeguard had become a potential labour force from which the postmaster supplemented his regular complement of men when more hands were required. At Rupert House each summer half a dozen men were engaged for six weeks to cut hay in the marshy lowlands along the river and transport it to the post where it was stored for winter use as feed for the livestock. Members of the homeguard also were hired to transport ammunition, salt, and barrels to distant goose-

Haying, Rupert House, 1884. A complement of coastal Indians was employed each summer in various tasks around the post.

hunting sites by boat and sled and to collect the geese when the season was finished. And as we have seen, the Rupert House homeguard provided many of the inland voyageurs each summer. Almost all of the local hunters were engaged at one time or another by the company. Indian women, too, were often employed at the posts to trap game, fish, and gather berries. Frequently Indians who had had a poor fur season, instead of being given food or credit, were given part-time jobs as an opportunity of earning additional income. It seems probable as well that favoured Indians were the ones given work, thereby making employment with the company a form of social control which the masters exerted over the Indians. For their part the homeguard seem to have viewed periodic employment as an alternate income source to be exploited when traditional resources failed.

While homeguard, and to a much lesser degree inland, Indians engaged with the company on a part-time basis, the mixed blood population in eastern James Bay provided a large proportion, usually more than one-half, of the full-time employees. Company officials decided very early in the century to cultivate at the bayside posts a "small Colony of very useful Hands" which ultimately would replace servants recruited in Europe (A.6/17: 76). To this end the officials recommended that "it would be advisable to instruct the Children belonging to our Servants in the principles of Religion and teach them from their Youth reading, writing, arithmetic and amounts which we would hope would attach them to our Service" (ibid.). This was the general policy throughout the Hudson's Bay Company domain (Brown 1977). Initially most mixed blood employees were confined to general labouring jobs, but by the 1840s they were competent at the full gamut of trades as well and men such as George Atkinson Jr and Thomas Wiegand were undertaking important expeditions on behalf of the company (A.12/2: 218d). The impetus for this change of policy was partly economic but it must also have had a psychological motive. As European-born servants acquired native families, they naturally developed certain aspirations for their children, aspirations which included tutoring in the Christian religion and a basic level of literacy, especially if employment with the company was contemplated. It was 1840 before a missionary was posted to James Bay, but spelling books were sent out in 1794 "for the purpose of teaching the Children at your Factory to read" and in 1808 James Clouston was posted to Eastmain House as a schoolmaster, the first on the east coast (A.6/15: 105d; Davies 1963, 341). The school was intended for mixed blood children of servants, but if "the Chiefs of the Trading Tribes" wished to enrol any of their children, the schoolmaster was instructed to receive them as "a means of cultivating the Friendship & Goodwill of the Parents and Children" (A.6/17: 119d). When missionaries arrived later in the century, they assumed the responsibility of educating the mixed blood and Indian children.

Mixed blood servants did not always or to the same degree shed their "Indianness." George Atkinson Jr, for example, who in 1803 had been sent north to Big River to establish a post in opposition to the Nor'westers and who remained in the company's service until 1821, often passed the winter tenting away from the post hunting to support his family. Though on occasion proving less energetic on the company's behalf than officials desired, particularly when it came to expanding the trade northward, Atkinson was a valued employee entrusted with a series of responsibilities including the whale fishery and northern exploration. Yet after his

Portraits of Mr and Mrs
Joseph Gladman, taken in a
studio at Port Hope, Ontario.
Gladman was chief trader
of the Rupert River district
from 1844 to 1864.

retirement from the service he settled on the modern Poplar River near where it empties into Moar Bay and proceeded to counsel the local Indians to demand better prices for their furs and services. James Clouston at Big River Post reported that in the spring of 1823 Atkinson told the coast Indians "not to hunt geese for the Englishmen 'till they be paid for it'" (B.77/e/5: 2). The postmaster went on to complain that "most of those Indians who wintered at the Coast are very dissatisfied which is attributed to George Atkinson Senr. having told them the Englishmen cheat them in trade by giving so little for their Furs and suggested to them not to hunt Furs 'till they are better paid for it'" (B.77/e/5: 5). The company's response to Atkinson's opposition was to try and induce him to retire to the Red River colony, an offer he initially refused but finally accepted in 1829, a year before his death at the age of sixty (Davies 1963, 341).

The records contain no other comparable example of a mixed blood of Atkinson's distinction encouraging a group of disaffected hunters to resist the company, but there are frequent examples of mixed blood servants being considered too sympathetic with the Indians. At Mistassini in 1836, for instance, Joseph Aideeson was censured because "he drinks Rum with the Indians when ever an opportunity occurs" and because "he had more the ways of an Indian than that of a European" (B.133/e/14: 7). At the same post, Thomas Cooper, another mixed blood servant, was found to have "too much to say to the Indians. He was even gone so far as to tell them that were he in their line and could hunt and procure furs as well as them, that he would not cum for any of the Masters but would go and Trade his furs with any person who could give the most goods for them" (ibid.). Obviously, the native servant was expected to identify his interests with those of his employer. And most did; these instances of opposition were exceptional. More usual was the contribution of such men as Andrew Moar, master at Rupert House during the 1820s, whose three surviving sons, Thomas, John, and Peter, all entered the company's service. Or Thomas Wiegand, educated at the Eastmain House school, who went on to become a sloopmaster at Fort George and an explorer of the Belcher Islands. Or Joseph Gladman, whose grandfather George was Rupert House postmaster in the 1780s and who himself superintended the company's Rupert River district for twenty years between 1844 and 1864. The list could be extended indefinitely and would include the majority of the Hudson's Bay Company servants in eastern James Bay during the century. The "small colony of very useful hands" had become an accomplished fact.

By no means all servants' sons joined the service, of course. George Atkinson's son, George III, engaged with the company after being educated in England but later resumed "his Indian mode of life" (B.135/c/2:

66; Davies 1963, 341). Jacob Atkinson, brother of George Atkinson Jr, sometimes worked in the summer as a sloopmaster but otherwise preferred the woodlands to the factory (B.59/a/109: 8d). A hunter named Chizzo, brother of the inland servant Thomas Beads, hunted geese and furs from his tent on the Eastmain River, and the brothers Jack and Hugh Hester, descendants of the Eastmain House postmaster who suffered a mental breakdown in 1767, were accomplished trappers but never employees. Once again the list continues indefinitely. The names are less important than the fact that full-time employment with the company was an option many mixed bloods, even the formally educated ones, found less appealing than the traditional life-style of the Indian hunter.

While the education and employment of mixed blood servants provided a reliable supply of men for the posts, native recruitment proved to have a significant drawback from the company's point of view. The servants' families, wives and children, gathered in the vicinity of the post and formed an almost permanent population of dependants. At certain times of the year the women could feed themselves and their children by fishing and trapping small game but in general they relied on their servant husbands for support. When the men were unwilling or unable to meet their responsibility, it devolved to the company, and inevitably officials balked at the expense. Furthermore, it was not unusual for European-born servants to retire from the country leaving their families with no means of support whatsoever, save company charity. As the numbers of dependants increased, regulations were passed to curb desertion and nonsupport. First, men were forbidden to marry without the postmaster's permission. Next, in 1827, it was decided that no servant "be allowed hereafter to take a woman without binding himself down to leave 1/10 of his annual wages in the hands of the Company as a provision for his family in event of Death or retirement" (B.135/k/1: 38d). Still not satisfied, a decade later the company endeavoured to reduce the number of dependants by ruling that boys at fifteen years of age be taken into the service as apprentices and sent to a distant post for employment. If the father did not agree, he would be fired (B.135/k/1: 95–95d). These measures apparently did not solve the problem of indigent dependants and, ironically enough, by 1870 the company had come full circle on the question of native servants, finding that the "small colony" included too many expensive dependants, and was again looking to Europe as the best source of recruits (D.9/1: 639).

In James Bay, unlike to the west (see Brown 1980 and Van Kirk 1980), the mixed blood servants and their families never came to constitute a separate Métis society. In the latter part of the 1800s their identification seems to have been with the coastal people whose life-style was becoming increasingly divergent from that of the inlanders. For James Bay, though, this is a subject and a time period that awaits investigation.

At the same time as Indians were becoming more involved in the functioning of the fur-trade post, their subsistence activities remained substantially unaltered. This was especially true of the inland hunters who from time to time engaged as voyageurs but otherwise did not participate in wage employment at the posts. At Rupert House most of the homeguard men were hired for the summer months, but by the end of August all the Indians congregated at the first rapids above the post, called Smoky Hill, for the traditional fall fishery, which carried on through October. Fish not consumed on the spot were dried and stored at the post, and during the winter Indians would come in to claim their supply as needed. In September the customary goose hunt took place after which fishing resumed. When the snow came, the families dispersed to their hunting grounds. Frequently during the winter the coastal people came in with their furs to barter more supplies and, depending on the success of the hunt along the shore, in January they often moved inland where furs were more plentiful, returning in time for the spring goose hunt, if not sooner. For a few months each year, then, a small number of Indians supplemented their income from furs by taking employment with the company. This was a significant change in the Indians' economic strategy but the numbers of people involved should not be exaggerated.

The involvement of the home Indians with the Hudson's Bay Company was further increased towards the middle of the century by what appears to have been a decline in food resources along the coast. Company records are not specific or reliable on this point, but the situation seems to have conformed to Robert Miles's complaint that "at Rupert's House the local resources are very contracted, the Goose Hunts not being to be depended upon, and in the winter season few or no fish to be procured" (B.186/b/36: 10d). The local Indians relied on hare and ptarmigan to see them through the winter, and when these failed and the stock of dried fish was expended, they had to fall back on the company's store. This predicament was exacerbated by company attempts to have the Indians reduce their beaver hunts. The meat of this animal was a traditional preferred food resource, and hunters often told Miles they had been forced to ignore the company's beaver restrictions because they needed the food. The post journals contain frequent and recurring petitions similar to the following:

Jan. 5, 1843: Woppunaweskums Wife and Widow Pullackataway belonging to Indian's who proceeded Inland the 12th Ulto. came here for the remainder of their dried fish (which is very little) having already exhausted what they took away in consequence of finding no other food, which since leaving the Coast, now upwards of 20 days, three large families have procured only two Rabbits, one Partridge one Marten and one Lynx. They request from me nearly a fifth of a

Barrel of Oatmeal and a dozen Geese, to enable them to proceed farther in quest of subsistence, and which I cannot withhold without running the risk of their either returning on our hands here, or what would be still more painful, allowing them to perish. (B.186/a/66: 34)

The degree of reliance on the post for provisions differed from homeguard family to homeguard family and from winter to winter and should not be exaggerated. Bishop has concluded in his study of northwestern Ontario that changed trade policies and a decline in animal resources meant that "the Northern Ojibwa were dependent upon the store by the mid-nineteenth century" (1974, 190). However, such a generalization does not conform to the complexity of relationships at Rupert House. There were usually half a dozen widows, elderly Indians, and indigents dependent on the company for support year round and two or three families, like Woppunaweskum's, which returned regularly to the post during the winter for provisioning. Other hunters came in for supplies from time to time and others not at all. And, of course, inlanders almost never appeared at the post during the winter.

An incident relating to apparent starvation among the coast Indians took place at a small company outpost at Hannah Bay in January 1832 – the so-called Hannah Bay massacre. On 20 January a party of about a dozen Indians, usually attached to Rupert House, visited the outpost. According to one witness the Indians were "in a Starving and Naked State" and had come to request provisions, which they were given (B.135/a/137: 15). Two day later, apparently as planned, the visitors murdered the occupants of the post – the mixed blood master William Corrigal, his wife, and seven other Indians – plundered it of furs, trade articles, and foodstuffs, and disappeared (B.135/a/138: 2). Four survivors of the attack fled to Moose Fort where a search party was organized and dispatched in pursuit of the murderers, eventually identified as an elderly man, Quapakay, his sons Shaintoquaish and Stacemow, his son-in-law Bolland, and their families. The company men returned empty-handed and for two months nothing was heard of the fugitives. Then, late in March, Shaintoquaish and Bolland appeared at Rupert House with their families, again in a starving condition, and confessed to postmaster Joseph Beioley their part in the Hannah Bay murders (B.135/a/138: 5). Beioley conducted the two men to Moose, and although Bolland escaped enroute, his brother-in-law agreed in return for his life to lead a posse of Hudson's Bay Company men in search of the other accused (B.135/a/138: 7). This party left Moose early in April. Shaintoquaish, who appeared to be lame, was hauled on a sled until he was thought to be too much of a burden on the expedition and was summarily executed (B.135/a/138: 9). William Swanson, the party's leader, reported that three days from Moose his men came up with two Women and a Boy, they proved to be Stacemow's Wife, his son and Quapecay's Daughter, they informed us their Tent was close by and that Quapecay and Stacemow were out hunting, none being at the Tent except Stacemow's son ... and the Women and Children. She led us to the tent, Stacemow's son came out, seized him and lashed his hands and placed him in a separate Tent. (B.135/a/138: 9d)

One by one Quapakay, Stacemow, and a young brother were captured and one by one all the mature males, five in number, were executed on the spot. The youngest was fifteen years old. The women and young children were given provisions and the Hudson's Bay Company men returned to Moose. Later in the month Bolland was apprehended at his father Artawayham's tent and also executed (B.186/a/45: 41). The Hannah Bay incident had resulted in the deaths of sixteen people.

The reasons for such an atypical outbreak of violence are obscure. Certainly privation played a role and quite possibly the Indians were not being treated satisfactorily by the postmaster at Hannah Bay. An oral account of the incident collected at Rupert House suggests this explanation. "A group of people decided to kill the manager because they were not satisfied with the little he gave them" (Cree Way Project 1975). We have seen in the case of Henley House that starvation and what the Indians considered to be unsympathetic treatment had contributed to violence in the past. According to Joseph Beioley, the Indians themselves proffered a religious explanation for their behaviour. Shaintoquaish, reported Beioley, explained that his family had been

ordered by the "Spirit above" to do what they had done; that they had striven hard to get the "Spirit above" not to enforce the task on them, because they had a disinclination to do what they thought to be wrong but that the "Spirit above" threatened and assured them that except they obeyed they should have all their children taken from them ... He then said that they had conjured, or practised divination repeatedly and separately, that is to say, his father, his brother, and Bolland and himself in order to have the task of executing the orders of the Spirit above taken from them. (B.135/a/138: 6–6d)

Evidently conjuring took place but whether some form of messianic movement was involved is impossible to tell from the evidence. The version of the incident related by John McLean, a Hudson's Bay Company employee serving at the time in the Ottawa Valley, suggests this interpretation. He was told that the attack was planned by

an individual who had acquired considerable influence among his tribe, from his pretending to be skilled in the art of divination. This man told his fellows that he had had a communication from the Great Spirit, who assured him that he would become the greatest man in Hudson's Bay if he only followed the course prescribed to him, which was, first, to cut off their own trading post, and then with the spoil got there to hire other Indians, who should assist in destroying all the other posts the Company possessed in the country. (1932, 99)

James Anderson, a servant involved in the capture of the Indians, indicated in his account that Quapakay and his family intended the attack on Hannah Bay to be the first step in a program of resistance against the company's posts in eastern James Bay. Anderson stated:

From the women it was afterwards ascertained that the Indians intended to have cut off the different small posts in the interior of Rupert's River District – then Rupert's House and lastly, Moose Factory. They expected to be joined by all the E. Main Indians and had even contemplated the possibility of capturing the vessel from Europe and murdering the crew. (Anderson Papers, 7)

Apparently a mixture of religious and economic motives sparked the Hannah Bay murders. The available evidence is too fragmentary and one-sided to allow a more definite explanation. If a general rebellion against the company was contemplated, it did not materialize. According to the archival sources, the accused did not enjoy the support of other local Indians – in fact Bolland's father alerted Beioley to his son's presence in the neighbourhood (B.186/b/22: 16; B.186/a/45: 41).

The Hannah Bay murders were unique in eastern James Bay. In general the Indians had evolved a different, more peaceable strategy for coping with changes in the trade and in local animal resources. Some opted out of the traditional life-style, choosing not to be hunters at all but instead joining the Hudson's Bay Company as full-time servants. Others, and this included most of the homeguard, chose to supplement their fur returns with brief periods of wage employment. Others, and again this included most of the homeguard, began to utilize the company store as an alternate food resource during specific seasons of the year or when certain game animals failed. And still others, the majority of the James Bay Indians, continued to subsist quite independently of the post, visiting it only to trade their furs as usual.

Towards 1870, the end of the period covered by this book, a new era was beginning in eastern James Bay, an era initiated by the arrival of Christian missionaries. Missionaries, of course, had been the first Europeans to penetrate the interior of the James Bay region. Father Albanel visited the area twice in the 1670s and he was followed by several of his fellow Jesuits. Their influence was greatest among the Mistassini people who lived within easy reach of the mission at Chicoutimi. However, no clergymen ever established a permanent residence on the shores of the bay in these early years, and even Jesuit influence among the Mistassini waned in the mid-eighteenth century when the Chicoutimi mission was transferred to Tadoussac (Angers 1971, 61). It was not until the next century that the Christian church began to minister to the Indian people at the bay on a permanent basis. A study of the full impact of these missionaries would take us beyond the limits of this inquiry, but it is possible to describe when and where they first established themselves and to suggest the contours of their influence.

Coincident with the arrival of schoolmasters in the bay, that is, about 1810, the Hudson's Bay Company decided to station clergymen at some of its posts. It was intended that the clergy would minister to the servants and their families and only secondarily carry on missionary activity among the Indians (A.6/17: 76). But the company found it difficult to find clergymen willing to come to Rupert's Land, and when the first one, sponsored by the Wesleyan Methodist Missionary Society, did arrive in James Bay in 1840, his preoccupation was the spiritual life of the Indians as much as the acculturation of mixed blood servants (Methodist Missionary Society [MMS] 11: 271). As we shall see presently, this led to ambiguity in the company's response to the missionary presence, since officers were not convinced that a Christian Indian population served their best interests.

The Reverend George Barnley settled at Moose Factory, but since his responsibilities included the whole of James Bay, he visited Fort George and Rupert House often. He had three favoured projects which he attempted to implement during his stay. The first was to teach the Indians to read and write a syllabic script of his own devising; the second was to establish a party of Indians on an agricultural settlement near Moose Factory; and the third was to open a residential school for Indian children surrounded by at least ten square miles of land on which the pupils would be taught both agricultural and hunting skills. None of these projects came to fruition before Barnley was recalled to England in 1847 following a rupture in personal relations between himself, his English wife, and the company officers (A.12/4: 82d).

The next missionaries to reside in James Bay were Anglicans sent from England by the Church Missionary Society. John Horden was stationed at Moose in 1851 and supervised the bottom of the bay, while his colleague E.A. Watkins was stationed a year later at Fort George with an eye to pursuing missionary activity among the Inuit further north. Watkins's mission was a disappointment to himself and his superiors. The simple provision of food for himself and the natives he took on as potential interpreters and teachers was a constant problem in such an inhospitable climate. Travel to the Whale rivers was frustrated again and again by lack

Mission church, Fort George, 1888. First attempted in 1855 but beset by many difficulties, missionary activity at Fort George is shown here to be firmly entrenched by the 1880s.

of supplies and willing guides. At Fort George itself, there was seldom more than a handful of Indians present at any one time and a permanent settlement would have been unable to sustain itself. "If I were to induce Indians to settle here they would depend entirely on the Society for grain which would be a most heavy expense," Watkins complained (Church Missionary Society [CMS] reel A-97, 18 July 1853). In 1855 he managed to complete a small cottage which doubled as a church and a school, but Watkins never fooled himself that he was having much success among the northern Indians who "feel no interest whatever in the sacred truths which it is my duty to proclaim"; in the summer of 1856 he was removed from Fort George to Red River (CMS reel A-97, 10 Jan. 1856; reel A-98, 3 Aug. 1856). Two years later the Missionary Society dispatched the Reverend T. Hamilton Fleming to the post at Little Whale River where he remained only four months, and there were no further attempts to establish a permanent mission in the north during this period.

At Moose, on the other hand, John Horden was able to accomplish far more than the northern missionaries, since a larger number of Indians were present at the post, at least seasonally. A year after his arrival he imported a printing press and began producing a steady stream of religious works in the syllabic script developed earlier in the century by the Methodist missionary James Evans. In 1854 a schoolhouse was built and before long Horden was training a native clergy. At Rupert House, postmaster Joseph Gladman's daughters were enlisted to teach syllabics to the Indians, and in the 1860s a church was constructed, partly financed by Indian donations. Thanks to Horden's activities, the Anglican religion was firmly established in James Bay, and when the diocese of Moosonee was created in 1872, he was made first bishop.

Nowadays it is customary to view traders and missionaries as partners in a common assault on Indian culture – while traders were transforming the Indians' traditional life-style and eroding their economic independence, missionaries were undermining their religious and moral beliefs. Yet initially the Hudson's Bay Company officers looked with a sceptical eye upon the activities of the churchmen. As good Christians themselves, the officers could not have objected to a "reform" of the Indians' religious ideas nor to the "improvement" of their manners. However, these good works often required a prolonged unwelcome presence of the Indians about the post. Master Robert Miles explained in 1842:

June 10: Every Indian here is Settled with, but they seem to hang about to hear the Revd Mr. Barnley, although most of them are destitute of food, and under existing circumstances, I do not like to order them off. Our Goose Casks & Oatmeal Barrels must however suffer in Consequence, as no fish are caught here at this season of the Year, and I imagine I would be censured did I permit them to Starve under the immediate eye of our Pastor. (B.186/a/62: 43)

Any attempt at a settlement of Indians, a project never far from a missionary's mind, was quickly squelched by the company. Barnley's scheme for a residential school which would train Indian children in agricultural skills (A.12/2: 218d) was considered by Governor Simpson "very prejudicial to the Hon. Company's interests," and the governor's objections to the permanent settlement of Indian hunters were made clear in 1848 in a letter to the Catholic bishop of Montreal:

Should a permanent R.C. mission be established at any given point on the shores of Hudsons Bay, I am apprehensive it would attract so large a population of Indians as to incur the danger of starvation, not only to themselves, but to the establishment or trading post in the neighborhood of which it might be erected, as the inhospitable character of the climate renders it quite impossible to raise agricultural produce to any extent, & the natural resources of the country in fish & game are quite inadequate to the support of the natives, even during their transient visits to the posts, without the aid of imported supplies from Europe. (A.12/4: 87d)

Another reason for Simpson's refusal was his belief that if Catholic and Protestant missionaries were permitted to reside at the same post, their conflicting doctrines would simply confuse the Indian people (B.186/b/43: 51). Two years earlier the governor had allowed the construction of Catholic chapels at Waswanipi and Migiskan where no Protestant missionaries were active (B.186/b/53: 1).

In 1862 the matter of Catholic missionaries arose again, this time at Nichikun. The postmaster there, Robert Chilton, wrote to the district chief at Rupert House that an Indian had arrived "from the frontier" with a message from Catholic missionaries inviting all the Indians there for instruction. Chilton did not favour such an action and suggested to his superior that inasmuch as the Indians wanted to be baptized, he could send them down to Rupert House to see the minister. Another plan he had was to have the Indian preacher named Jacob come from Rupert House to preach to the Indians (B.186/b/69: 38d). Jacob is the first native Christian preacher to appear in the records for James Bay but little else is known about him. He did not travel to Nichikun, however, because Gladman, the district chief, did not think he would be respected there, being "one of them" (B.186/b/70: 16).

Moreover, when Christian morality and company interest conflicted, Hudson's Bay Company men were not always wholehearted in their endorsement of the former. Divorce was a case in point. Some Indian hunters traditionally had more than one wife. When missionaries began conducting Christian marriages and separating second wives from their husbands, leaving the women at least temporarily without support, Miles was obliged to report that "I have in no manner interfered in the separations of these young families, which hereafter it is not improbable will be thrown on the protection of the Company for clothing and support" (B.186/a/66: 69). Hudson's Bay Company men were instructed to make the missionaries welcome at the various posts, but there were subtle ways in which relations might be soured. Necessary supplies could be overpriced at the company's store; accommodation could be inadequate; transportation could be unreliable. However, by 1870 differences seem to have been resolved and company officials seem to have accepted the benefits of a missionary presence.

If fur traders viewed them with ambivalence, it is more difficult to ascertain how the missionaries impressed the Indians. As far as religious beliefs are concerned it is impossible to say with any certainty the extent to which traditional Indian beliefs were extinguished and Christian beliefs adopted. Definitely the missionaries were antipathetic to aboriginal religion and attempted to convert their charges by sermon, individual counselling, and the determined destruction of ritual manifestations such as conjuring poles and drums. Evidence from the east coast suggests that often they met resistance – conjurers who refused to cease their customary practices and hunters who held to a belief in the efficacy of the venerable ways. Yet at the same time the missionaries met quick acceptance, so that just two years after his arrival Horden could report eighty-two baptisms and seventy-four native communicants (CMS reel A-88, 20 Feb. 1855). For whatever reason an Indian may have converted outwardly to Christianity, and evidence from eastern James Bay sheds no light on this process, it was not unusual for him to retain elements of his traditional religion. Often religious beliefs became an amalgam of Christian and native concepts. One example is offered by a man at Rupert House who Horden said "had a great influence over some of his brethren whom he told that he had been to heaven and received directions how to act, and that he intended to buy a fine blue cloth coat that he might appear respectable when he again went there" (CMS reel A-88, 3 July 1854).

A more unfortunate example occurred on the west coast in the early 1840s. In the summer of 1841 the Reverend Mr Evans arrived at York Factory and commenced preaching among the Indians there. Some time thereafter an Indian named Abishabis and a confederate appeared at the post claiming to have visited heaven and hell and proclaiming a new religion. According to James Hargrave, postmaster at York, Abishabis "by his bold blasphemies" convinced his fellows that he was "High Priest of the Tribe" and began demanding from them presents of clothing and ammunition (A.12/2: 295). However, Hargrave continued, Abishabis went too far when he began coveting other men's wives, and his followers "fell from him one by one, – his wives starved and forsook him, – and he was last Spring (1843) left in a state of as great beggary, as that from which he had at first arisen." That summer, Hargrave reported, he murdered five members of an Indian family at York, then fled along the coast to Severn House where, after terrorizing the population for a short while, he was killed by a local hunter and his body burned with the full support of the others (A.12/2: 295d).

Meanwhile, that spring, the "new religion" had been carried down the coast to Albany by an elderly woman from Severn House. Barnley, who went to Albany to stamp out the doctrine, explained that Abishabis had produced a chart "exhibiting representations of a path which branched off in two directions, passing by the Sun and Moon; the one leading to Heaven and the other to Hell" (MMS 14: 95). Each follower had a similar chart from which, postmaster Thomas Corcoran said, "they were taught to believe they had only to look to obtain everything they required in this life or the next" (B.3/b/70: 27). The charts were traced on wood or paper and were referred to as the "Great Book." "A person at a distance," reported Corcoran, "will scarcely believe how rapidly and widely this pernicious doctrine has spread" (ibid.).

In the spring of 1844, when word reached Albany of the death of Abishabis the previous fall, the new doctrine seemed to lose its attraction and the Indians burned their charts. In August Barnley baptized a number of Albany Indians, "amongst the latter is the old Severn Priestess who has been the cause of much mischief here. She came forward as a penitent and promised never to be guilty of the Sin of propagating errors again" (B.3/a/150: 7). The new doctrine spread as far south as Abitibi and as far east as Moose, where Barnley reported that "most of the natives had fallen into the same snare, though among them only two or three of their dogs had been destroyed whereas on the West Main scarcely one of these very useful animals has survived the proscription of their race by the Prophets" (MMS 14: 95). Apparently the enthusiasm for the new doctrine did not influence the Rupert House Indians, though they must have been aware of it. At any rate the incident illustrates the confusion created to one degree or another at all posts by the rapid introduction of a new and seemingly powerful religion. Recently Jennifer Brown (1981) has examined the Abishabis cult and analyses in more detail the factors promoting its initial widespread acceptance.

Turning from religious beliefs to social life, the Christian missionaries proposed nothing less than a complete transformation of Indian society. The most trivial of the white man's customs – eating from a table, for example, or drying themselves with a towel – were urged on the natives as necessary elements of their salvation (MMS 14: 95). More importantly, the missionaries sanctioned monogamy and required the dissolution of polygamous relationships; they interrupted traditional social events, such as feasts, which embodied religious elements and instead encouraged prayer meetings and hymn sings; they despaired at the Indians' wandering ways and attempted to influence Hudson's Bay Company policy in favour of small settlements.

The missionaries, much more so than the traders, denied any value to Indian customs. As their counterparts to the west (Fisher 1977, 124), they attacked native belief systems as evil and superstitious and undermined Indian self-respect and cultural pride. This at any rate was their intention. But the James Bay people were not resourceless or defenceless. Over the past two centuries they had taken the fur trade and in many ways adapted it to their own needs and aspirations. As this study ends, they were preparing to cope with yet another threat to their cultural survival.

CHAPTER THIRTEEN

Conclusion

The history of eastern James Bay from 1600 to 1870 tells the story of the meeting of two peoples. Disparate though they were in life-style and outlook, the two peoples recognized that it was in their common interest to coexist peacefully. The production of furs was their common bond and whatever animosities or mistrust may have developed from this contrived partnership were subordinated by both parties to achieving that end. Since the relationship was economic in origin, it changed each time new elements were added to or subtracted from the economic equation. Essentially the object of this history has been to examine these changes.

The term "fur trade" is a bit of a misnomer. It suggests a monolithic enterprise, uniform at all times in all parts of the country. Regional studies, such as this one, indicate that this view is too inflexible. In practice there were a number of different fur trades, differing over time depending on economic situations and differing from place to place depending on geography, ecology, and relationships with the Indian people. Regional history allows the researcher to examine the conduct of the trade in one area in some detail and to test certain generalities which have been taken for granted about the continental trade.

The primary object of our own work has been to study the relationship between the Indians and the fur traders in eastern James Bay. Until recently it has been common to describe this relationship in almost servile terms. The Indians, defenceless in the face of a technologically superior civilization, surrendered their independence for a gun and a kettle. This is not the place for an extensive survey of the literature, but the following extract from Rich is representative of this point of view:

European supplies were necessities, not luxuries, for the Indians who traded to the Bay, and to many times that number of Indians living inland. Within a decade of their becoming acquainted with European goods, tribe after tribe became utterly dependent on regular European supplies. The bow and arrow went out of use, and the Indian starved if he did not own a serviceable gun, powder and shot. (1967, 102)

Because of their abject dependence on European goods, the Indians lost all freedom of action and control over their own destinies. Recently this point of view has been challenged by, among others, Ray (1974, xi) who writes of a "partnership," Bishop (1974), and Fisher (1977). Significantly, each of these studies deals with regions rather than with the country as a whole. Fisher's conclusions in his study of the British Columbia region regarding the consequences of the fur trade mirror our own.

Readers of this history will know that we do not accept the notion of Indian dependence, believing that it does not reflect the variety and complexity of Indian responses to European traders. For one thing, the word is misleading if at the same time it is not accompanied with a record of European dependence on the Indian. The journals and correspondence from eastern James Bay show clearly that the traders relied on Indian hunters for most of their food supplies. Furthermore, local hunters carried out a number of tasks which made the trade possible. They served as couriers, carrying mail between the isolated posts; as guides and teachers; as manufacturers and suppliers of essential equipment such as snowshoes and canoes; as labourers around the post; at times as a potential defence force in case of attack; and as voyageurs transporting goods inland and furs back to the coast. White traders were simply incapable of accomplishing most of these tasks themselves. As for the Indians' dependence on European technology, it was neither as rapid nor as complete as Rich implies. The nature of the subsistence economy and the distance from a trading post were both factors which affected the degree to which different Indian groups came to rely on the white man's trade goods.

The Indians did not surrender their freedom of action to the trader. The records are full of examples of their refusing to bend to the will of the Hudson's Bay Company. On the contrary, as long as competition existed among traders, the Indians were able to manipulate trade practices to their own advantage. This is not to deny that the Hudson's Bay Company profited handsomely from the trade or that the company callously manipulated the Indians or that it was able to bring tremendous pressures to bear on its Indian suppliers. All these things are true. But so is the fact that the Indians were active participants in the trade, not hapless victims.

This sanguine view of Indian-white relations must be qualified when we reach the first quarter of the nineteenth century. At that time in eastern James Bay, as elsewhere in the Hudson's Bay Company's domain, animals became scarce and competition almost nonexistent. Ray, writing of the southern Manitoba area, found the production of furs and the engagement in fur-trade activities coming to an end. He outlined the new modes of adaptation developing whereby increasing numbers of hunters took up residence in the Red River colony and engaged in seasonal agricultural employment, a pattern repeated later in Saskatchewan and eastern Alberta (1974, 218–19). In northern Ontario, an ecological zone having greater similarity to the eastern James Bay region, the northern Ojibwa, as a result of depletion in the numbers of moose, caribou, and beaver turned to a subsistence based on fish and hare. This shift, Bishop explains, resulted in socio-economic changes which left the Indians more reliant on the trading post in the post-1821 period (1974, 186, 297).

In eastern James Bay animal resources declined but did not disappear. This decline was accompanied by certain socio-economic changes made possible by the end of competition. For example, the trading captain system was replaced by a more egalitarian system in which individuals were rewarded by the company on the basis of the number of furs they produced and not the number of hunters they brought to the post. Still, local and coresidential groups continued to be the bases of the social organization with no evidence of a trend to larger band structure as occurred later. The land tenure system of individually owned hunting territories persisted but probably as a more clearly defined system owing to dwindling resources and the company's austerity measures. The trend towards a dependence of sorts on the post perhaps had its origins at this point but was never realized within the period under study. Although the end of competition had drastically reduced the James Bay people's ability to manipulate the fur trade, most of them, that is, the inlanders, had dealings with the traders just once a year when they came to exchange their furs for their hunting requirements. Although this contact was brief, the company did have the power and ability to exert control over its producers through the extension of credit, determination of prices, and dictation of the kinds of furs and other commodities traded. These were not inconsiderable controls. However, it was not in the company's interest to destroy the fur trade, and it continued to attempt to increase its output during a time of depleted resources by encouraging individual initiative. The records as late as 1865 indicate that the Hudson's Bay Company men were still giving presents as a means of encouraging trade and discouraging the hunters from taking their trade to posts in other districts. None of this would have been necessary if the company was in complete control and the hunters at their mercy. Nor were the traders, much to their annoyance, ever able to discontinue the practice of extending credit. As well, the Indians knew they would always be able to receive some support from the company in dire times. The company needed a healthy, content, and productive population. The fact that the hunters and traders worked together in instituting the beaver preserves and other conservation measures indicates a working relationship to fulfil common objectives.

Reviewing the Indians' participation in the European fur-trade complex reveals its relatively minimal disruption to their own cultural system. The first seven decades of the nineteenth century was not a period in which the James Bay people depended on the Hudson's Bay Company for food. This food dependence continued to work in the opposite direction. Employment as voyageurs and summer labourers supplemented hunting or trapping activities as means of acquiring European goods and drew the families to a summer residence closer to the post, but they were not in residence at the post and were not receiving food from the post. Subsistence activities for all the Indians still were of far greater significance than were hunting or trapping activities associated with exchange. Moreover the Indians still brought in as many pelts as they wanted, not the number the company would have liked. European technology continued to be used because the metal goods provided in some cases more efficient hunting tools, but hunting was still (as it is even today) based on age-old methods. The use of guns and steel traps did not predominate and in fact they were used sparingly for practical reasons. The political, social, and religious life of the James Bay people continued outside the direct influence of the Europeans, though it was not unaffected by occurrences in the economic sphere. The arrival of missionaries in James Bay marked the beginning of deliberate attempts by external agents to alter the ideological system and social patterning. Unlike northern Ontario, directed cultural change did not occur in James Bay until a much later period.

Changes however did take place in the nineteenth century that were a direct result of events associated with the fur trade. The changes are best described as greater involvement in all aspects of the fur trade. The proliferation of posts inland brought more people into direct contact with the European trading system and European life-styles. Seasonal employment was available for some and in fact men were pressured by the company to work as labourers or voyageurs. As some mixed bloods who were members of Indian families became employees of the company, the everyday operation of the fur trade became more familiar to the James Bay people. Then, the fur trade offered some individuals an alternative to the traditional life-style. This was the beginning of the development of a whole class of James Bay Indians which arose to service the fur trade, a class that continued to exist for one hundred years or so. Primarily it was the coasters who were involved in the transformation; the inlanders were relatively immune to the changes. The decline in animal resources, a reduced and more distant competition, and a changing fur market in London would have heralded for the Indians the beginning of the realization that their lives were intricately connected with the fortunes of the Hudson's Bay Company.

All these factors altered the nature of the partnership between the Indians and the traders in their midst but it did not drastically transform their culture, as happened in other areas of the Hudson's Bay Company's domain. Greater social change occurred in the period after this study ends as missionaries and governments introduced concepts and institutions developed for the southern industrial social setting, also a finding of Fisher's (1977, 145, 174). However, the James Bay Cree today continue to maintain a distinct culture still very much attuned to and dependent on living off the land. This fact strongly suggests that although events in the nineteenth century altered the Crees' relationship to the traders, they did not radically change or destroy their relationship to the land. But that is another story.

Appendix

Population of James Bay in 1838 and 1858
(Includes Men, Women, and Children)

Post	1838	1858
Rupert House	205	250
Mistassini	95	200
Temiskimay	19	75
Waswanipi	101	150
Migiskan	58	75
Nichikun	74	80
Kaniapiskau	42	75
Pike Lake	–	80
Fort George	399*	†
Total	993	985‡

Sources: 1838 census from B.186/b/36: 2d; 1858 census from *Census of Canada, 1876*.

* This figure would have included all those who formerly traded at Eastmain House, closed in 1837. Among these numbers would be those who were later trading at Great Whale River and Little Whale River.

† The records do not give the total population for the northern posts. However, the number of hunters trading is given at two of the posts: 57 at Fort George in 1869 (B.77/z/1: 98) and 22 at Little Whale River in 1867 (B.373/d/9: 6). Great Whale River Post had been closed in 1869 so its former hunters would have been trading at either of the other posts. The total population of the north would have been, then, somewhere between 316 and 395.

‡ The total Indian population of James Bay and southeastern Hudson Bay in the 1860s would have been about 1300.

References

MANUSCRIPT SOURCES

All manuscript collections cited here are on deposit at the Public Archives of Canada (PAC).

ANDERSON, JAMES. Transcripts, 1849–63 (MG 19 A29)

ARCHIVES NATIONALES DE FRANCE
Archives des Colonies (AC) (MG 1)
   Series B, C11A, C11E, F2A, F3

Archives de la Marine (MG 2)
   Series B2, B4

Bibliothèque nationale de Paris (MG 7)
   Collection Clairambault
   Collection Margry (includes Normandin journal)

CHURCH MISSIONARY SOCIETY (CMS) (MG 17 B2)
   Journals and Correspondence, 1851–70

FALCONER, WILLIAM. Records of, 1768–76. Originals and Transcripts.
   (Catalogued under Severn House) (MG 19 D2)

METHODIST MISSIONARY SOCIETY (MMS) (MG 17 C1)
   Correspondence: Maritimes, 1840–5

HUDSON'S BAY COMPANY ARCHIVES (MG 20)
A. *Headquarters' Records (selected volumes)*
A.5 London Correspondence Books Outwards – General Series

A.6 London Correspondence Outwards – Official
A.11 London Inward Correspondence from Hudson's Bay Company Posts
A.12 London Inward Correspondence from Governors of Hudson's Bay Company Territories
A.16 Officers' and Servants' Ledgers

B. *Post Records*

B.3/a/1–29	Albany Post Journals, 1705–40
B.3/b/1–23	Albany Correspondence Books, 1742–86
B.3/d/1–88	Albany Account Books, 1692–1780
B.3/k/1	Albany Minutes of Council, 1783
B.19/a/1–3	Big Lake Post Journals, 1818–21
B.19/e/1	Big Lake Report on District, 1818–19
B.59/a/1–122	Eastmain Post Journals, 1736–1837
B.59/b/1–33	Eastmain Correspondence Books, 1781–1837
B.59/c/1	Eastmain Correspondence Inward, 1804
B.59/d/1–44	Eastmain Account Books, 1783–1815
B.59/e/1–18	Eastmain Reports on District, 1814–36
B.59/f/1–9	Eastmain Lists of Servants, 1804–15
B.59/z/1–2	Eastmain Miscellaneous Items, 1806–26
B.77/a/1–38	Fort George (Big River) Post Journals, 1805–71
B.77/b/1–4	Fort George Correspondence Books, 1837–49
B.77/c/1	Fort George Correspondence Inward, 1849–70
B.77/d/1–30	Fort George Account Books, 1810–74
B.77/e/1–10	Fort George Reports on District, 1817–40
B.77/z/1	Fort George Miscellaneous Items, 1855–71
B.98/a/1–4	Kaniapiskau Post Journals, 1836–44
B.133/e/1–16	Mistassini Reports on District, 1816–40
B.135/a/1–44	Moose Post Journals, 1730–68
B.135/a/137–8	Moose Post Journals, 1832–3
B.135/b/1–23	Moose Correspondence Books, 1768–94
B.135/c/1–2	Moose Correspondence Inward, 1732–1808
B.135/d/1–20	Moose Account Books, 1732–51
B.135/h/1	Moose District Fur Returns, 1825–71
B.135/k/1	Moose Minutes of Council, 1822–75
B.135/z/1–2	Moose Miscellaneous Items, 1810–70
B.142/a/1–9	Nemiskau Post Journals, 1794–1809
B.143/a/1–21	Neoskweskau Post Journals, 1793–1820
B.143/e/1–5	Neoskweskau Reports on District, 1814–18
B.147/a/1–11	Nichikun Post Journals, 1834–41
B.147/e/1	Nichikun Report on District, 1834–5
B.182/a/1–11	Richmond Post Journals, 1750–9
B.182/b/1	Richmond Correspondence Book, 1754

B.182/d/1–9	Richmond Account Books, 1751–9
B.186/a/1–96	Rupert House Post Journals, 1777–1871
B.186/b/1–70	Rupert House Correspondence Books, 1817–70
B.186/c/1	Rupert House Correspondence Inward, 1820–70
B.186/d/1–6a	Rupert House Account Books, 1810–65
B.186/e/1–24	Rupert House Reports on District, 1817–40
B.186/z/1	Rupert House Miscellaneous Items, 1818–70
B.187/a/1	Rush Lake Post Journals, 1821–2
B.227/e/1–13	Waswanipi Reports on District, 1820–36
B.233/a/1	Windsor House Post Journal, 1799–1800
B.372/a/1–6	Great Whale River Post Journals, 1814–65
B.372/b/1	Great Whale River Correspondence Books, 1857–60
B.372/c/1	Great Whale River Correspondence Inward, 1866
B.372/d/1–3	Great Whale River Account Books, 1813–68
B.372/e/1–3	Great Whale River Reports on District, 1815–16
B.373/a/1–5	Little Whale River Post Journals, 1857–74
B.373/b/1	Little Whale River Correspondence Books, 1867–78
B.373/c/1	Little Whale River Correspondence Inward, 1853–70
B.373/d/1–11	Little Whale River Account Books, 1858–76

D. *Governors' Papers*

| D.4/89–112 | Simpson's Official Reports, 1826–43 |

PUBLISHED SOURCES (Selected Works)

Abbe, Ernest C., and Gillis, Frank J.
  1965   "Henry Hudson and the Early Exploration and Mapping of Hudson Bay, 1610–1631." In *Merchants and Scholars: The History of Exploration and Trade*, edited by J. Parker, pp. 87–116. Minneapolis: University of Minnesota Press.

Adams, A.T., ed.
  1961   *The Explorations of Pierre Esprit Radisson*. Minneapolis: Ross and Haines.

Anderson, J.W.
  1961   *Fur Trader's Story*. Toronto: Ryerson Press.

Angers, Lorenzo
  1971   *Chicoutimi: Poste de traite, 1676–1856*. Ottawa: Leméac.

Asher, G.M., ed.
  1860   *Henry Hudson the Navigator*. London: Hakluyt Society.

Bailey, Alfred G.
  1969   *The Conflict of European and Eastern Algonkian Cultures, 1504–1700*. 2nd ed. Toronto: University of Toronto Press.

Banfield, A.W.F.
1974   *The Mammals of Canada*. Toronto: University of Toronto Press.
Batty, Beatrice
1893   *Forty-Two Years amongst the Indians and Eskimo – Pictures from the Life of the Right Reverend John Horden ...* London: Religious Tract Society.
Bell, R.
1879   "Report of an Exploration of the East Coast of Hudson's Bay in 1877." *Annual Report, 1877–78, Geological Survey of Canada*. Ottawa.
Biays, P.
1964   "Quelques aspects de la géographie des glaces marines dans l'est du Canada." In *Le Nouveau Québec*, edited by J. Malaurie and J. Rousseau. Paris: Mouton.
Biggar, H.P., ed.
1922   *The Works of Samuel de Champlain*. Vol. 1. Toronto: Champlain Society.
Bishop, Charles A.
1970   "The Emergence of Hunting Territories among the Northern Ojibwa." *Ethnology* 9: 1–15.
1972   "Demography, Ecology and Trade among the Northern Ojibwa and Swampy Cree." *Western Canadian Journal of Anthropology* 3(1): 58–71.
1974   *The Northern Ojibwa and the Fur Trade: An Historical and Ecological Study*. Toronto: Holt, Rinehart & Winston.
1976   "Henley House Massacres." *Beaver* 307 (Autumn): 36–41.
Bishop, Charles A., and Ray, Arthur J.
1976   "Ethnohistoric Research in the Central Subarctic: Some Conceptual and Methodological Problems." *Western Canadian Journal of Anthropology* 6(1): 116–44.
Blackned, John, and Craik, Brian
1975   *The Beaver*. Rupert House: Cree Way Project.
Bodilly, R.D.
1928   *The Voyage of Captain Thomas James for the Discovery of the Northwest Passage, 1631*. London: Dent.
Borins, Edward H.
1968   "La Compagnie du Nord, 1682–1700." MA thesis, McGill University, Montreal.
Brassard, J.M., and Audet, R.
1977   "Historique et répartition des troupeaux de caribous dans la région de la baie James et du centre de l'Ungava." In *Environnement – Baie James – Symposium*, pp. 595–615. Montreal: Société de développement de la baie James.

Brown, Jennifer S.H.
1977   "'A Colony of Very Useful Hands.'" *Beaver* 308 (Spring): 39–45.
1980   *Strangers in Blood: Fur Trade Company Families in Indian Country*. Vancouver: University of British Columbia Press.
1981   "The Track to Heaven: The Hudson Bay Cree Religious Movement of 1843." Paper presented to the Thirteenth Algonquian Conference, 23–5 Oct., Toronto.

Burgesse, J.A.
1947   "Jolliet in James Bay." *Beaver* 277 (Dec.): 12–15.

Campbell, Marjorie W.
1957   *The North West Company*. Toronto: Macmillan.

Canada
1876   *Censuses of Canada, 1665–1871*. 4 vols. Ottawa: King's Printer.

Caron, Ivanhoë, ed.
1918   *Journal de l'expédition du Chevalier de Troyes à la baie d'Hudson, en 1686*. Beauceville: l'Eclaireur.

Chappell, Edward
1817   *Narrative of a Voyage to Hudson's Bay in His Majesty's Ship Rosamund*. London: J. Mawman.

Charlevoix, F.-X. de
1744   *Histoire et description générale de la Nouvelle-France ...* 3 vols. Paris.

Chism, James V.
1977   "James Bay Archaeology: Prehistoric and Historic Settlement Patterns." In *Environnement – Baie James – Symposium*, pp. 741–50. Montreal: Société de développement de la baie James.

Christy, Miller, ed.
1894   *The Voyages of Captain Luke Fox of Hull, and Captain Thomas James ...* 2 vols. London: Hakluyt Society.

Coats, William
1852   *The Geography of Hudson's Bay*. London: Hakluyt Society.

Cooke, Alan
1969   "The Ungava Venture of the Hudson's Bay Company, 1830–1843." PHD dissertation, University of Cambridge, Cambridge.
1976   "A History of the Naskapis of Schefferville." Presented to the Naskapi Band Council of Schefferville, Quebec. 87 pp.

Cooper, John M.
1946   "The Culture of the Northeastern Indian Hunters." In *Man in Northeastern America*, edited by F. Johnson, pp. 272–305. Andover: R.S. Peabody Foundation for Archaeology.

Craig, B.G.
1968   "Late Glacial and Postglacial History of the Hudson Bay Region." In *Earth Science Symposium on Hudson Bay*, edited by P.J. Hood. Ottawa: Dept. of Energy, Mines, and Resources.

Cree Way Project
  1975   Untitled Oral History Accounts. Collected, transcribed, and trans-
          lated at Rupert House, Quebec. Typescripts.
Crouse, Nellis M.
  1924   *Contributions of the Canadian Jesuits to the Geographical Knowledge
          of New France, 1632–1675*. Ithaca: Cornell Pubs.
Curtis, S.C.
  1977   "Waterfowl Ecology of the Quebec Coast of James Bay." In *Envi-
          ronnement – Baie James – Symposium*, pp. 701–24. Montreal: Soci-
          été de développement de la baie James.
Damas, David, ed.
  1969a   *Contributions to Anthropology: Band Societies*. National Museum of
          Man, Bulletin 228. Ottawa.
  1969b   *Contributions to Anthropology: Ecological Essays*. National Museum
          of Man, Bulletin 230. Ottawa.
Davies, K.G., ed.
  1963   *Northern Quebec and Labrador Journals and Correspondence, 1819–
          35*. London: Hudson's Bay Record Society.
  1965   *Letters from Hudson Bay, 1703–40*. London: Hudson's Bay Record
          Society.
Deer, Brian
  1974a   *Bibliography of the Cree, Montagnais and Naskapi Indians: Ethno-
          graphic*. Rupert House: Cree Way Project.
  1974b   *Bibliography on the History of the James Bay People Relating to the
          Cree People*. Rupert House: Cree Way Project.
Delanglez, Jean
  1944   "The Voyage of Louis Jolliet to Hudson Bay in 1679." *Mid-America*
          26: 245–50.
  1948   *Life and Voyages of Louis Jolliet, 1645–1700*. Chicago: Institute of
          Jesuit History.
Denton, David
  1981   "Variation in the Size of Prehistoric Co-Residential Groups in the
          Eastern Sub-Arctic: Evidence from the Central Interior of Quebec-
          Labrador." Paper presented to the Canadian Archaeological Associa-
          tion, 27–30 Apr., Edmonton.
Désy, Pierrette
  1968   "Fort George ou Tsesa-sippi: Contribution à une étude sur la
          désintégration culturelle d'une communauté indienne de la baie
          James." PHD dissertation, Université de Paris, Paris.
Dionne, Jean-Claude
  1976   "L'action glacielle dans les schores du littoral oriental de la baie de
          James." *Cahiers de géographie de Québec* 20: 303–26.

Dobbs, Arthur
  1744   *An Account of the Countries Adjoining to Hudson's Bay* ... London: J. Robinson.
Dunbar, M.J.
  1968   *Ecological Development in Polar Regions*. Englewood Cliffs: Prentice-Hall.
Dunning, R.W.
  1959   *Social and Economic Change among the Northern Ojibwa*. Toronto: University of Toronto Press.
Ellis, Henry
  1748   *A Voyage to Hudson's Bay by the Dobbs Galley and California in the Years 1746 and 1749* ... London: Whiteridge.
Elson, J.A.
  1969   "Late Quaternary Marine Submergence of Quebec." *La Revue de géographie de Montréal* 23(3): 247–58.
Elton, Charles
  1942   *Voles, Mice and Lemmings*. Oxford: Clarendon Press.
Ewers, John C.
  1972   "Influence of the Fur Trade on Indians of the Northern Plains." In *People and Pelts: Selected Papers of the Second North American Fur Trade Conference*, edited by M. Bolus, pp. 1–26. Winnipeg: Peguis.
Feit, Harvey
  1969   "Mistassini Hunters of the Boreal Forest." MA thesis, McGill University, Montreal.
  1973   "The Ethno-Ecology of the Waswanipi Cree." In *Cultural Ecology*, edited by B. Cox, pp. 115–25. Toronto: McClelland and Stewart.
Fisher, Robin F.
  1977   *Contact and Conflict: Indian-European Relations in British Columbia, 1774–1890*. Vancouver: University of British Columbia Press.
Foster, J.E.
  1977   "The Home Guard Cree and the Hudson's Bay Company: The First Hundred Years." In *Approaches to Native History in Canada*, edited by D.A. Muise, pp. 49–64. National Museum of Man, Mercury Series, History Paper 25. Ottawa.
Francis, Daniel
  1976a   "Cree-Iroquois Conflict in the Seventeenth Century." Presented to Direction de l'archéologie et de l'ethnologie, Ministère des Affaires culturelles, Quebec. 13 pp.
  1976b   "An Historical Chronology of Eastern James Bay, 1610–1870." Presented to Direction de l'archéologie et de l'ethnologie, Ministère des Affaires culturelles, Quebec. 73 pp.
  1976c   "An Historical Chronology of Southeastern Hudson Bay, 1739–1870."

182   References

Presented to Direction de l'archéologie et de l'ethnologie, Ministère des Affaires culturelles, Quebec. 40 pp.

1977   "Whaling on the Eastmain." *Beaver* 308 (Summer): 14–19.

1979   "Les relations entre Indiens et Inuit dans l'est de la baie d'Hudson, 1700–1840." *Etudes Inuit* 3(2): 73–83.

Frégault, Guy

1944   *Iberville le conquérant*. Montreal: Pascal.

Georgekish, Fred

1976   "Traditional Cree Construction." Presented to Direction de l'archéologie et de l'ethnologie, Ministère des Affaires culturelles, Quebec. 82 pp.

Goldstein, R.

1969   *French-Iroquois Diplomatic and Military Relations, 1609–1701*. The Hague: Mouton.

Graham, Andrew

1969   *Andrew Graham's Observations on Hudson's Bay, 1769–91*. Edited by G. Williams. London: Hudson's Bay Record Society.

Hadlock, W.S.

1947   "War among the Northeastern Woodland Indians." *American Anthropologist* 49: 204–21.

Hardy, Léon

1976   "Contribution à l'étude géomorphologique de la portion québecoise des basses terres de la baie de James." PHD dissertation, McGill University, Montreal.

Heidenreich, Conrad

1973   *Huronia: A History and Geography of the Huron Indians, 1600–1650*. Toronto: McClelland and Stewart.

Heidenreich, Conrad, and Ray, Arthur J.

1976   *The Early Fur Trades*. Toronto: McClelland and Stewart.

Hillaire-Marcel, Claude

1976   "La déglaciation et le relèvement isostatique sur la côte est de la baie d'Hudson." *Cahiers de géographie de Québec* 20: 185–220.

Hodge, F.W.

1913   *Handbook of Indians of Canada*. Ottawa: King's Printer.

Hoffman, Bernard G.

1961   *Cabot to Cartier: Sources for a Historical Ethnography of Northeastern North America, 1497–1550*. Toronto: University of Toronto Press.

Hunt, G.T.

1940   *The Wars of the Iroquois*. Madison: University of Wisconsin Press.

Hunter, J.G.; Kidd, B.T.; Greendale, R.; Baxter, R.; and Morin, R.

1977   "Fisheries Resources of the Lower Reaches and Coastal Regions of

Eastmain, La Grande, Roggan and Great Whale Rivers from 1973 to 1975." In *Environnement – Baie James – Symposium*, pp. 299–321. Montreal: Société de développement de la baie James.

Innis, Harold
1956   *The Fur Trade in Canada*. Toronto: University of Toronto Press. (First published in 1930.)

Isham, James
1949   *Observations on Hudson's Bay, 1743*. Edited by E.E. Rich. Toronto: Champlain Society.

Johnson, Alice M.
1964   "Old Nemiscau and Cheashquacheston." *Beaver* 295 (Spring): 40–3.

Jolliet, Z., and Denis, I.
1914   "Prise de possession de Nemisco." *Bulletin de recherches historiques* 20: 390. (Original text.)

Judd, Carol M., and Ray, Arthur J., eds.
1980   *Old Trails and New Directions: Papers of the Third North American Fur Trade Conference*. Toronto: University of Toronto Press.

Lafitau, L.
1724   *Mœurs des sauvages amériquains*. 2 vols. Paris.

Laliberté, Marcel
1980   "Rapport sur l'adaptation, le mode d'organisation et de subsistance des populations préhistoriques de la région de Kanaaupscow." Presented to Service du Patrimoine autochtone, Ministère des Affaires culturelles, Quebec. 93 pp.
1981a   "Rapport d'analyse des sites GaGd-1, GaGd-8, GaGd-11 et GaGd-16 du lac Kanaaupscow, baie-James, Québec." *Interventions archéologiques*, n° 3. Quebec: Direction générale du patrimoine, Ministère des Affaires culturelles.
1981b   "Rapport d'analyse des sites GaGc-1, GaGd-4 et GaGd-13 du lac Kanaaupscow, baie-James, Québec." *Interventions archéologiques*, n° 4. Quebec: Direction générale du patrimoine, Ministère des Affaires culturelles.

Lamontagne, Roland
1974   *La baie James dans l'histoire du Canada*. Montreal: Beauchemin.

Larnder, M.M.
1968   "Ice." In *Science, History and Hudson Bay*, edited by C.S. Beals and D.A. Shenstone, 1: 318–41. Ottawa: Dept. of Mines and Resources.

Leacock, Eleanor
1954   *The Montagnais "Hunting Territory" and the Fur Trade*. American Anthropological Association Memoir 78.

Lee, H.A.
1968   "Quaternary Geology." In *Science, History and Hudson Bay*, edited

by C.S. Beals and D.A. Shenstone, 2: 503–43. Ottawa: Dept. of Mines and Resources.

Lehoux, Denis, and Rosa, Jacques
1973   'Description des principales unités physiographiques de la région de la baie James." Ottawa: Canadian Wildlife Service, Dept. of the Environment. 25 pp.

Lips, Julius E.
1947   *Naskapi Law. Transactions of the American Philosophical Society,* new series, vol. 37, pt. 4.

Long, John
1791   *Voyages and Travels of an Indian Interpreter and Trader ...* London. (Facsimile ed., Toronto: Coles, 1971.)

Low, A.P.
1887–8   "Report on Explorations in James Bay." In *Annual Report, Geological Survey of Canada.* Ottawa.
1900   "Report on an Exploration of the East Coast of Hudson Bay." In *Annual Report, Geological Survey of Canada.* Ottawa.

MacKenzie, Marguerite
1977   'Montagnais Dialectology – One More Time." Paper presented to the Ninth Algonquian Conference, 28–30 Oct., Worcester, Mass.

McLean, John
1932   *John McLean's Notes of Twenty-Five Year's Service in the Hudson's Bay Territory.* Edited by W.S. Wallace. Toronto: Champlain Society.

Mailhot, José
1981   "A moins d'être son Esquimau, on est toujours le Naskapi de quelqu'un ..." Paper presented to the Thirteenth Algonquian Conference, 23–5 Oct., Toronto.

Mandeville, Jean
1980   "Rapport des excavations du site archéologique, FjFp-4, Réservoir LG-3 Jamesie." Presented to the Service du Patrimoine autochtone, Ministère des Affaires culturelles, Quebec. 152 pp.

Mansfield, A.W.
1968   "Seals and Walruses." In *Science, History and Hudson Bay,* edited by C.S. Beals and D.A. Shenstone, 1: 378–87. Ottawa: Dept. of Mines and Resources.

Martijn, Charles A., and Rogers, Edward S.
1969   *Mistassini-Albanel: Contributions to the Prehistory of Quebec.* Centre d'études nordiques, Travaux divers 25. Quebec: Université Laval.

Masson, L.F.R., ed.
1960   *Les Bourgeois de la Compagnie du Nord-Ouest.* 2 vols. New York: Antiquarian Press. (First published in 1889–90.)

Mitchell, Elaine Allan
1977   *Fort Timiskaming and the Fur Trade*. Toronto: University of Toronto Press.
Morantz, Toby
1976   "L'organisation sociale des Cris de Rupert House, 1820–1840." *Recherches amérindiennes au Québec* 6(2): 56–64.
1977   "James Bay Trading Captains of the Eighteenth Century: New Perspectives on Algonquian Social Organization." In *Actes du Huitième Congrès des Algonquinistes*, edited by W. Cowan, pp. 77–89. Ottawa: Carleton University.
1978   "The Probability of Family Hunting Territories in Eighteenth Century James Bay: Old Evidence Newly Presented." In *Papers of the Ninth Algonquian Conference*, edited by W. Cowan, pp. 224–36. Ottawa: Carleton University.
1980   'The Impact of the Fur Trade on Eighteenth and Nineteenth Century Northern Algonquian Social Organization: An Ethnographic-Ethnohistoric Study of the Eastern James Bay Cree from 1700–1850." PHD dissertation, University of Toronto, Toronto.
1982   "Northern Algonquian Concepts of Status and Leadership Reviewed: A Case Study of the Eighteenth Century Trading Captain System." *Canadian Review of Sociology and Anthropology*, in press.
Morton, A.S.
1939   *A History of the Canadian West to 1870–71*. London: Thomas Nelson & Sons.
Naroll, R.
1969   "The Causes of the Fourth Iroquois War." *Ethnohistory* 16: 51–81.
Nute, Grace L.
1943   *Caesars of the Wilderness*. New York: Appleton.
Oldmixon, John
1931   "The History of Hudson's Bay." In *Documents Relating to the Early History of Hudson Bay*, edited by J.B. Tyrrell, pp. 371–410. Toronto: Champlain Society. (First published in 1708.)
Pentland, David, and Garson, Emile
1978   "A Historical Overview of Cree-Montagnais Dialects." In *Papers of the Ninth Algonquian Conference*, edited by W. Cowan, pp. 104–26. Ottawa: Carleton University.
Perrot, Nicolas
1864   *Mémoire sur les mœurs, coustumes et relligion des sauvages de l'Amérique septentrionale*. Paris: A. Franck.
Peterson, R.L.
1966   *The Mammals of Eastern Canada*. Toronto: Oxford University Press.
Preston, Richard J.
1975   *Cree Narrative: Expressing the Personal Meaning of Events*. National

Museum of Man, Mercury Series, Canadian Ethnology Service Paper
30. Ottawa.

Quebec

1973   "Faune du Québec: Le Caribou." Quebec: Service de la Faune,
Ministère du Tourisme, de la Chasse et de la Peche. 8 pp.

Ray, Arthur J.

1974   *Indians in the Fur Trade: Their Role as Hunters, Trappers and
Middlemen in the Lands Southwest of Hudson Bay, 1660–1870.*
Toronto: University of Toronto Press.

1975a   "The Factor and the Trading Captain in the Hudson's Bay Company
Fur Trade before 1763." In *Proceedings of the Second Congress,
Canadian Ethnology Society*, edited by J. Freedman and J.H. Bar-
kow, pp. 586–602. National Museum of Man, Mercury Series. Ottawa.

1975b   "Some Conservation Schemes of the Hudson's Bay Company, 1821–
50." *Journal of Historical Geography* 1(1): 49–68.

1976   "The Early Hudson's Bay Company Account Books as Sources for
Historical Research: An Analysis and Assessment." *Archivaria* 1:
3–38.

1980   "Indians as Consumers in the Eighteenth Century." In *Old Trails and
New Directions*, edited by C.M. Judd and A.J. Ray, pp. 255–71.
Toronto: University of Toronto Press.

Ray, Arthur J., and Freeman, Donald B.

1978   *"Give Us Good Measure": An Economic Analysis of Relations between
the Indians and the Hudson's Bay Company before 1763.* Toronto:
University of Toronto Press.

Rich, E.E.

1958   *The History of the Hudson's Bay Company, 1670–1870.* Vol. 1, *1670–
1763.* London: Hudson's Bay Record Society.

1959   *The History of the Hudson's Bay Company, 1670–1870.* Vol. 2, *1763–
1870.* London: Hudson's Bay Record Society.

1960   "Trade Habits and Economic Motivation among the Indians of North
America." *Canadian Journal of Economics and Political Science* 26:
35–53.

1967   *The Fur Trade and the Northwest to 1857.* Toronto: McClelland and
Stewart.

Rich, E.E., ed.

1942   *Minutes of the Hudson's Bay Company, 1671–1674.* Toronto: Champlain Society.

1945   *Minutes of the Hudson's Bay Company, 1679–1684: First Part, 1679–
82.* Toronto: Champlain Society.

1946   *Minutes of the Hudson's Bay Company, 1679–1684: Second Part,
1682–84.* Toronto: Champlain Society.

1948   *Copy-Book of Letters Outward &c ... 1680–1687.* Toronto: Champlain Society.

1954   *Moose Fort Journals, 1783–85.* London: Hudson's Bay Record Society.

1957   *Copy Booke of Letters, Commissions, Instructions Outward, 1688–1696.* London: Hudson's Bay Record Society.

Robinson, J.L.

1968   "Regional Geography." In *Science, History and Hudson Bay*, edited by C.S. Beals and D.A. Shenstone, 1: 201–35. Ottawa: Dept. of Mines and Resources.

Robson, Joseph

1752   *An Account of Six Years Residence in Hudson's Bay, from 1733 to 1736 and 1744 to 1747.* London: T. Jefferys.

Rochemonteix, C. de

1906   *Les Jésuites et la Nouvelle-France au XVIIIe siècle.* 2 vols. Paris: Picard.

Rochemonteix, C. de, ed.

1904   *Relations par lettres de l'Amérique septentrionale.* Paris: Letouney et Ané.

Rogers, Edward S.

1963   *The Hunting Group–Hunting Territory Complex among the Mistassini Indians.* National Museum of Man, Bulletin 195. Ottawa.

1967   *The Material Culture of the Mistassini.* National Museum of Man, Bulletin 218. Ottawa.

1973   *The Quest for Food and Furs: The Mistassini Cree, 1953–54.* National Museum of Man, Ethnology 5. Ottawa.

Rotstein, Abraham

1967   "Fur Trade and Empire: An Institutional Analysis." PHD dissertation, University of Toronto, Toronto.

Rousseau, Jacques

1950   "Les voyages du Père Albanel au lac Mistassini et à la baie James." *Revue d'histoire de l'Amérique française* 4: 556–86.

1964*a*   "Coupe biogéographique et ethnobiologique de la péninsule Québec-Labrador." In *Le Nouveau-Québec*, edited by J. Malaurie and J. Rousseau. Paris: Mouton.

1964*b*   "Le Canada aborigène dans le contexte historique." *Revue d'histoire de l'Amérique française* 18: 39–63.

Rousseau, Madeleine, and Rousseau, Jacques

1948   "La crainte des Iroquois chez les Mistassins." *Revue d'histoire de l'Amérique française* 2: 13–26.

Rowe, J.S.

1972   *Forest Regions of Canada.* Canadian Forestry Service Pub. 1300. Ottawa: Dept. of Environment.

Roy, P.-G.
1917   "A la mer du nord par le Saguenay en 1661." *Société de géographie de Québec* 2(3): 163–5.

Ruttle, Terence
1968   *How to Grade Furs*. Dept. of Agriculture Pub. 1362. Ottawa.

Séguin, Jocelyne
1980   "Rapport des excavations du site archéologique FlFo-1. Réservoir LG-3 Jamesie." Presented to the Service du Patrimoine autochtone, Ministère des Affaires culturelles, Quebec.

Sharp, Henry
1977   "The Caribou-Eater Chipewyan: Bilaterality Strategies of Caribou Hunting and the Fur Trade." *Arctic Anthropology* 14(2): 35–40.

Skinner, Alanson
1911   *Notes on the Eastern Cree and Northern Saulteaux*. Anthropological Papers of the American Museum of Natural History 9(1). New York.

Skinner, R.G.
1973   *Quaternary Stratigraphy of the Moose River Basin, Ontario*. Geological Survey of Canada, Bulletin 225. Ottawa.

Speck, Frank G.
1923   "Mistassini Hunting Territories in the Labrador Peninsula." *American Anthropologist* 25: 452–71.

1935   *Naskapi: The Savage Hunters of the Labrador Peninsula*. Norman: University of Oklahoma Press.

Tanner, Adrian
1973   "The Significance of Hunting Territories Today." In *Cultural Ecology*, edited by B. Cox, pp. 101–14. Toronto: McClelland and Stewart.

1979   *Bringing Home Animals: Religious Ideology and Mode of Production of the Mistassini Cree*. London: C. Hurst.

Thompson, H.A.
1968   "Climate." In *Science, History and Hudson Bay*, edited by C.S. Beals and D.A. Shenstone, 1: 263–86. Ottawa: Dept. of Mines and Resources.

Thorman, George E.
1961   "An Early Map of James Bay." *Beaver* 291 (Spring): 18–22.

Thwaites, Reuben Gold, ed.
1896–   *The Jesuit Relations and Allied Documents*. 73 vols. Cleveland.
1901

Tooker, Elisabeth
1964   *An Ethnography of the Huron Indians, 1615–1649*. Washington: U.S. Govt. Printing Office.

Traversy, Normand
1977   "Etude du castor à la baie James." In *Environnement – Baie James –*

Symposium, pp. 569–94. Montreal: Société de développement de la baie James.

Trigger, Bruce

1969   *The Huron*. New York: Holt, Rinehart & Winston.

1976   *The Children of Aataentsic: A History of the Huron People to 1660*. 2 vols. Montreal: McGill-Queen's University Press.

Turner, Lucien M.

1894   *Ethnology of the Ungava District. Eleventh Annual Report, Bureau of Ethnology*. Washington, DC: Smithsonian Institution.

Umfreville, E.

1790   *The Present State of Hudson's Bay*. London: C. Stalker.

Van Kirk, Sylvia

1980   *"Many Tender Ties": Women in Fur-Trade Society in Western Canada, 1670–1870*. Winnipeg: Watson & Dwyer.

Vincent, J.S.

1977   *Le quaternaire récent de la région du cours inférieur de la Grande Rivière, Québec*. Geological Survey of Canada, Paper 76-19. Ottawa.

Voorhis, Ernest

1930   *Historic Forts and Trading Posts of the French Regime and of the English Fur Trading Companies*. Ottawa: Dept. of the Interior.

Wallace, W.S.

1947   "The Nor'Westers Invade the Bay." *Beaver* 277 (Mar.): 33–4.

Wallace, W.S., ed.

1934   *Documents Relating to the North West Company*. Toronto: Champlain Society.

Weinstein, Martin S.

1976   *What the Land Provides: Report of the Fort George Resource Use and Subsistence Economy Study*. Montreal: Grand Council of the Crees.

Williams, Glyndwr

1963   "Captain Coats and Explorations along the East Main." *Beaver* 294 (Winter): 4–13.

Zarnovican, R.; Gerardin, V.; Ducruc, J.P.; Jurdant, M.; and Audet, G.

1976   "Les régions ecologiques du territoire de la baie James." Project ETBJ. Ste-Foy: Service des études ecologiques régionales, Environnement Canada. Typescript, 12 pp.

Index

Page numbers in italics refer to the illustrations.